Reading
Nonfiction

Kylene Beers & Robert E. Probst

Reading
Nonfiction

Notice & Note
Stances, Signposts, and Strategies

Heinemann
Portsmouth, NH

Heinemann

361 Hanover Street

Portsmouth, NH 03801–3912

www.heinemann.com

Offices and agents throughout the world

The authors and publisher wish to thank those who have generously given permission to reprint borrowed material:

Excerpt from *World History*, Student Edition. Copyright © 2006 by Holt, Rinehart and Winston. Reprinted with permission from the publisher, Houghton Mifflin Harcourt Publishing Company. All rights reserved.

Abstract from "Americans' Attitudes Toward the Affordable Care Act: Would Better Public Understanding Increase or Decrease Favorability?" by Wendy Gross, Tobias H. Stark, Jon Krosnick, Josh Pasek, Gaurav Sood, Trevor Tompson, Jennifer Agiesta, and Dennis Junius. Copyright © 2012. Reprinted with permission from Jon Krosnick, Stanford University.

See page 301 for additional credits.

Library of Congress Cataloging-in-Publication Data

Names: Beers, G. Kylene, author. | Probst, Robert E., author.

Title: Reading nonfiction : notice & note stances, signposts, and strategies / Kylene Beers & Robert E. Probst.

Description: Portsmouth, NH : Heinemann, [2016] | Includes bibliographical references and index.

Identifiers: LCCN 2015034861 | ISBN 9780325050805

Subjects: LCSH: Reading comprehension—Study and teaching.

Classification: LCC LB1573.7 .B44 2015 | DDC 372.47—dc23

LC record available at http://lccn.loc.gov/2015034861

Editor: Debra Doorack

Production Editor: Patty Adams

Cover and Interior Designs: Lisa Fowler

Typesetter: Gina Poirier Design

Manufacturing: Steve Bernier

Printed in the United States of America on acid-free paper

19 18 17 16   EBM   3   4   5

Dedication

This book is dedicated to the people
who most inspire our thinking:

Our nation's teachers
Who show up each day to do the hard work

And to Lesa Scott
For never losing sight of what matters most

And to Melvil Dewey
Because, after all, to discuss nonfiction without remembering
Melvil makes no sense at all

Contents

Introduction

We Begin Again

The title for this introduction includes the word *again* as a nod to the title of the introduction in *Notice and Note: Strategies for Close Reading* (Beers and Probst 2013), which is simply "We Begin." At one point we wanted to title this introduction "We Continue," but that suggested that we would have to write a third book, and it would have to begin, "We End." Beginning a book with "We End" didn't sound like a good idea for a plethora of reasons.

So, we began *again*. Beginning again was hard, perhaps even harder than beginning the first book. The challenge wasn't only that of writing another book, though that certainly was challenging. It was also the problem of telling a second story in a way that would seem as new as the first. It required us to challenge ourselves as writers and you as readers.

And we do want this book to challenge you. We want you to pause to consider new ideas, mull over comments we make, and mark passages you want to reread and discuss with colleagues. We want you excited to start online conversations, discard what you know isn't true for you, make better what you see you can revise for your students, or adopt intact what seems immediately applicable. This book was ours as we wrote it, but now that it's finished, it's yours. Your reading is what will make it meaningful.

> For those of you wondering, "What third book?" our plan as of this writing is to follow this book on reading nonfiction with a book about helping reluctant readers. If, however, we become reluctant *writers*, that might change. Perhaps we'll write a pamphlet.

This book was ours as we wrote it, but now that it's finished, it's yours. Your reading is what will make it meaningful.

You

And because it's your reading that counts, you should know that we had you in mind while we were writing this book. We saw you in classrooms, standing before twenty or thirty or sometimes forty students (and that's only one class). We saw you arriving early, staying late, listening intently to students, laughing with them, guiding them, urging them, steering them, and always teaching them.

We saw you nod as states promised that these new Common Core State Standards are the standards we've been waiting for, only to be told within a year, that, well, we're not actually going to use these standards but are going to adopt our own, only to discover that these new standards look a lot like the CCSS. We watched you face new assessments, endure new evaluations, and accept new policies that demanded your salary be tied to how individual children performed on a test. We watched you teach through salary freezes, increased class sizes, decreased time for professional development, and endless onslaughts of negative public opinion (coming often from politicians who seem to know very little about the public schools). Through it all, you kept doing what matters most: teaching kids. Every day. Like postal workers who deliver the mail no matter the weather, you delivered instruction even when facing a blizzard of new challenges.

> **Through it all, you kept doing what matters most: teaching kids. Every day. Like postal workers who deliver the mail no matter the weather, you delivered instruction even when facing a blizzard of new challenges.**

Your Students

Not only did we have you in mind while writing this, but we had your students in mind, too: diverse, quirky, funny, solemn, noisy, quiet; monolingual, bilingual, trilingual; selfie-snapping, snapchat-chatting, text-messaging kids. This is the generation that has declared that email is "too slow" (and we had just figured out how to add attachments), that Facebook is for old people (and suddenly we aren't quite as proud of our Facebook pages), and that the one-second video is "just about the right length."

> By 2016, every student in school will have been born in the 21st century. They will have grown up with the world at their fingertips, almost literally. The ubiquitous smart phone, with its countless apps and the Web's search engines, put, if not everything, then at least information *about* almost everything in their pockets.

There are the kids who make headlines for all the wrong reasons, and as we were writing, we were thinking of them too. What have we not done? What else should we be doing? Those kids who hurt others, who bully some to suicide, who strike out with knives and guns, were kids who sat in someone's classroom. They answered questions (or did not); they turned in homework (or did not). They walked our nation's schoolhouse hallways, and nobody noticed that something was amiss?

Those kids make the headlines, while far bigger groups of children and teens go about their lives making a difference. They stand up for those who are put down. They join teams, not gangs. They show up for car washes and school math/sports/band/drama/art/debate/FFA competitions.

This is also the generation that cares deeply about the environment, has logged more volunteer hours in universities than any other generation, has started gay-straight alliances on their school campuses, and has used the Internet to let people know about child labor issues, child poverty, and the plight of child immigrants. These are the kids who start antibullying campaigns in their schools, who raise money to dig wells for clean drinking water in Africa, who bring to our awareness horrific conditions of children who are forced to work for the cocoa bean industry along the Ivory Coast, who cut their hair in solidarity with their friends in chemotherapy, who believe in stamping out injustice and intolerance.

These kids you teach hate conformity and simultaneously work hard to always fit in. Like zebras moving across the Serengeti, they run as a herd, changing directions seemingly as one group, and yet, when they pause and you look closely, you see that each one has stripes that make it unique from the next. These kids you teach desperately need outstanding teachers and simultaneously need, desperately, not to admit this to anyone.

These kids you teach desperately need outstanding teachers and simultaneously need, desperately, not to admit this to anyone.

We watch kids from all walks of life enter your schools, some ready to work in your classroom, some already working in the world outside. Some leave to attend afternoon arts classes or sports events or participate in school clubs; others leave to rush home to watch siblings, sitting behind locked doors waiting for a parent to arrive home from job number two or three.

And some simply wait. They wait for a better tomorrow; they wait to discover how something they are learning in school will help them escape the street they live on. They wait for someone to notice it's winter and they have no coat; it's summer and they have no lunch; it's the start of school and they have no one to take them to the store for school supplies. They wait for a teacher to show them why knowing more will make them hunger less.

And Nonfiction

Writing this book also meant thinking about what nonfiction is, about how we would explain that to children and teens, about how we read nonfiction differently than we read fiction. Writing this book has meant reading a vast amount of nonfiction about things we had never considered. So, if any of you want to talk about the role of the dung beetle in curbing global warming problems, we are here for you! It meant reading about one topic from various perspectives. It meant thinking about what it means to read history texts, science texts, political texts, technical texts, math texts, autobiographies, biographies, human interest stories, essays, op-eds, how-to books, and anything else that falls into the very large category called nonfiction.

It meant asking you how you teach with nonfiction, asking kids what they do or don't like about reading nonfiction, and asking ourselves how we as literature teachers feel about this push from the universe to teach more nonfiction. It meant turning to colleagues who know far more about books than we ever will (that's you, in particular, Teri Lesesne).

So, with those three characters in mind (you, your students, and nonfiction), we set about telling our story—a true one, mind you— about the teaching of nonfiction.

What You Will Find in This Book

At first, this was going to be a book only about nonfiction signposts. We began thinking about them while writing *Notice and Note*, and we wondered if the signposts we had found in the novels would show up again in nonfiction.

But as we were looking for nonfiction signposts, we realized that this book had to do more than *Notice and Note* did, that it had its own story to tell. This book had to discuss a stance that's required for the attentive, productive reading of nonfiction. It's a mindset that is open and receptive but not gullible. It encourages questioning the text but also questioning one's own assumptions, preconceptions, and possibly misconceptions. This mindset urges the reader both to draw upon what he does know and to acknowledge what he doesn't know. And it asks the reader to make a responsible decision about whether a text had helped him confirm his prior beliefs and thoughts or had enabled him to modify and sharpen them, or perhaps to abandon them and change his mind entirely. How did we finally begin to help students to adopt such a mindset? We taught them to keep what we came to call "Big Questions" in mind as they are reading. Those big questions opened up reflection about nonfiction in a powerful way.

> So, with those three characters in mind (you, your students, and nonfiction), we set about telling our story—a true one, mind you— about the teaching of nonfiction.

We also discovered that we wanted this book to share strategies we've always found helpful for getting kids into nonfiction texts, helping them through the texts, and then extending their thinking after they've finished reading those texts. We added some new twists to some old strategies and found that with a little tweaking, some strategies that we—and perhaps you—had set aside could become powerful tools in a student's toolbox of strategies.

Stances. Signposts. Strategies. Those three topics form the heart of this book. We begin now with an overview of how we share these tools with students and how you might do the same. Then, as we did in *Notice and Note*, we look at some major issues confronting us all. And we conclude with what we hope are words of encouragement for all of you.

Into Practice

Reading a book is different from putting the ideas it conveys into practice in your classroom. We realize that and thought it important, up front, to share what it might look like when you start to combine stances, and the questions they imply, with signposts and strategies. What does it look like to put the ideas presented here into practice?

Stances. Signposts. Strategies. Those three topics form the heart of this book.

To answer that, we want to share with you a bit of a lesson we heard from a teacher. This teacher, burdened by constraints he felt from his district, had set aside what he told us he knew were *best practices* to instead use "*test practices* that I know will show the administration I did all I could to get kids ready for the almighty test." So, his lesson on a topic (any topic will do) basically followed this pattern:

- ▸ Show students an interest-building clip on the topic from the web.

- ▸ Tell kids what they need to know about the topic. They take notes.

- ▸ Have some discussion on the topic.

- ▸ Give kids a test on the topic.

Show. Tell. Discuss. Test. Do you notice what's missing? Where's the reading kids do to learn about the topic? When we asked the teacher that question, he pointed out that when he begins his series of lectures about the topic (lectures lasting from one day to several weeks), he often has short articles from the web up on the whiteboard for all to read. We asked him if that was enough reading to help students become savvy readers of nonfiction. He stared at us for a moment and then responded that "the textbook is worthless, and frankly I don't have time for kids to read in class. And they don't want to read. They don't care about the topics we discuss, so if I gave them something to read, if they did anything it would be just a surface-level reading." We asked if he assigned reading for home. "Are you kidding?" he replied. "They wouldn't do it." Then he asked us, "So, if you were going to try to get kids into reading some nonfiction, how would you do it?"

Combining Stances, Signposts, and Strategies

We appreciated his invitation and began a series of lessons.

Day 1: We taught kids the Big Questions we want them to keep in mind as they read any text and had them practice this with a short text. These are the questions that help create questioning, curious, slightly skeptical stances.

Big Questions are discused in Part II.

Extreme or Absolute Language is discussed on p. 136.

Possible Sentences is found on p. 185 and KWL 2.0 on page 193.

Day 2: We taught them one signpost—Extreme or Absolute Language—and pointed out to them that noticing this signpost would help them think about the Big Questions.

Day 3: We introduced the topic they would be reading about by having kids do Possible Sentences and KWL 2.0. At the end of the lesson, they were asking (literally) when they would get to read the text. The teacher was stunned.

Day 4: Kids read the text (short, one page, single spaced), marking examples of Extreme or Absolute Language. Then they paired up with one other student and discussed what they both noticed. The class was abuzz with kids sharing, comparing, rereading, asking us if something was/was not a signpost (a pretty typical first-time response since kids are conditioned to look for "the right answer"), and more rereading as they kept thinking about why the author used that particular word or phrase.

Day 5: Kids continued their paired discussion, this time talking with each other about how noticing the Extreme or Absolute

Language informed their thinking about the Big Questions. We wrapped up by asking what they thought about this week. The comments ranged from "This was cool. I liked getting to read and figure out stuff" to "I didn't know about extreme, and I heard my brother using it" to "The Big Questions are easy but hard. They make you think differently about the text" to "Can we just do it like regular next week? That's easier."

After Day 5

At the end of the week, we had the chance to debrief with the teacher. He said that after Days 1 and 2, he wasn't too impressed because we had not covered any of the content he needed to get covered. He said that at the end of Day 4 he was surprised at the level of engagement he saw from this class of kids who were mostly disengaged from learning in general and from reading in particular. He said that when a few (well, two) students actually came into class a little before the bell rang (twenty seconds) and asked, "Do we get to use that article again and keep discussing it?" he knew he wanted to give this a try.

He was also impressed, he said, that we didn't have to do all the teaching. He pointed out that while we were busy all the time, moving from group to group, calling kids together for brief reminders, urging them to think more about something by rereading and talking again, we weren't the only ones doing all the talking. He did express reservations about how long it took to get into the text that had the content he needed his students to learn. We pointed out that once kids learn the Big Questions, the signposts, and some strategies, those days turn back to content days.

> This is important to us. We can't create independent readers, actually, independent *learners*, if we never give them a chance to work independently and never give them a chance to read.

The teacher saw that firsthand when the following week he decided to repeat our pattern and realized he didn't need to spend Days 1 and 2 teaching the Big Questions or Extreme or Absolute Language. When he later wanted to add a signpost, he was obligated to build back in a day to do so. And when he taught the Fix-Up strategies in Part IV, he did spend about thirty minutes showing kids how to use each one.

The chart that follows offers an idea for how your time might look as you initially share these questions, signposts, and strategies with students. The following chart offers a slower pace.

THE FIRST 6 WEEKS	
Week 1 Students learn and practice reading with Big Questions in mind.	As you are teaching these, you are using the content your kids need to be reading. So, you are still moving forward with your content.
Weeks 2–6 Students learn one signpost per week. As they learn new signposts, they continue thinking about the others they've already learned.	Kids use the signposts to help them get to the Big Questions. Our most disengaged readers need the signposts to push them into deeper reflection about the text. As kids are learning to be alert for these signposts, you're asking, "How do these help you think about the Big Questions?"
Weeks 4–6 Students learn the three main Fix-Up strategies we use.	Although we present seven strategies in the book, three of them are great for students to use on their own to fix up confusions: Somebody Wanted But So (SWBS), Sketch to Stretch, and Syntax Surgery. Take a look at the ways we introduce them to students, and decide how you want to do it.
Throughout Weeks 2–6 You use the other strategies with students as needed/wanted.	The remaining four strategies should be used throughout this time—and the year—as you see fit.

What You'll Find Online

As you read this text, you will occasionally see QR codes in the margin. These codes take you to some videos that highlight students using the Big Questions, Signposts, or Strategies. We'd like to thank teachers Jeff Williams, Eileen Ours, Angie Rosen, Elizabeth Snevily, and Lauren Maynes who helped considerably and generously shared the smart thinking of their students.

Additionally, online you will also find templates that support the strategies and the teaching texts that support all the lessons. URLs and a QR code for these materials are provided throughout this book.

Accessing the Teaching Texts Found in Appendix B

To access these files digitally, you need a Heinemann account.

1. Enter the URL http://hein.pub/readnfres2 or scan the QR code and enter your email address and password.

2. Click "Sign In."

If you need to set up a new account, click "Create a New Account."

3. Enter the key code **READNF** and click "Register."

Teaching Materials You'll Find Online

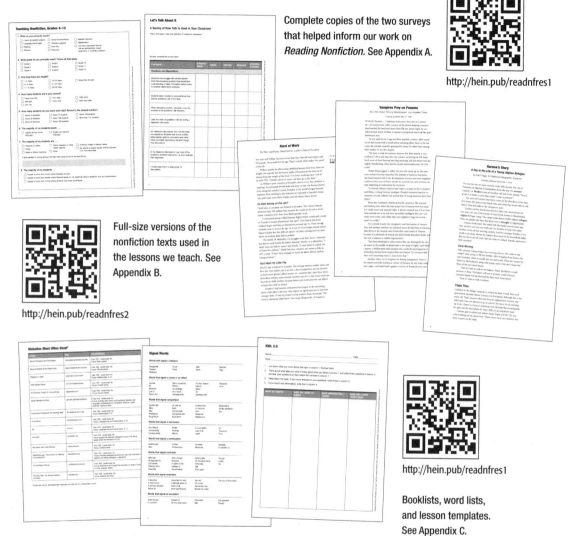

Complete copies of the two surveys that helped inform our work on *Reading Nonfiction*. See Appendix A.

http://hein.pub/readnfres1

Full-size versions of the nonfiction texts used in the lessons we teach. See Appendix B.

http://hein.pub/readnfres2

http://hein.pub/readnfres1

Booklists, word lists, and lesson templates. See Appendix C.

Before You Begin

We invite you now to think with us. In some places we hope you'll nod and agree. In other places, we hope the ideas will cause you to stop and wonder. And when you find places where you disagree, mark them, and when our paths cross—virtually or at a conference—let's do what colleagues do: talk and wonder together. But mostly, we hope you'll find something that will be helpful in your classroom. We believe you make a critical difference not only in the classroom, but in the very lives of your students.

And so, let's begin—again.

Issues to Consider

In Part I, we share ten issues that directed our thinking while writing this book. At the end of each section you will find "Talking with Colleagues." We encourage you to use these prompts to guide faculty conversations. But before we begin we want to tell you . . .

A True Short Story of Why We Wrote This Text

Once upon a time, a long time ago, printed texts existed to record critical historical events or explain man's relationship with God. As a result, what was written was expected to be factual and was, therefore, perceived that way. No one wondered if a text was fiction or nonfiction—first, because those terms were not yet used and, second, because if a text was written it was expected to be true.

And that makes sense. Creating a printed text took a long time. When people first started creating printed records, their "high-tech tools" consisted of the chisel and stone, later to be replaced by a clay or wax tablet. Eventually there was a monk in a dank, candlelit room with a scroll and a quill. Although writing on a scroll was certainly faster than chipping into a clay tablet, there still was no delete key. As a result, writing was laborious. If that monk made a mistake, then, well, actually we aren't sure what happened to those error-prone scribes of long ago. What we do know, however, is that those early writing efforts were not intended to create entertaining texts. The entertainment waited until evening, around the fire, provided by storytellers. If anything was written, it was to record. To inform. To educate. To illuminate. No flying carpets, trips to Hogwarts, or escapes through a magical wardrobe.

But, to paraphrase Bob Dylan, the times were changing. In China, then in Korea, and eventually in Germany, people were figuring out faster ways to produce written texts. The Chinese were early inventors of a moveable-type printing press, around 1040. Koreans had developed their own system by the early 1200s. And in 1450, a German, Johannes Gutenberg, invented a printing press with moveable type that allowed for the rapid (relatively speaking) reproduction of printed documents, making assembly-line book production possible for the first time.

"WE ARE REQUIRED TO READ BEYOND THE FOUR CORNERS OF THE TEXT; WE ARE REQUIRED TO LET NONFICTION INTRUDE; WE ARE REQUIRED TO WONDER WHAT IT MEANS ON THE PAGE, IN OUR LIVES, AND IN THE WORLD."

A detailed history of moveable type is available online
at http://en.wikipedia.org
/wiki/Movable_type.

It seems logical that as printing became less time-consuming it could be used for less weighty tomes than those devoted to understanding man's (and we mean *man's*) relationship with God.

Enter: Fiction

It's only a little before Gutenberg's invention that we see another invention. This time it's a word: *fiction*. There had been no need for this word previously because what was told around the fire was simply part of the experience of sitting around the fire. Tales of ogres and heroes, of wicked witches and fairy godmothers, of dragons and knights were *told*. They weren't labeled fairy tales or chivalric romances or epics. They were just tales told. There was no need to classify them.

But enough of these imaginative tales had made it into print by the early 1400s that in 1412 we see for the first time the word *fiction* used in print to describe work that is "an invention of the mind." In 1599 the definition of fiction changes from "invention of the mind" to "imaginative literature," and "fiction" as a particular type of written text—those texts that were not just imaginative but were created primarily for entertainment—becomes a more commonly used term (see *American Heritage Dictionary* 2000/2003).

Fiction comes from the Latin word *fictio*, meaning "fashioning," and that word came from an older Latin word, *fictus*, which means "feigned" or "false." *Fictus* comes from an even older word, *fingere*, which means to "adapt," "transform into," and "make up."

Next Up: Libraries

Over the next several centuries, not only do we see more and more printed fiction, but we also see a development in libraries, which had existed since early Roman times. They changed from being repositories of books (and previously, scrolls) that were accessible for reading only by the learned (and frequently were chained to desks—the manuscripts, not the readers—lest anyone decide to take one home), to public libraries that were open to everyone.

Additionally, by the early eighteenth century, an increasing number of libraries in England had become what were called *lending* libraries. The texts no longer stayed chained to a desk but could be borrowed with only the sincere promise that they would be returned. Those lending libraries contained that growing body of work called "fiction." Indeed, by 1797, a publication titled "The Use of Circulating Libraries" explained that "for a successful circulating library, the collection must contain 70% fiction" (http://en.wikipedia.org/wiki/Public_library).

Figure 1 While arrangement by height made all look neat, when books began to be circulated to the public, this proved to be a silly shelving system.

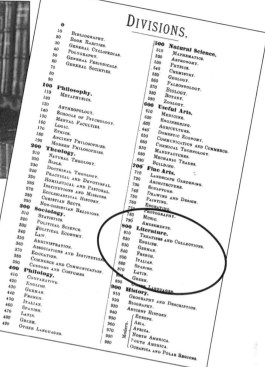

New Thinking: Melvil Dewey

In 1871, twenty-one-year-old Melvil Dewey, while working as a student assistant in the library at Amherst College, decided that the current way of shelving books in a library just wasn't workable. The system at that time was to arrange books by height or date of acquisition. He believed that a more workable system would be to arrange books by topic: philosophy, theology, sociology, natural science, and literature, to name a few of the categories he suggested. We have to say, we agree. (See Figure 1.)

This system, refined by Dewey and colleagues over many years, resulted in what is now called the Dewey Decimal Classification (DDC) system. Though Dewey did other notable work—he was a founder of the American Library Association; became the librarian of Columbia College; created traveling libraries, and worked to reform education—it is the Dewey Decimal Classification system for which he is best known. (See Figure 2.)

Figure 2 Dewey's original classifications. Notice that the 800s were for literature.

John Dewey

Melvil Dewey

Many folks think the Dewey Decimal Classification system came from John Dewey. That's a different Dewey known for different reasons.

> We see the term *nonfiction* or *nonfictional* being used in libraries by 1909 and would do well to remember that its first use was simply to designate the work as "not fiction," not a novel.

A New Addition: Nonfiction

By the early 1900s, public libraries had indeed become public (well, as public as anything was in the early 1900s), and more and more librarians agreed that keeping novels separate from all the other books made sense. This way, the public could more quickly find books by their favorite authors. So novels were placed in a newly established section, and the books were referred to as *fiction*. That left the remaining books to be called *nonfiction*, or literally, "not fiction."

We see the term *nonfiction* or *nonfictional* being used in libraries by 1909 and would do well to remember that its first use was simply to designate the work as "not fiction," not a novel. Somewhere along the way, though, this original intent of the word was lost, and a new definition emerged: *fiction*, educators began to tell their students, means "false or imaginary," and so *nonfiction* came to mean "not false, and therefore true."

Shift Happens

The meanings of many words have shifted over time. *Awful*, at one time, meant "full of awe." *Dogma* literally meant "an opinion." *Investment* came from the Latin *vestere*, meaning "to clothe." As you might predict, early on this word had nothing to do with where to put money but instead meant to put clothes on someone. *Naughty* meant "nothing" as in "He had naught." And a *spinster* was a woman who—you guessed it—spun yarn. Word meanings shift. That's part of the fluidity of language.

It's really not surprising that the meaning of *nonfiction* has shifted as well. What was once a term used by librarians to signify that the text simply wasn't a novel morphed into meaning "not false" and even "informational." While not surprising, we do wonder if this shift has served us well.

The Plot Thickens

Between 2013 and 2014 we conducted two surveys of teachers, the first for teachers in grades 4–12 and the second for teachers in grades 1–12. Our first survey yielded 1,627 responses; the second yielded 788 responses. In the second survey, we asked teachers to tell us how they define nonfiction for their students. This was an open-ended question, so teachers were required to write their answers. When we studied the 788 responses (an open-ended question for 788 folks was not one of our smartest moves), we discovered that the number one definition from *all* teachers across *all* grades was "an informational text." That was closely followed by definitions that included the words or phrases "facts," "true," "real," and "not fake." (See Figure 3, which shows a word cloud revealing the top twenty responses.)

When we examined responses by grade level and by content taught, the top twenty responses remained unchanged across all grades and disciplines. High school seniors were told that nonfiction means "informational texts," exactly what they had been told when they were kindergartners.

In late 2014, we surveyed 1,300 students, across all the grades, and we asked them to define *nonfiction* (and again we used that open-ended format, proving that the adage "You learn from your mistakes" doesn't hold true for us). If you ever wonder if kids are listening, we at least now know they are listening to our definitions of nonfiction, because their top responses were "information books," "true stories," "things that are real," and "not fake."

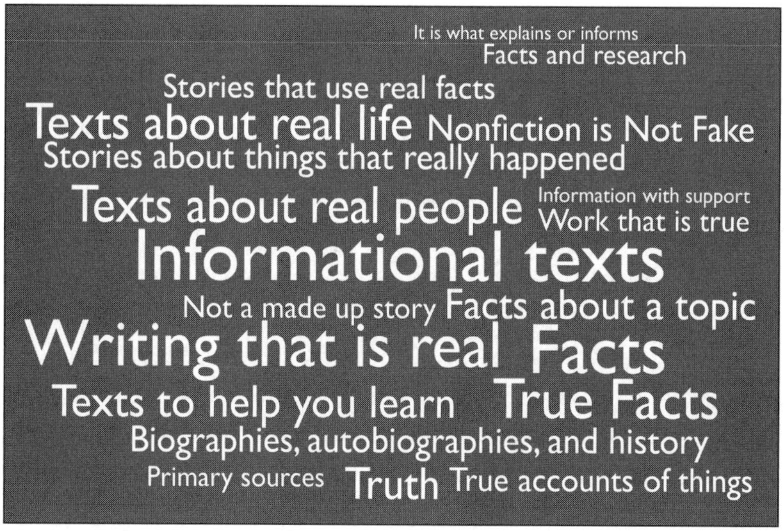

Figure 3 A word cloud of teachers' most common definitions of nonfiction. Remember that the larger a word's font, the more often it was used by respondents.

The Conflict Emerges

We wouldn't argue with telling students that nonfiction texts offer information. But when we tell students that nonfiction means "true," then we have created potential conflict for them because there is a great deal that is classified as nonfiction that happens to be inaccurate, untrue, and occasionally even deceitful. We understand the temptation to offer that definition: *non* means "not" and *fiction* means "imaginary," so something that is not imaginary leads us directly to the words *factual*, *real*, and *true*. The logic for this shift is certainly more understandable than the shift that transformed *awful*, at one time a synonym for *awesome*, into a synonym for *terrible*.

> Many texts contain information that once was cutting edge and deemed accurate but later was deemed "old" and incorrect. The Earth was flat. Leeches were once an important part of the fight against infection. And some people were only three-fifths of a person.

But when we tell students that *nonfiction* means *true*, we inadvertently have excused them from the task of deciding if the text is accurate, if the author's biases have skewed information, if new information now contradicts "old" information in that text or in our own thinking. By telling students that *nonfiction* means *true*, we've implied that their job, when reading nonfiction, is simply to learn and absorb the information in the text, not to question it. The logic is syllogistic:

Nonfiction is true.

This text is nonfiction.

Therefore this text is true.

So it's no wonder that when we ask kids to examine the author's biases, many stare back confused. If nonfiction is true, then how can there be biases? Our oversimplified definition of nonfiction has perhaps misled kids into thinking that reading nonfiction is simply a matter of learning the text, assimilating the information it provides. The reader's role, given this simplistic definition, is to accept.

> The role of the reader of nonfiction texts is to be active, to challenge the text, and to invite the text to challenge him.

In actuality, the role of the reader of nonfiction texts is to be active, to challenge the text, and to invite the text to challenge him. We must read with an eye skeptical enough that we see in the text the places we must question the author's assertions. But at the same time we must read with a mind open enough that we will be able to, when warranted, change our understandings—about the text, about ourselves, about the world around us. Reading nonfiction is, we have come to believe, some of the most important and valuable reading we all do. *Reading Nonfiction* is at its heart about challenge and change.

Defining Nonfiction

The easiest, simplest, most straightforward, if inelegant, definition of *nonfiction* is probably, as the history of the term suggests, "If it isn't a novel, it's nonfiction." After all, the genre's very name, *nonfiction*, seems to admit that we know less about what it *is* than about what it *isn't*, and what it isn't is novels and short stories. But that definition isn't very helpful. It's about as useful as it would be to divide up the entire world of living creatures into human and nonhuman. If we did that, we'd have everything from amoebas to zebras, bacteria to blue whales, lumped together in one huge, unmanageable group.

So we discarded that definition and wondered if we might agree that nonfiction is a group of texts about the real world or real people. This definition is close to the one offered in many dictionaries and is better than simply saying, "Nonfiction means not fake." Ultimately we found it lacking because it emphasized the content of the texts and neglected the obligation imposed by such texts on the reader. Nonfiction isn't merely a group of books; nonfiction makes some demands on readers, and we wanted a definition that considered those demands.

Demands of Reading Nonfiction

At first glance, one might conclude that nonfiction works hard *not* to place demands upon readers. Flashbacks rarely occur; multiple narrators rarely intrude; unreliable narrators are almost never seen (though the deceptive author often rears his head). Steps in a process are often numbered. Signal words—*first, by contrast, another reason, consequently*—help readers determine text structure.

Maps, figures, graphs, headers, timelines, sidebars, photos, and illustrations—all devices meant to make texts "considerate" and support comprehension—appear in many texts of nonfiction. But those supports often create their own problems for some readers. All must be read in tandem with the prose, sometimes without any explanation in the text telling you when to turn to the diagram, study the map, consider the chart, or look at the sidebar. With any Dorling Kindersley *Eyewitness* book, one could argue that reading no longer proceeds top to bottom, left page to right page, because pages are filled with short paragraphs, eye-catching graphics, and timelines that sprawl across pages. Yes, graphics, labels, sidebars, and fonts of different sizes are all meant to enhance reading and aid comprehension. Text features such as these are important and students should be reminded to attend to them. And for some students, we need to teach them how to read these aids. (See Figure 4.)

Furthermore, often it seems that nonfiction doesn't want the reader to suffer through the thinking required to make an inference. So authors tell us directly: "The Westward expansion benefited the young United States for many reasons . . ." or "Wolves should be

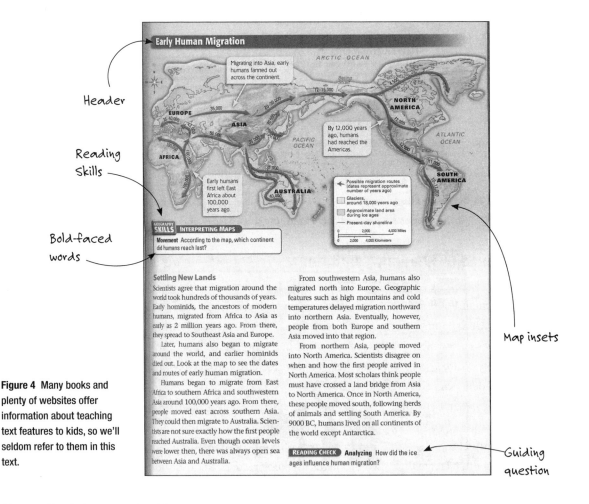

Figure 4 Many books and plenty of websites offer information about teaching text features to kids, so we'll seldom refer to them in this text.

reintroduced into these protected areas." No inferences required here. This direct language appears to ease the demands made upon us as readers, but then you realize that if you are going to read about how the Westward expansion benefited the United States, you should know who is providing those reasons, and before you accept that wolves should become a part of the wildlife in a particular area, you might want to hear what ranchers in that region have to say. You realize (or should) that the direct language might be used to discourage you from making an inference so that you will be less likely to dispute the author's point. That should raise all sorts of questions.

The reality is that the reading of nonfiction places many demands upon the reader. Not only does it require that we be on the lookout for biases, but it often requires more background knowledge than the reading of fiction does. Many times that required knowledge is technical, specific, and complex. The vocabulary can be intimidating, the syntax can be daunting, and the concepts can be abstract. For example, for those of us who are not physicists (such as your average eleventh grader), consider this sentence from a high school physics textbook: "Although both a simple pendulum and a mass-spring system vibrate with simple harmonic motion, calculating the period and frequency of each requires a separate equation" (*Holt Physics*, Holt, Rinehart and Winston 2002). Right.

Reading nonfiction, in many ways, requires an effort not required in the reading of fiction. We must question the text, question the author, question our own understanding of the topic, and accept the possibility that our views will change as a result of the reading we're doing. All those demands mean that the *reader* has great responsibility when reading nonfiction.

The Reader's Responsibility

Our job as readers of nonfiction is to enter into a text recognizing that the author is not offering *the* truth, but *one* vision of the truth. It is the reader's responsibility to resist the lure of the seemingly authoritative—or highly persuasive—text that the author wants us to accept without questioning. We must be alert to times when the author has purposefully—or not—made a statement we should challenge. And it is the reader's responsibility to question his or her own beliefs and assumptions while struggling with determining what's true—or not—in the text.

The Role of Truth

The United American Indians of New England celebrates a "National Day of Mourning" on the Thursday Thanksgiving is celebrated. This day, celebrated since 1970, is meant to bring to the public greater awareness of the misrepresentation of the Native Americans and the colonial experience (http://bit.ly/1GXq3zl).

But truth is an elusive quality. The author's perspective, her consideration of her audience, and sometimes mundane realities such as the amount of space available for the text all shape what a writer says and probably affect the truthfulness of any piece she writes. For example, an article in *National Geographic for Kids* about the first Thanksgiving paints a more realistic view of that gathering than some other children's accounts, but it still omits mention of the devastation of smallpox on the indigenous people (http://kids.nationalgeographic.com/explore/history/first-thanksgiving/). The consideration of audience (young readers) presumably helped shape what the author chose to share.

But is this account *true?* Can it be accurate when many events are glossed over if not completely skipped? Do those omissions call into question the truthfulness of this brief account? Should the omissions be an indication of personal biases? The United American Indians of New England offers a perspective on Thanksgiving rarely (if ever) taught in our classrooms and certainly not presented in the *National Geographic for Kids* article. Does that mean that article is "wrong?" Does that mean it shouldn't be read?

Thinking through issues such as these helped us conclude that the author of nonfiction should, at the very least:

- ▶ Have a commitment to honest representation of its subject matter, to logic, and to evidence.

- ▶ Avoid carelessly or deceitfully misrepresenting as actual and true what is invented or false.

But "honest representation" for a second grader might be inadequate for a seventh grader and oversimplified, if not misleading, for a senior in high school.

And the Definition Is . . .

We've come to realize that in spite of all the headers and photographs, all the chapter titles and indexes, in spite of all that we do to make nonfiction look neat and navigable, *there is nothing neat and tidy about nonfiction.*

Nonfiction is the stuff of real life—life with all its contrasts and contradictions, all its tough questions and aha moments, all its half-truths and little white lies, its moments when we have to say, "Well, let me clarify" or "That was taken out of context" or "What I really meant"—so, of course, there is nothing neat and tidy about it. Our job as readers of nonfiction is to enter into that potentially messy reading as a co-constructor of meaning. We're more likely to take on that role if we have adopted a definition of nonfiction that not only tells us what the author is doing, but reminds us that we, too, have a job. Much of our job in reading nonfiction is to evaluate what the author has done in the text.

> **Our job as readers of nonfiction is to enter into that potentially messy reading as a co-constructor of meaning.**

Understanding all this, we eventually agreed upon a definition:

> Nonfiction is that body of work in which the author purports to tell us about the real world, a real experience, a real person, an idea, or a belief.

Notice—we don't say it is a text about something real. We say the author is purporting to tell us something real.

Is this definition too abstract for a seven-year-old child? Probably (not including *your* seven-year-olds). The seven-year-old needs to be given trustworthy texts and needs to learn to take information from them. But the mnemonic "NF stands for *not fake*" is too simple (too deceptively simple) for the twelve-year-old. Nonetheless, this is the definition that guided our thinking as we came to understand what it means to read nonfiction.

TALKING WITH COLLEAGUES

▶ You might start a conversation by sharing with others your definition of nonfiction. Discuss with others how nonfiction is defined in your school. Is there consensus? Are you comfortable with your definition? If the definition suggests to students that nonfiction is "true" or "real" or "not fake," how do you reconcile with students all the nonfiction that is not true?

▶ Next, you might discuss what you want students to understand about nonfiction by the time they leave your school, and make sure *that* understanding is reflected in changes seen across the school years.

▶ The word *purports* is important in this definition. Identify a few examples of nonfiction that only pretend to tell you about the real world but that, in fact, are deceptive or fraudulent, and discuss these with your colleagues.

▶ Flip through some of the textbooks—or articles or trade books— used in your school. Talk with others who teach your same content about any examples offered to students that you think are incomplete or grossly oversimplified. Make a plan for addressing those shortcomings.

Developmental Demands

We shared our definition of nonfiction with some seventh graders and asked them what they thought of it. Put politely, they responded, "Not much." When we asked what the problem was they said, "We don't get it. Why don't you just say that nonfiction is not fake?" When we headed into a second-grade classroom, we were quickly bombarded by the twenty-three students who felt compelled to tell us (simultaneously) "Look, look, look at this. This is my story I wrote" and "Did you get that pen at the store across the street?" and "I got a cut on my arm yesterday and . . ." They did not seem interested in exploring the nuances of our definition. Some eleventh graders looked at us and said, "Whatever."

The honesty of those seventh graders and the rapid-fire questions of the second graders reminded us that definitions must attend to the developmental needs of the learner. (The eleventh graders reminded us that high school teachers are due a huge salary increase). Embarrassingly, we knew better than to assume that what works at one age group will work for another. So we returned to our definition and rewrote it with the developmental needs of primary, upper elementary, middle school, and high school students in mind. In essence, the definitions we'll now share constitute a gradual change from the concrete and simple to the more abstract and complicated.

> We learn so much every time we enter a classroom and teach a lesson. To each of you who invited us into your schools and let us teach your students, thank you.

Primary Grades

We recognize that our youngest students—kindergartners, first graders, and second graders—are eager to learn everything even though, for them, learning doesn't look like learning. It looks a lot like play (or it should). These students are just *beginning* to understand rules of logic, and they still see the world through egocentric eyes. Not too long ago (when they were three or four years old) if you had asked them which glass held more water, a tall skinny glass or a short fat glass, they would

have picked the tall skinny glass—even after watching you pour the water from one glass to the other, demonstrating that they held the same amount. But by around age seven, they realize they hold the same amount. And if three-year-olds cover their own eyes, they may announce to you that you can't see them. Your primary-age children laugh at that idea. Developmentally, primary-age children are concrete learners who mostly understand the world from their own point of view.

These developmental markers suggest that simply rewriting our definition by replacing difficult words with easier ones isn't enough. Our youngest students don't yet have the ability to follow an author's logic or to recognize if the author is implying anything beyond what he or she is directly stating. (That's a blanket statement and is probably disproved by your particularly precocious second graders.) For these less mature students we need a more concrete, reader-centered definition. Better yet, a description will help students more than a definition. *Descriptions* of abstract concepts—goodness, justice, photosynthesis, democracy, irrational numbers, and nonfiction—better serve concrete thinkers. With that in mind, we're more likely to tell our youngest students,

> A book about real people or real things is called nonfiction. There won't be any talking animals or flying people in a book about real things. A counting book and books about trucks or dinosaurs or the planets are examples of nonfiction. When you read nonfiction ask yourself, "What did I learn?"

> Notice that we tell them what it is, tell them what it isn't, give them an example, and have them ask a question that puts them—not the author or the text—at the center.

Upper Elementary

By about third grade and certainly by fifth, most students have had enough experience with the world so that the way they think has shifted—somewhat. Two specific shifts ought to be considered as we rethink what a definition of nonfiction should be for these more sophisticated students.

First, students at this stage can apply some rules of logic to a situation or a task as long as the task is still concrete. For example, if you say to a five-year-old: "*A* is greater than *B*; *B* is greater than *C*; therefore *A* is greater than *C*," it's likely her response will be something like, "Nope. I think *M* is the greatest because my name starts with the letter *M*." By fourth grade, that same child will certainly understand it if you say, "The blue cup is taller than the red cup. The red cup is taller than the yellow cup. So, the blue cup is taller than the yellow cup." Some children will still need a blue, red, and yellow cup in front of them to move around before they can really grasp this, and others will be able to simply see it in their minds. And some will have already realized that *A* in our first example is represented by the blue cup.

Second, upper-elementary students can think about a problem from another's perspective. The toddler who once covered his own eyes to hide from you now realizes that *his* vision (in this case, literally) doesn't determine *yours*. As the child matures, he is able to see things from other perspectives. For instance, imagine showing a four-year-old these pictures shown below.

In the first frame, Jill places her pencil on her desk. In the next frame, we see Jill leave the room, and then Jack takes her pencil and places it on the bookshelf. In that final frame, Jill returns to the room to retrieve her pencil. But unbeknownst to her, jokester Jack has moved it.

If you ask the four-year-old where Jill will look for her pencil, the child is likely to say that Jill will look for it on the *bookshelf*, because that's where it now is. The four-year-old is not likely to realize that although he—as the viewer—saw the pencil moved, Jill (who was out for recess) did not.

Girl places pencil on her desk.

Boy moves her pencil to bookshelf.

Girl returns. Where will she look for her pencil?

But if you show this child the same series of drawings when he is in the third grade, he is very likely to tell you that Jill will look for the pencil on her *desk* where she left it. The third grader will realize that Jill did not see Jack move it and therefore has no reason to look elsewhere.

These developments—the growing ability to reason and apply some rules of logic and the increasing ability to see things from another's perspective—enable us to offer a slightly more sophisticated definition of nonfiction:

> Nonfiction books are about real people and real events. Some nonfiction might be about ideas or beliefs. A book about your favorite sports player or a book about a musician is nonfiction. So is a book about how the weather is changing. When you read nonfiction, you should ask yourself, "What does the author want me to understand?"

Middle School

By *around* age eleven, students develop the ability to think abstractly, apply rules of logic to real-life situations, and reflect on their thinking.

For example, if you give a toddler a small board and a prop to serve as a fulcrum so that she can improvise a balance scale, and you ask her to place various-sized weights on the board to balance the scale, she may build a tower with the weights and then show you that she can stand on one foot (after all, you said the word *balance).*

By second grade, she understands "balance" in a limited way. If she puts two weights on one side, she puts two weights on the other. Through trial and error she may choose weights that have the same heft, but she originally tries to create balance by having the same number of weights on each side. (This limited understanding of "balance" shows up when distributing cookies to eight-year-olds. Though you might recognize that a particular cookie is twice the size of two others, when you give one child the bigger cookie and another child the two smaller ones, the child who received the larger cookie feels slighted. *Balance,* for a while, literally means "the same.")

What a second grader won't realize is that the distance from the center of the fulcrum matters as much as the heft of each weight. A two-pound weight placed six inches from the fulcrum will be more-or-less balanced by a one-pound weight that is twelve inches from the fulcrum.

Notice that even the first sentence has shifted some. Students' ability to classify objects and apply some rules of logic means "nonfiction" can become an immediate descriptor of "books." The definition still needs an example. We can also shift the question that students should ask while reading from focusing on the reader to instead focusing on the author.

By around fifth grade, the child will begin to grasp that location matters (and she'll be more willing to agree that one big cookie is the same as two small ones—but she would still prefer to have the two). And she's still most likely to figure things out by a haphazard trial-and-error method.

Around middle school, she'll begin thinking in the abstract and will be able to apply some rules of logic. For instance, she will solve complex problems using if-then logic (rather than trial and error): "If I place this weight here, then this will happen." She can hypothesize, and she can visualize the outcomes and even make adjustments before actually placing weights.

This ability to hold several competing images in mind is helpful as we increasingly need the child to understand the claims the author is making and call to mind evidence that might counter—or support—those claims. She will need to be able to spot faults in logic, compare what this text says to what others have said, and compare what's being said to what she already understands about that topic. This is complex thinking, and our definition can honor the more complex cognitive work these students can now do:

> Nonfiction is the group of texts in which the author makes claims or assertions to readers about the real world, real people, real experiences, ideas, or beliefs.

> This more compact definition requires that the reader unpack a lot—which developmentally, she can do. She recognizes that texts can be classified. Finally, she can consider the text from the author's point of view and weigh that viewpoint against her own.

High School

By high school, what we see is a continually increasing sophistication—more than an actual shift—in students' thinking (although impulse control will continue to develop for several more years). For high school students our definition might be framed in slightly more sophisticated and abstract language:

> Nonfiction is that body of work in which the author purports to tell us about the real world, a real experience, a real person, an idea, or a belief.

> The critical shift is that now we're asking kids to recognize that the author *purports* to tell us. Of course, this means we'll have to define *purports*.

This is the definition toward which we have been gradually moving.

Notice that this definition presumes that students have been thinking about what nonfiction is over many years. This thinking began with a *description* that included examples and only later shifted to the more direct definition. This is an example of a spiraling curriculum.

So if you're a high school teacher (or middle school teacher) and your students seem to have latched onto the definition "nonfiction means not false, and thus true," then handing them this more sophisticated definition will confuse more than help. Those students who haven't developed an increasingly complex understanding of a concept over the years need to begin their thinking about that concept with descriptions, attributes, visuals—to honor the concrete thinking that precedes abstract understanding—before moving to a more formal definition.

"Developmentally Appropriate"

Our definition (or perhaps more accurately, our evolving series of definitions) should take us some distance from "Nonfiction means not fake." We felt it important to share how a definition changes over time for two reasons. First, we kept remembering the responses of those seventh graders. Just because a definition works for us does not mean it will work for the kids we teach.

Too often we think that we've made something developmentally appropriate by simply choosing easier vocabulary for younger children. That's the equivalent of speaking slower and louder to someone who doesn't speak your language.

Second, we believe one problem with education is that far too often we toss in the term "developmentally appropriate" without considering what it means about how students think and what, therefore, instruction should look like. Too often we think that we've made something developmentally appropriate by simply choosing easier vocabulary for younger children. That's the equivalent of speaking slower and louder to someone who doesn't speak your language. Slowing down does help that listener distinguish sounds better, but it doesn't help him grasp concepts that are outside his intellectual reach. Likewise, more accessible vocabulary might be necessary, but it won't be sufficient. In this case, we had to make sure that the definition didn't require students to think in ways that they simply—developmentally—could not.

We encourage you—with colleagues—to work together to consider what a developmentally appropriate definition of nonfiction might be for your students in your school. If inclined, use our thinking as a starting point.

The Common Core State Standards

If you are rushing to pull out your Common Core State Standards document (or whatever your state has now chosen to call them) to see how these definitions correlate with the anchor or benchmark standards, stop now. They don't.

We didn't try to correlate with standards. We correlated our definitions with what cognitive psychologists have shown us about how thinking develops, and with what we as teachers of many decades have learned about how kids make sense of the world. We trust you to make the adjustments needed, a trust that we find some educational policymakers lack.

TALKING WITH COLLEAGUES

▶ If you have not yet jotted down or thought about your own definition of *nonfiction*, do. Next, think about how your understanding of this term has been challenged or changed. Talk with others about how their thinking has changed.

▶ Is there a consensus in your school about the definition and characteristics of nonfiction? Does that definition change, become more sophisticated, from lower to higher grades? If not, what changes should be made?

▶ The idea of fiction (more accurately, *the fictitious*) in nonfiction is important. Spend some time examining short sections of the nonfiction your students read. Do you see some places where the author obviously or less obviously has inserted fictitious matter? Talk with colleagues about how you discuss those parts of the text with students.

Democratic Requirements

One teacher told us that he didn't have time to have kids read the text-book in his world geography class:

> "Most of them wouldn't read it; some of them can't read it. It would take too much time, and then I'm not sure what they would understand. They will learn it faster if I just tell them what they need to know."

We understand his comments and admit that at times we've reached the same conclusion about the kids before us. High-stakes tests and pacing guides that demand we move at a break-neck speed means we all understand the need to help students "learn it faster." But we can't confuse faster with better. No matter the inclination to simply tell kids what they need to know, we must give them many opportunities to struggle with the content and figure it out themselves. This was affirmed for us after reading a national study about the public's attitudes toward the Affordable Health Care Act (Gross et al. 2013). To understand our conviction, take a look at this brief excerpt from the executive summary of the study's findings.

> National surveys conducted in 2010 and 2012 suggest the following conclusions:
> - American understanding of what is and is not in the ACA [Affordable Care Act] has been far from perfect.
> - Older people and more educated people have understood the elements we asked about better than have younger and less educated people.
> - Between 2010 and 2012, public understanding of the bill did not change notably.
> - Most people have favored most of the elements of the ACA that we examined, but not everyone recognized that these elements were all in the plan.

> ▶ Most people opposed the elements we asked about that were not in the ACA, but some people thought these elements were in the plan.
>
> ▶ If the public had perfect understanding of the elements that we examined, the proportion of Americans who favor the bill might increase from the current level of 32% to 70%.
>
> Taken together, all this suggests that if education efforts were to correct public misunderstanding of the bill, public evaluations might increase considerably in favorability. (Gross et al. 2013)

So there it is: if the public correctly understood the bill, their attitude toward it might be more favorable. The public's understanding is critical because more times than not, legislators decide whether or not they will support a bill based on public opinion (Gross et al. 2013; Anand and Krosnick 2003; Krosnick 1988). Too often, we all presume that public opinion is formed from knowledge that is accurate and complete. But what happens when public opinion is formed on omissions, distortions, half-truths, or blatant misinformation? In this case, we see that the public was so uneducated or *mis*-educated that some people did not know that elements they would have found favorable were actually *in* the bill; nor did they realize that elements they found unfavorable were *not* included, as they had been informed.

Where did the majority of the public go to get information about this critical bill? Mainstream news sources such as ABC, NBC, CBS, and CNN as well as Fox News, MSNCB, radio news, and Internet news were the sources for information.

Do you see what's missing? No one *read* the bill (including the two of us and, we fear, members of Congress). We—too many of us—turned over our understanding of this critical piece of legislation to news commentators (and we have no knowledge of whether or not they read the bill). Furthermore, in all likelihood, we each listened to the commentator whose personal political views matched ours, and we let those folks tell us what was in the bill, or wasn't in the bill, and what we should think about it. We let their commentary become our knowledge, form our opinions, direct our thinking. *Public* opinion was, in actuality, the opinion of a very few that was adopted and then parroted by many. We let others tell us what *they* wanted us to know. We fear this is often the case.

And That's Why We Can't Just Tell Kids What They Need to Know

The major problem with simply telling kids what they need to know is that for the rest of their lives, there will be a great many people happy and eager to do precisely that. There's no doubt that this would be a faster, more efficient way of getting content to them. But in the long run, although this very direct type of instruction might help raise test scores, it won't help raise students who are independent thinkers.

> The major problem with simply telling kids what they need to know is that for the rest of their lives, there will be a great many people happy and eager to do precisely that.

Once they leave school, our students' days are going to be filled with people who want to tell them what they need to know, how to think, and what to do. If your students wanted to, they could walk off the stage at graduation and never bother to think again. The vacuum in their brains would be enthusiastically filled by a great many people—the unscrupulous politicians, advertisers, salespeople, and religious leaders—who see the easily led as a source of profit.

And so, students need to learn to do something more than take notes on our explanations and our lectures. That note-taking is a useful skill, but what it gives the student is the ability to capture *someone else's* ideas and to make a record of what *someone else* has thought. Far more important than the ability to capture the teacher's information and thoughts is the ability to acquire information on ones' own, to test ideas against one another, and to decide for one's self what notions have merit and which should be rejected or abandoned.

> While we've had a hunch that most teachers use lecture and explanation as a way to deliver content, our survey—reported in a following section—supports that. Be sure to take a look at Figure 11 on page 36.

When we use lecture and explanation as our primary way of sharing information in the classroom, we imply that someone else knows, and all students have to do is listen. This disenfranchises them and leaves them vulnerable. They will have had little practice in sorting through information and ideas on their own and coming to judgments about them. That leaves them capable of doing little more than following someone else, and if they have not been taught to evaluate what is presented to them as knowledge, not been taught to respect evidence and logic, then they won't even be qualified for the task of choosing whom to follow.

If in school our students are not given the opportunity to develop the stamina needed to struggle successfully through difficult texts with complex ideas, then when confronted with those difficult texts in their adult lives, they will again look up, say "I don't get it," and wait for someone else to tell them what they should know. And thus their education will have prepared them to be the ready-made victims of the cult leaders, political manipulators, commentators offering their views thinly disguised as "news," and anyone else ready and eager to take advantage of their vulnerability.

Look ahead to Figures 9 and 10 on page 36 to see how much (or actually how little) reading of nonfiction students are doing in and out of class.

For their own protection, and for the protection of the society, of our democracy, our students need to learn *how to learn*. They need to learn to resist, intelligently, efforts to tell them what they need to know. They need to develop intellectual standards that open them up to new possibilities and challenging ideas and that give them the courage and resilience to change their minds when they see persuasive reasons to do so.

They need to develop intellectual standards that open them up to new possibilities and challenging ideas and that give them the courage and resilience to change their minds when they see persuasive reasons to do so.

TALKING WITH COLLEAGUES

▶ How much of your own reading is nonfiction? How much of what you read is about controversial topics or issues? How much do you trust what you read?

▶ Think of a recent national issue that captured your attention. Where did you go to find out information about that topic? What did you do to consider this topic from another perspective?

▶ As you read this section, did you identify any passages or ideas as surprising? Did any challenge your own thinking? If so, discuss those with colleagues. Did any passages confirm your own beliefs?

Research Findings

The survey, along with some demographic data on the respondents, is provided in the Appendix on page 259.

Curious about how nonfiction is used in schools, in 2013 we put an electronic survey in the field. About 1,600 teachers in grades 4–12 responded. This online survey was announced on Twitter, Facebook, email bulletins from the National Council of Teachers of English and the National Council of Literacy Education (which includes the science, math, and social studies professional organizations), and the Heinemann website.

Two limitations of this survey must be acknowledged. First, this survey reached those who had digital access, had Twitter or Facebook accounts that linked to Kylene's accounts, were members of the targeted professional organizations, or who looked at the Heinemann website on the days it was advertised. We realize that responses might change considerably if we had been able to reach teachers who did not fit that profile.

Second, we make no claims that the responses offer a representative, and therefore generalizable, sample. Instead, the responses are simply what over 1,600 teachers told us about how they use nonfiction in their classrooms. We encourage you to view these findings as a lens through which you might view yourself and your school.

With those limitations, why do we even bother to report the findings? First, we think responses from over 1,600 teachers are worth considering, especially when looking for patterns of responses. Second, we think this survey might form the basis for a second survey that reaches more teachers. With those parameters in mind, let's look at three trends that emerged from this study.

Trend One: Trade Book Reading Declines Across the Grades

We asked teachers to tell us what type of nonfiction they assign their students to read. Magazine articles? Trade books? Textbooks? Figure 5 reveals the responses of teachers in grades 4 and 5. Here we see a heavy reliance on trade books, with 38% of the fourth- and fifth-grade teachers choosing this as their primary source. When we move into grades 6 through 8 (see Figure 6) the use of trade books drops considerably, with only 11% of the teachers marking this as their primary source of materials. Magazine articles, though, climb to 27%, and textbooks are up to 22%.

> Trade books are those books you might buy in a book store or find in a library.

At the high school level (Figure 7), we saw trade book reading dwindle even further, with teachers turning first to materials from the web (25%), then to articles from magazines (23%), and then from primary source documents (17%). If we eliminated English teachers from respondents, we saw that textbooks were used most often (see Figure 8).

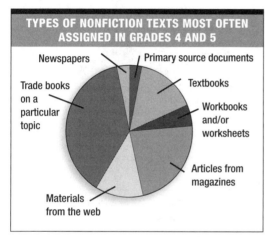

Figure 5 Teachers in grades 4 and 5 use trade books more than any other source of nonfiction.

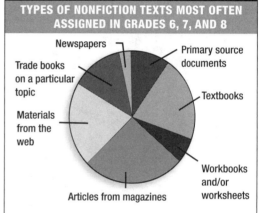

Figure 6 In middle school we see trade book use decline as article, web-based materials, and textbook use increases.

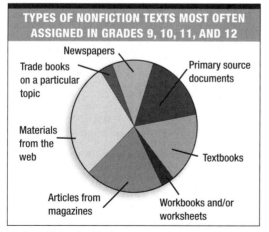

Figure 7 High school students rarely read trade books as a source for learning new information.

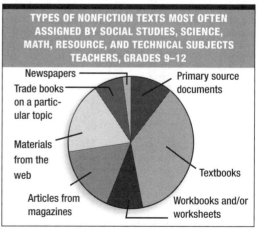

Figure 8 Textbooks are the number one source of nonfiction for social studies, math, and science teachers.

Trend Two: Nonfiction Reading Is Minimal

Teachers reported that they actually don't assign much nonfiction for students to read. Roughly 57% of all the teachers reported that they spend thirty minutes or less having their students read nonfiction *in class* (see Figure 9), and 85% reported that they ask their students to read fewer than ten pages of nonfiction a week *outside of class*. About half of those teachers said they assign no nonfiction at all to be read outside of class (see Figure 10).

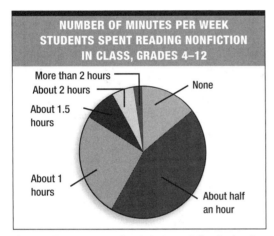

Figure 9 Teachers don't give students much time in class to read nonfiction.

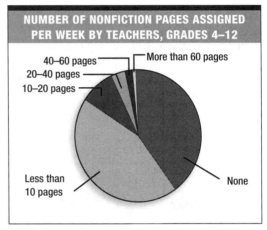

Figure 10 And this shows that they aren't expected to read much nonfiction at home, either.

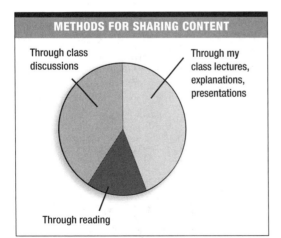

Figure 11 Perhaps one problem students have on state assessments is that those assessments expect that students learn via reading, and our classroom instruction does not.

Removing the English language arts and reading teachers from the group did not change the numbers significantly. Of the teachers in the other disciplines, disciplines where we would have thought nonfiction reading would be significant, 84% still reported that they assign only ten pages or fewer per week, and again, about half of those assign none.

If we accept the commonsense idea that practice is important in developing any skill, then it is reasonable to suggest that these students are not getting enough practice with nonfiction. This finding was corroborated when we asked teachers how they share content with students. A look at Figure 11 shows that only 17% said students learn content by reading it, while 43% said that students learn material through class lectures, and 40% said through class discussion.

Trend Three: Our Lower-Performing Students Are Taught Lower-Level Skills

When we asked teachers what reading skills they taught their struggling readers, they said they spend most of the time on identifying and paraphrasing the main idea (see Figure 12). On the other hand, when they are working with students perceived as or identified as more skilled readers, they reported spending most of their time teaching these students to draw logical inferences and think about the author's point of view (see Figure 13).

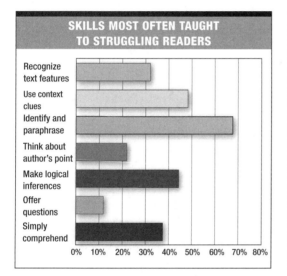

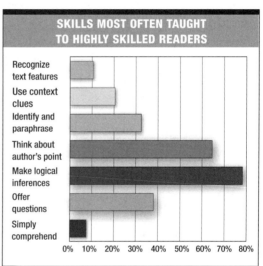

Figure 12 If students are seen as struggling readers, instruction is focused on finding and paraphrasing the main idea.

Figure 13 We wonder if one reason these students have higher skills is because they are taught higher skills.

In other words, the students who probably need the most practice at such higher-order thinking as inferential reasoning, assessing authorial intent, and evaluating the evidence for claims made, are getting the least instruction in these skills, skills that are critical for the responsible reading of nonfiction. We assume that there is a belief that lower-performing students need practice with more basic reading skills and that the higher-order thinking will just have to wait. But it is the skills involved in more sophisticated thinking that students will need most as

Primary grade teachers: we didn't include you in the survey because our work in your grades showed a heavy reliance on nonfiction. If you aren't sure this is true in your school, you migh reproduce the survey in the Appendix for the K–3 teachers in your building.

they confront more and more complex texts. If our assumption is accurate, we wonder if this mindset best serves our underachieving students or if it might, instead, result in a segregation by intellectual rigor that is potentially as harmful as segregation by color.

And So What?

The survey showed us some trends to consider. We saw trade books used more often in lower grades and less often in higher grades, especially in content areas. Not surprisingly, we saw textbooks used less frequently in lower grades and more frequently in higher grades. We saw that teachers use lecture and class discussions as the main way of sharing content and they spend little time during the week on in-class reading. Additionally, they assign little nonfiction reading to be done at home. Some of the research suggests that we might want to rethink our use of time.

TALKING WITH COLLEAGUES

▶ Do any of these results we've shared here reflect practices in your school? In your classroom? If so, are there any actions you and your colleagues might like to take? If not, what differences do you see in the circumstances in your school?

▶ We're particularly interested in the decline in the use of trade books over the school years. Is that a pattern that you think is repeated in your district? If so, would you identify that as a concern?

▶ The focus on lower-level skills for underachieving students is something we see in many schools. Do you agree with this practice? Is there research justifying this stance? Does the self-fulfilling prophecy inform this situation in any way?

▶ The reliance on lecture and class discussion is interesting. Are we doing students a disservice when we do not require more reading? Do we require vast amounts of reading from certain groups of students (AP, IB, honors) and less from others? Is it possible that our highest-achieving students are better at reading in large part because they practice reading more than our underachieving students?

Issue *5*

Invitations and Intrusions

FROM KYLENE: Early in our discussion of this book, we kept pushing each other to define the most critical difference between fiction and nonfiction. We discarded the idea that one was true and the other not because we read a great deal of nonfiction that we know is not based on facts or truths. Then, during the 2014 Boothbay Literacy Retreat, Bob made the following comment: "Fiction invites us into the writer's imagined world; nonfiction intrudes into ours and purports to tell us something about it."

Everyone in the room stopped taking notes and looked up, and I knew we (well, Bob) had said something that resonated with many. People broke into groups and began discussing this. During dinner that night, Lester Laminack wanted to know more about this idea. Over the next several months, Bob and I continued to discuss this vision of how fiction and nonfiction differ. Eventually, we agreed that his comment captured something we find critically important.

> Fiction invites us into the writer's imagined world; nonfiction intrudes into ours and purports to tell us something about it.

****

Perhaps fiction allows (at times) a more relaxed reading because it acknowledges that it's inviting us into an imaginary realm. It may ask us to regard as true, for the moment, what we know to be unreal. When we enter the novel we agree to accept many of the inventions. When the author presents to us a character, we accept him or her and pretend for the moment that the character is a living person. When the author shows us something happening, we accept that it happens. Some genres within fiction ask us to accept more than others. In a work of science fiction or fantasy, for example, we may be asked to believe—temporarily, of course—that one can travel through time or upon the back of a dragon. If we are to read that novel with enjoyment, we probably have to say to ourselves, in essence, "All right, while I'm in the pages of this book, I'll pretend that dragons do exist."

This momentary suspension of disbelief does not require us to leave our values and understandings behind, nor does it deny us the right to make our own judgments about the fictional text. Indeed, we may doubt whether the motivations and the behaviors depicted are believable, we may question the ethics of the characters, and we may condemn the morality of their choices. Or the reverse may be true. We may find that reflection upon the fictional text causes us to question some of our own understandings of human behavior, perhaps question our own ethics and some of our own choices. But if we don't accept, momentarily, some of the author's invention, we may as well not read the novel in the first place.

Writing that enters our world so directly needs to be read with a questioning stance, one that reminds us to be somewhat skeptical of that person intruding into our world.

Developing That Skeptical Eye

Nonfiction, on the other hand, enters our world and tells us something about it. It *must* enter our world if it is to be meaningful to us. We aren't invited into the author's invented world to mingle with her invented characters and witness her invented happenings; the nonfiction writer intrudes into our very real world, tells us about real people, describes real events. At least, we want to trust the writer to do so.

The nonfiction text may tell us about the newest tech tool, what caused World War II, how dinosaurs evolved, whom we should vote for in the next election, or how to fix dinner. No matter the content, it will give us information or make some argument about the world we inhabit. Writing that enters our world so directly needs to be read with a questioning stance, one that reminds us to be somewhat skeptical of that person intruding into our world.

We don't raise that question about the flying brooms in the Harry Potter novels, but texts about health care, climate change, Ebola, women's reproductive rights, cyber-bullying, testing mandates, marriage equality, or the lengthening of the school year deserve that consideration. Perhaps we have a better opportunity at holding on to that skeptic's eye if we remember we aren't guests in the author's world; he is a guest in ours.

That intrusion requires that we approach nonfiction with rigor that is perhaps not always as necessary in the reading of fiction. We explore this idea next.

TALKING WITH COLLEAGUES

▶ The two of us are avid readers of fiction and maintain that the truths that are examined in fiction have direct bearing upon lives. And yet we've just said that it is nonfiction that intrudes into our lives. Do you agree that nonfiction is the more intrusive of the genres? Perhaps non-fiction begins as more intrusive, but fiction, if it comes to resonate with us, enters and shapes our world as powerfully. What do you think?

▶ We struggled a long time with the word *intrude* because that word has a negative connotation, and we don't think of nonfiction in a nega-tive way (save for our income tax forms). Eventually (obviously), we decided to use the word. Would you have chosen this word? If not, what's the word that works best for you?

▶ For us, recognizing that writers of nonfiction intrude upon our real world reminds us to be attentive, careful, questioning—a bit of a skeptic. Talk with colleagues about this stance. Would you agree or disagree that there is some benefit in reading with a skeptic's eye?

Rigor and Relevance

If music artist Meghan Trainor (with her hit song "All About That Bass") were a teacher, we could easily imagine her singing, "It's all about the rigor." Since the release of the Common Core State Standards, education has indeed been all about the rigor, to the point that we now offer a workshop titled "It's Rigor: Not Rigor Mortis."

That title might lead you rightly to infer that we are frustrated with what we consider to be an overemphasis on the word *rigor*. Do we want to see rigor in classrooms? You bet. Do we think there are times when all of us must recognize that a particular lesson wasn't what anyone would deem rigorous? Of course. Should each lesson and every activity of each and every day be "rigorous"? We aren't sure what that would look like, but we think it would be overkill—and that's what results in rigor mortis.

We do agree that we have an obligation to make sure kids are doing meaningful work. We want them engaged, focused, and curious. We want to see them working independently some of the time and cooperatively at other times. We want to see them participating in student-led discussions. We want to see them asking questions in the classroom—questions about the content they've read and not merely about whether a particular topic will be on the test.

We want to hear students making connections from one topic to another and from one class to another. And we want them reading more and more complex texts as the year progresses. Actually, just reading *more* as the year progresses, whether the texts grow more complex or not, surely would increase their stamina. For many kids "more" is a critical step toward becoming a reader—but it's a missing step in many schools (Anderson et al. 1988; Beers 1996; Criscuola 1994; Fielding et al. 1986; Greaney 1980; Greany and Hegarty 1987; Hafner et al. 1986; Krashen 1993; Searls et al. 1985; Taylor et al. 1990; Watkins and Edwards 1992).

If you haven't seen the excellent derivative music video created by talented high school students at Bar Harbor High School as they sing "All About Those Books," take a look at www.youtube.com/watch?v=g2pu8nsUtCQ. Of course, after watching, you'll have that tune in your head for days.

If we could encourage you to read one report on the value of more reading for students, it would be Bernice Cullinan's research summary titled "Independent Reading and School Achievement" (2000). The report is available online at http://www.ala.org/aasl/sites/ala.org.aasl/files/content/aaslpubsand journals/slr/vol3/SLMR_IndependentReading_V3.pdf.

The Importance of Rigor in Nonfiction Reading

If rigor is important in our attention to fiction, it may be even more vital in our reading of nonfiction. We have to admit that we read much of the fiction in our lives somewhat casually, even lazily. When we pull out a book to read on the plane, we may not push ourselves very hard. We want to be entertained. The more energy we put into it, of course, the more we'll get from it, and if it's a book that resonates with us, we may find ourselves thinking very seriously—rigorously—about the moral and ethical issues it raises. We may find ourselves pausing, staring out at the tops of clouds passing by below, trying to analyze the implications of accepting the vision of human life the novelist is offering. But if we don't, if we just sit back and enjoy the telling of the tale, the only consequence is likely to be that we will have missed an opportunity for reflection. If we are that lazy with every work of fiction we read, our intellectual growth may be stunted, but the world will go on.

Our reading of nonfiction—*some* nonfiction—prepares us for participation in this society. What we know affects not only us; it potentially affects those around us.

On the other hand, if we read nonfiction with that same laziness, there may be serious consequences. Not all nonfiction, of course. If we read the recipe carelessly, our cornbread may not rise. If our reading of the repair manual is less than rigorous, the only consequence is that we'll have to take the lawnmower to the shop so that a more competent mechanic can undo whatever damage we have inflicted upon it (or sell us a new one). But if we read the political speech carelessly—without rigor—we may end up voting for someone who will do more harm than good to our community. If we read the reports on anthropogenic climate change inattentively, we may find ourselves supporting damaging environmental policies and decisions. If we read the reports on the Affordable Care Act superficially, we may end up condemning something we actually—if we knew better—would support. Our reading of nonfiction—*some* nonfiction—prepares us for participation in this society. What we know affects not only us; it potentially affects those around us. And so, some nonfiction demands a rigorous reading.

The Role of the Reader

The recent focus on rigor has encouraged an examination of the level of difficulty of the texts we ask kids to read. We should, we are told, push kids to read more complex texts. The logic seems to

> Rigor isn't achieved by giving the student a harder text; rigor resides in the energy and attention the reader brings to the text.

be that if we give kids harder material, we will have increased the rigor.

In actuality, all we may have done is increase the frustration. We'll have an easier time raising the rigor if we focus more on the reader's engagement with the text. As we argued in *Notice and Note: Strategies for Close Reading*, rigor resides in the transaction of the reader and the text. It is achieved not simply by selecting a challenging text, but rather by deepening the reader's engagement with that text. The more rigorous reading will be done by the reader who is committed to doing the best job he can to make sense of the text, to seeing and exploring its implications, and to understanding what he as a responsible reader should think and do as a result of reading the text. Rigor isn't achieved by giving the student a harder text; rigor resides in the energy and attention the reader brings to the text.

If the text is too tough, all that happens is that students struggle through the words or the syntax. They aren't struggling with the issues, concepts, or ideas. Handing students a text with a higher Lexile measure might raise the difficulty of the syntax or the vocabulary; it won't, though, automatically raise the rigor of the thinking. It might have the unintended consequence of actually lowering the rigor of the reading experience.

Text complexity deserves its own section. You can read more about this on pages 47–55.

If it is the energy and attention that the student brings to the text, then we must pay attention to developing relevance.

The Role of Relevance

Relevance is the foundation, the necessary element, for any rigorous reading. Reading a text a prescribed number of times when it's irrelevant, when one has no interest in it, when it doesn't really matter what it means, is just hard labor. No teen has ever needed to be admonished to reread a text message from a new love interest. Each emoticon is considered and reconsidered. Each abbreviation is seen from various perspectives (Is there any chance *LOL* could mean "lots of love" and not "laugh out loud?"). Every word is parsed, every punctuation mark examined. Those text messages are read rigorously because they are so relevant.

Relevance and Interest

We have often made the mistake of confusing relevance with interest and have therefore worked hard to make a lesson interesting. We've shown video clips or brought in photographs of a location (obviously this was pre–Google Earth—now we can virtually fly students to the polar ice caps). We've baked food (OK, Kylene has) that was representative of a particular time or place; we've asked students to "imagine living for months in a wagon about the size of these eight desks pushed together." We've tried hard to make topics *interesting*.

Getting kids' attention is about creating interest; keeping their attention is all about relevance.

And most of the time, most of the students have nodded appreciatively, watched our videos, eaten our hush puppies (a food used by escaping slaves to keep barking dogs quiet), and perhaps even commented, "Wow! That's interesting." Then, though, as soon as that moment has passed, the excitement is gone. We think that's because, we have finally realized, interest and relevance are different.

Interest is about something out there, out in the world. The video is interesting. The photographs are interesting. Interest is often fleeting, lasting about as long as the video clip we provided for kids to watch. *Relevance*, by contrast, is always personal. Relevance is about what matters to you. It starts with observing something in the world, but then it shifts to a thought or a feeling inside of *you*. Something that is relevant is inherently interesting; but something that is interesting isn't always relevant. In short, getting kids' attention is about creating interest; keeping their attention is all about relevance.

If we have a class that is reading about the causes of the Civil War, and the Civil War just doesn't matter to a particular student, she's unlikely to do more than fulfill the assignment and perhaps take some notes (if she's committed to getting a decent grade). She may just not care enough to speculate about the possibility that there might have been other causes besides those listed, or that the textbook's assessment of cause and effect might be oversimplified. She might not think hard enough about the text to begin wondering if there are any similarities between the circumstances that led to our Civil War and the conditions that are yielding so much unrest in other parts of the world today. If she were somehow enticed to wonder about such matters, the Civil War might grow more relevant for her, and she might attack that text with more energy. Even so, she may not feel compelled to ask if the disagreements and dissensions we are dealing with in the United States today could conceivably grow severe enough to catapult us into another civil war in this twenty-first century. If she contemplated that possibility, the Civil War might be more relevant and she might read about it with more rigor.

This student was in an American History class we visited. She wasn't impressed that we were there and certainly didn't seem awed that we were teaching her class. So we called it a success when we managed to move her from "IDK" responses to saying the words "I don't know."

Now, if this student doesn't read with rigor, if all she does is plod through our assignment, then she will have done her homework, she will have taken some notes, she'll be able to demonstrate that she read the text (at least at some minimal level), and she'll be able to pass a test at the recall level of understanding without much of a problem (maybe). But she will have reinforced a pattern of reading texts carelessly and superficially, and she will have missed the opportunity to exercise her intellectual powers. She will have had no practice in raising questions and speculating about the author's intentions, and, in sum, she will have, at best, missed an opportunity to improve her thinking and, at worst, reinforced habits that will disable her as a reader and a thinker.

Rigor is important, but we don't get to rigor solely by increasing text complexity. We get to rigor by increasing students' interactions with the texts. And as those interactions develop, then we have the opportunity—and responsibility—to place before our students increasingly more complex texts. So let's turn to that topic next.

> We've used two strategies, Possible Sentences (p. 185) and KWL 2.0 (p. 193) to help create relevance for students before they read a text.

TALKING WITH COLLEAGUES

▶ We make the claim that rigor isn't about the difficulty of the text; instead, it is about the energy and the attention that students bring to the text. Do you agree with this? If so, what examples would you offer that support this claim? If not, what examples would you offer to challenge our statement?

▶ We say that relevance is critical for getting to rigor. Do you and your colleagues agree or disagree with this statement? Some would argue that kids just have to learn some things despite their utter irrelevance; others would argue that there's relevance in anything worth learning, and all we have to do is figure out what it is. Where do you stand on that spectrum?

▶ We've suggested that rigor requires talk, but we are also painfully aware that much talk is rambling, unfocused, and undisciplined. What do you and your colleagues think about the role of conversation in raising the rigor of thought about nonfiction texts in the classroom? Talk with others about the characteristics of a rigorous conversation.

Complexity and Readability

In a workshop for about 200 novice teachers, we shared a strategy and modeled it with an article we liked. Teachers liked it, too, and several inquired about the Lexile level of the article. When we asked why, one spoke up and said that she couldn't use texts unless they were in a certain Lexile level band. Others said they would be reprimanded if they used texts below a student's Lexile level.

The Common Core State Standards have encouraged us to give students more challenging texts. But if we aren't careful, that may reinforce the commonly held misconception about rigor, which is that if we simply make the text harder we will make the student's reading more rigorous. That seems logical. The heavier the cart, the harder we will have to pull to move it. The more difficult the text, the harder we will have to work to comprehend it. To an extent this is true.

We want texts that kids can struggle *with*, rather than texts they must struggle *through*.

Text complexity is multidimensional. It involves vocabulary and syntax. And those factors are influenced by clarity, coherence, inferences the reader must make, ease in spotting author bias, the style of the writing, and most certainly the content discussed. And all that is affected by what the reader is expected to do with the text. We find, though, that most schools focus primarily on vocabulary and syntax— quantitative measures—so let's look first at that.

Quantitative Factors

We are loathe to see students' reading choices limited by a number, or a letter, or a color code. We want texts that kids can struggle *with*, rather than texts they must struggle *through*. Struggling with ideas is less likely to happen if kids are instead struggling through words they don't understand or struggling through syntax that is too complicated for them. Seen that way, it makes sense to look at a formula that gives us an idea about sentence length and word difficulty. With the Lexile formula, a higher number suggests that the sentences are longer and the word frequency is *lower*. A lower word frequency means the word isn't one readers will encounter often. *Verdant* has a lower frequency than *green*.

But reducing text complexity to a formula based on sentence length and word frequency isn't the solution. Such a limited view of "readability" misses the point that those formulas can't "gauge the clarity, coherence, organization, interest, literary quality, or subject matter adequacy of books" (Heibert et al. 2010, p. 65). Even information on the Lexile site confirms this: "It is important to note that the Lexile measure of a book refers to its text difficulty only. A Lexile measure does not address the content or quality of the book" (retrieved online from https://lexile.com/about-lexile/grade-equivalent/grade-equivalent-chart/).

The next time someone requires that you use a Lexile number to match a child to a book, encourage a conversation about the efficacy of this as a sole measure. Be quick to point out that word frequency and sentence length don't address many of the issues that make a text difficult or appropriate for a reader. Many times, difficulty—especially in nonfiction texts—is in the content. Consider this passage about Black soldiers fighting in the Civil War from a textbook titled *United States History: Beginnings to 1877* (Holt McDougal, 2012):

> As the war casualties climbed, the Union needed even more troops. African Americans were ready to volunteer. Not all white northerners were ready to accept them, but eventually they had to. . . . About 180,000 African Americans served with the Union army. They received $10 a month, while white soldiers got $13. They were usually led by white officers, some from abolitionist families. African Americans faced special horrors on the battlefield. Confederates often killed their black captives or sold them into slavery. In the 1864 election, Lincoln suggested rewarding African American soldiers by giving them the right to vote. (p. 531)

"High" word frequency means a word is used often; it would be what we would call a Tier I vocabulary word. "Low" frequency refers to a rare word, Tier II or III vocabulary. So *giving* in "giving them the right" is high frequency; *granting* would be a little lower; and *conceding*, even a lower-frequency word.

With a Lexile level of 810L, teachers who have been told to depend solely on the score to match kids to text would say this text belongs in fourth grade. We agree that the short and direct sentence structure and vocabulary put very few demands upon a reader; we don't agree that the content is appropriate for nine-year-olds. Very few fourth graders have the maturity to discuss the inequalities Black soldiers faced during the Civil War. Eighth graders, however, are ready to talk about why these particular troops made less money and were led by white officers. We want them to question why whites in the north didn't want them in the army. We want students to question why these soldiers would go to war for a country that did not grant them the opportunity to vote. If they could not vote, were they indeed emancipated? We want them to think about the racial tensions evident in our country today and wonder why some changes are so slow.

Text complexity is multidimensional. It involves vocabulary and syntax. And those factors are influenced by clarity, coherence, inferences the reader must make, ease in spotting author bias, the style of the writing, and most certainly the content discussed.

When districts tell us that they couldn't use this text because it would be "too easy" and they must "raise the rigor," we remind them that rigor is about relevance and not about a Lexile score.

Qualitative Factors

In *Notice and Note*, we shared a worksheet we created that helps us think through text complexity in fiction. We've revisited this worksheet and modified it for nonfiction texts (see Figure 14). As you look at this worksheet, pay special attention to the "Qualitative Dimensions." Qualitative issues we should consider when thinking about the complexity of a text include:

- ▶ Ideas presented
- ▶ Structure
- ▶ Language
- ▶ Prior knowledge required

For each of those areas on the worksheet, you'll see descriptors of signifiers of easier (less complex) texts on the far left side of the continuum and of demanding (more complex) texts on the far right. For instance, as you look down the left side of the worksheet, you'll see that easier texts offer readers a simple, direct, explicit idea and use an easily identifiable text structure. They use contemporary and familiar language and require no special knowledge, or new knowledge is explained.

Complex texts, by contrast (seen if you look down the far right side of the sheet), probably present subtle arguments with implied meanings; multiple text structures are used and are not readily apparent. They rely

Worksheet for Analysis of Text Complexity of a Nonfiction Text

Title of the text: _____

Quantitative Measures: Lexile (other) score _____ Grade level suggested by quantitative measures: _____

Qualitative Dimensions:

Ideas Presented			
Offers basic information. Simple, single meaning. Explicit and direct. Purpose or stance clear.	Mostly explicit, but moves to some implied meaning. Possibly two perspectives. Requires some inferential reasoning.	Probably requires weighing of multiple perspectives. Some analysis of bias and author's motivations. Some ambiguity.	Complex, subtle arguments, implied meanings. Author's intent may be concealed. Difficult ideas, evidence hard to assess; main idea must be inferred across many pages.

Easier ← ———————————————————————————→ More Demanding
Evidence:

Structure Used			
Easily identified text structure; photographs or illustrations help provide the meaning. Text features such as headings guide reading.	Primarily explicit; primarily one perspective; may vary from simple chronological order. Graphics and text features clarify points.	More complex, multiple perspectives may be presented; more deviation from chronology. Tables and figures support understanding.	Complex, multiple text structures and perspectives. In some texts, almost no graphics are used; in others overuse can interfere with reading.

Easier ← ———————————————————————————→ More Demanding
Evidence:

Language Used			
Explicit, literal, contemporary, familiar language. Vocabulary simple. Mostly Tier I words. Mostly simple sentence structure with one idea or fact presented. More similes than metaphors.	Mostly explicit. Tier II and III words are defined in context and used sparingly. Sentence structure more complex with perhaps more than one idea presented in a sentence.	Vocabulary not defined at point of use. Mostly Tier II and III words. Metaphor (rather than similes) used more. Multiple technical words may be used in one sentence.	Implied meanings, allusive. Language may hide speaker's biases or affiliations. Compound, complex sentences require much unpacking. In some texts, Tier III vocab is used extensively.

Easier ← ———————————————————————————→ More Demanding
Evidence:

Knowledge Required			
Requires no special knowledge or experience. Settings, problems familiar or easily envisioned.	Some references to events or other texts. Most of text deals with common or easily imagined experience.	More complex problems. Experiences may be less familiar to many. Cultural or historical references.	Explores complex ideas; refers to texts or ideas that may be beyond students' experiences. Expected prior knowledge is not explained in the text. May require specialized knowledge.

Easier ← ———————————————————————————→ More Demanding
Evidence:

Qualitative dimensions indicate text makes demands that are: Mostly easier . . . Mostly more demanding

Grade level suggested by qualitative assessment _____

Figure 14 The text complexity worksheet for nonfiction

Reader-Task Considerations

This is perhaps the most important element in judging the complexity of the text, and the most subtle. At issue is the suitability of a particular text for a particular reader. What follows are some questions to consider in making such a judgment. As you think about these questions with students in mind, make comments in the space provided.

Interest

▶ Is the student/class likely to be interested in the situation, theme, topic, issue, or subject matter?

Background and Ability

▶ Does the student/class have background knowledge or experience necessary to deal with the text?

▶ Is the student/class intellectually capable of dealing with the issues presented in the text?

▶ Does the student/class have vocabulary and inferential skills necessary for this text?

Attitudes and Maturity

▶ Is the student/class sufficiently mature and sophisticated to deal with the subject matter?

▶ Does the text raise issues that might embarrass readers or be in some other way problematic?

Potential for Stimulating Thought, Discussion, and Further Reading

▶ Is there potential in the reading of this text for good conversation among readers?

▶ Does this text raise issues or questions likely to inspire the student/class to further reading, research, and writing?

Comments Summarizing the Assessments on the Three Dimensions (quantitative, qualitative, and reader-task)

How much support will be needed with this text at grade _____ ?

Final Recommendation for Use and Placement of Text: _____

(Grade level? Early or late in the year? For independent reading, guided group instruction, full class?)

Figure 14 The text complexity worksheet for nonfiction, *continued*

upon implied meanings, allusions, and use complex vocabulary. Expected prior knowledge is assumed and not explained.

These qualitative demands cannot be measured with a Lexile score.

Reader and Task Considerations

The second page of the text complexity worksheet helps you contemplate how students will use the text in question. Do you expect them to read it with no support? Will it be read earlier in the unit or later? Are they using it to answer questions directly from the text, or is this a text that is a part of a text set, two or three texts students will read to synthesize across texts?

Addressing these issues helps you decide if this is a text students should be able to read on their own or with your support. Again, these critical issues can't be addressed by a formula.

If Rigor Is About What the Reader Does, Why Raise the Complexity of the Text?

An interesting study, *Reading Between the Lines* (ACT 2006), took a look at the types of questions that were missed on the reading portion of the college entrance exam called the ACT. This national test, a competitor of the SAT, has a top score of 36, with 21 points seen as a "benchmark" score. In other words, history has shown that seniors in high school who score below 21 have difficulty reading college-level texts; likewise, students who score above that benchmark have fewer difficulties and generally are not required to take a remedial reading class once in college.

The goal of the study was to determine why some students scored below the benchmark, while others score above it.

Findings

First, researchers looked at how students performed in answering two types of comprehension questions: literal and inferential. Students who scored below 21 and students who scored above 21 could answer *both* types of questions. The ability to make an inference was not the discriminating factor for scoring higher on the test. Next, they studied students' ability to answer questions that addressed particular reading skills: "main idea, supporting details, relationships (sequential, comparative, or cause and effect), meaning of words, and generalizations

> Texts earlier in a unit should be less complex than texts later in a unit. Texts earlier in the year should put fewer demands on readers than texts later in the year.

> You can access this study at act.org/research /policymakers/reports /reading.html.

and conclusions" (14). Again, they discovered that the type of question didn't account for why some kids scored above 21 and others scored below 21.

The differentiating feature, they discovered, was the *complexity* of the text, not the nature of the question. The ACT presents readers with passages that move from less demanding to more demanding; at each level of complexity the same *types* of questions are asked. It was the complexity of the text—not the type of skill or type of thinking—that differentiated students on this test. So all students could make an inference or use context to define unknown words if the text was straightforward enough. Students who scored below 21, however, were not able to apply those abilities to complex texts.

Questions and Implications

For us, these findings raise interesting questions. First, do our underachieving students get enough practice with complex texts? In most of the middle and high school remedial reading classes we visit, students spend time in skill-centered programs using texts that are at their instructional level. Thus, a ninth grader who reads at a fourth-grade level might spend his time in that class learning how to find the main idea in a passage written at the fourth-grade level. If he does well on the daily or weekly tests, then he is deemed ready to move to the next Lexile level. But he's likely to continue looking for the main idea, rather than move on to such higher-level operations as drawing inferences.

The remedial work in middle and high schools is too often focused on reading skills (and our survey research would suggest the basic skills); furthermore, the texts students use to practice those skills are simplistic. This might explain why we often hear frustration from teachers who share that kids are passing the work in the remedial reading class but still struggling in their regular classes. It's not that the kids forgot how to find the main idea; it's that the texts in their content classrooms are significantly more complex than those used in the remedial class. The implication is clear: unless kids practice what they are learning on more complex texts, they will have difficulty applying that knowledge to those texts.

Second, this report made us wonder if we are hurting our students more than we had realized by not requiring more reading. Do we place our struggling readers at an even bigger disadvantage when we limit the amount of reading they do? With the intense pressure to prepare

> So what is our position on giving students "instructional" level texts? We think this is important to do with three caveats. First, level cannot be determined solely by a Lexile. Second, instructional reading is not to be confused with choice reading. Third, students must be reading enough volume that you have many opportunities to increase complexity.

Students can't write a genre they've never read, and they can't read—with any fluency or ease—complexity they have never encountered.

students for high-stakes tests, we see a growing tendency to "fix" the reading problem by removing the burden of reading. Such a solution is likely to inadvertently create a downward spiral: kids who don't read are told what they need to know so they don't have a chance to practice reading, and so they don't read well. And we're back to just telling them what they need to know.

Eventually kids who aren't given a chance to read more complex texts—those texts with attributes closer to the descriptors on the far right side of Figure 14—leave school unprepared for the texts they will face in college and in the workforce. The landmark study "Why Johnny Can't Read" would perhaps have been more accurately titled "Why Johnny Can't Read Complex Texts." Students can't write a genre they've never read, and they can't read—with any fluency or ease—complexity they have never encountered.

We must require our students to read, not simply to listen to lecture and explanation, and as the year progresses, the texts they read must become more and more complex.

But Not Too Complex

But as we look for more complex texts, we must recognize that if we make the texts *too* hard, that will very likely make the reading less rigorous.

FROM BOB (because Kylene isn't lifting any barbells):

If you decided that I needed an exercise program and gave me a 10-pound barbell, I probably wouldn't be able to have a very rigorous workout with it. You might then give me a 100-pound barbell. That would probably be more suitable. But let us say that you decide I am in such bad shape that I need still more rigor in my exercise plan, and so you add a few plates and give me a 200-pound barbell. What is that going to do to the rigor of my workout?

It's going to reduce it to zero.

About all I could do with that 200-pound barbell would be to admire it. I could appreciate its sheer heft and weight and bulk, but I wouldn't be able to budge it from the floor. Making the work that much harder would have made the workout much less rigorous.

It's obvious that the same thing happens with texts. If we give an average seventh grader the equivalent of "See Spot run," he probably will not have a very rigorous experience. *The Outsiders* might be more appropriate and might offer him the opportunity for a rigorous experience reading, thinking, and analyzing. Giving him James Joyce's *Ulysses* would probably drop the rigor of his reading to somewhere below that evoked by "See Spot run." It would be roughly the equivalent of giving me that 200-pound barbell. Giving the student a 200-pound text when she can handle only 100 pounds is probably going to be counterproductive.

Rigor is more likely to be achieved by efforts to deepen the student's engagement with the text. If she is committed to making sense of it, if it matters to her, then she is more likely to read rigorously.

And many times that engagement is strengthened by the talk. Let's turn there next.

TALKING WITH COLLEAGUES

▶ Talk with others about how texts are selected in your school. We suspect that some of you have little input on some of the texts (such as a district-selected textbook); others might be left up to you. For the texts you choose, how do you determine the complexity of the text?

▶ With some others who teach the same content as you do, pull some texts about one topic and discuss the complexity you see in each. Use the text complexity worksheet shown in Figure 14 on pages 50 and 51.

▶ We suggest that if the text is too tough, the rigor might diminish. The struggle might increase, but the energy left to grapple with big ideas is less. Do you agree with this? When your students are faced with texts that are too tough, what do you do?

Classroom Conversations

Student-centered talk that's focused on creating understanding—rather than teacher-centered talk that checks for understanding—is an important best practice. The research is clear: when we shift from scenarios in which the teacher asks questions and students respond toward scenarios in which students ask questions and other students respond, we see increases in:

Before you read this section, take a moment to complete the questionnaire about classroom discussions found in the Appendix on page 256.

▸ On-task behavior

▸ Length of student responses

▸ The number of relevant responses volunteered by students

▸ The number of student-to-student interactions

▸ Student use of complete sentences

▸ Speculative thinking on the part of the students

▸ Relevant questions posed by students

▸ Higher performance on tests with lower-level questions and higher-level cognitive demands (Cotton 1988)

Nystrand and Gamoran (1991) sum it up nicely: talk to *create* understanding rather than *check* understanding raises student achievement, encourages higher-level thinking, and encourages teachers to raise their own expectations of what students can achieve. Figure 15 on page 59 offers our comparison of these two types of talk.

Talk to create understanding encourages students to develop an argument, offer their logic, listen to others, share their thinking, and when appropriate, change their minds. Cooperative more than combative, exploratory more than definitive, tentative more than assertive: this is

Let's Talk About It

A Survey of How Talk Is Used in Your Classroom

First, in this space, write your definition of "classroom discussion."

Second, complete the survey below.

STATEMENT	STRONGLY AGREE	AGREE	NEUTRAL	DISAGREE	STRONGLY DISAGREE
Practices and Dispositions					
Students who struggle with content benefit from first answering questions that reveal their understanding of basic information before trying to consider higher-level questions.					
Students seem to listen to one another as they answer questions I ask of the class.					
When discussing content, I generally know the answers to the questions I ask students.					
I plan the order of questions I will ask during a classroom discussion.					
My classroom discussions look a lot like great conversations: Students look at one another, listen intently, build on comments each other make, and reach aha's about the text through their discussions.					
In my classroom discussions I ask most of the questions, students respond to me, and I evaluate their responses.					
I mostly keep kids in a large group for discussions.					

continues

talk that challenges, clarifies, and changes thinking. With this talk, students are more likely to want to share their thinking, more likely to craft arguments that might persuade others, and more likely to listen respectfully to others. This is the type of talk that values students as co-constructors of their knowledge. It's conversation, not lecture, and it values the act of exploring a question more than answering it. In short, it is *dialogic* rather than *monologic*.

> **Cooperative more than combative, exploratory more than definitive, tentative more than assertive: this is talk that challenges, clarifies, and changes thinking.**

Monologic and Dialogic Talk and Questions

If we look at conversations and classroom discussions as "joint projects" (Clark 1996), then we are quick to realize that if one person is directing the flow, the pace, who speaks, the questions, the order of the questions, the content that is covered, and the evaluation of what is said, then there is very little that is "joint." In fact, those exchanges are more accurately called interrogations or *monologic talk*.

Monologic Talk

Monologic talk is the type of talk most often heard in classrooms and particularly classrooms of underachieving students (Nystrand et al. 2003; VanDeWeghe 2003). It's the talk of lecture, of explanations, of directions. It privileges one person's knowledge over others' knowledge as it sets one person as the dispenser and others as receivers.

Questions that emerge during monologic talk are almost always from the teacher and are rarely seen—by students—as authentic questions, those questions for which the student believes the teacher doesn't know the answer and is sincerely searching for an answer. So we ask, "What is the first step in cell division?" or "Why did Isabella and Ferdinand underwrite Columbus's explorations?" or "How do we figure out the area of the parallelogram?" Students recognize that we already know the answer (or the teacher's edition will supply it), and the motivation of our question isn't to clarify *our* confusion but to check *their* understanding. It's not a *real* question. Even when we insert the word *you* into the question, students still assume there's a right answer we're searching for: "Why do *you* think scientists developed a taxonomy of biological organisms?" Too often we have conditioned them to look for the answer they think we want.

Dialogic Talk

Dialogic talk, by contrast, is more representative of that *joint* project. There's a give and take, an exchange of ideas so that each person is for a moment "teaching" as she shares her ideas. Student-initiated questions are the strongest indicators of dialogic conversations. When a student feels free to raise his hand and say, "I don't get why Isabella and Ferdinand gave Columbus all the money. Why'd they do that?" you're hearing an authentic question, and the teacher's response sets the stage for what happens next. If the teacher provides an answer, she has remained the fount of all knowledge, and the student's role, reminiscent of Oliver Twist, is to stand and wait for whatever it is the teacher wants to dispense, asking, "Please sir, I want some more."

But if she returns the student's sincere question with, "Well, what do you think?" she's likely to get a shrug of the shoulders. After all, the student has just admitted he doesn't know. But research has shown that three small adjustments to the response can encourage a dialogic exchange: (1) validating the question, (2) using the student's name, and (3) pushing the conversation to analysis or speculation.

> **STUDENT:** I don't get why Isabella and Ferdinand gave Columbus all the money.

> **TEACHER:** That's an interesting observation, Marcus. I agree it seems odd. What do others think?

In this short exchange, the teacher has transformed the student's confusion into a validating experience: "that's an interesting observation" and "it seems odd." In using the student's name, she has refocused the class' attention toward the student and away from herself. Finally, she has encouraged speculation by asking what others think. If students needed

support to answer their classmate's question, she might have said, "Let's all look at paragraph 4. Talk with your partner about words in that paragraph that suggest to you that Ferdinand and Isabella were a little concerned about giving Columbus the money." Now, she has directed them to a specific paragraph for closer analysis, but she still doesn't provide the explanation. She expects students to reread and talk with partners to answer the question.

What If My Students Won't Ask the Question About Isabella and Ferdinand?

That's the problem. In too many classes we've taught, most questions that students ask are what we call procedural questions: When is this due? Is it for a grade? Do we have to write in complete sentences? In one class, we asked, "What questions do you have about this?" The students had read an article about the Black Plague—at a time when the United States had just experienced its first case of Ebola. We expected some connections to be made. The first response was silence. The second was silence with a shrug. Finally, someone asked, "Do we need to turn this [the photocopied article] back in?" When this happens, we turn to the one question that we've found gets at least a few kids

TALK TO CHECK FOR UNDERSTANDING	TALK TO CREATE UNDERSTANDING
Teacher directed (monologic)	Student directed (dialogic)
Generally does not encourage sustained on-task behavior	Encourages sustained on-task behavior
Encourages giving the answer the student thinks the teacher wants	Encourages questioning (by the student) what the student knows or doesn't know
Purpose of the questions is to see if students understand (remember) what teacher had taught/explained	Purpose of the questions is for students to work together to figure something out
These check-for-understanding questions are more the type of questions teachers ask underachieving students	These create-understanding questions are more often the type of questions teachers ask high-achieving students
Students report that these questions are "inauthentic" since the teacher already knows the answer. In other words, these aren't questions teachers ask because they seriously need help with the answer. They are asked simply to see if the students know what the teacher wants them to know.	Students report that these questions are "authentic" since the teacher does not know the answer. In other words, these are the questions that are asked when the person asking actually needs help figuring out an answer.
Answers are usually short (one word to short phrases) and directed back to the teacher	Answers are usually longer and are directed to other students
Answers are usually right or wrong	Answers are often tentative, speculative, and about deep thinking
Answers are evaluated by the teacher	Answers are evaluated by the student and other students
Talk is directed to the teacher so other students often don't listen	Talk is directed to other students so students are more likely to listen

Figure 15 When you listen to students as they are talking to create understanding, you'll hear students making predictions, summarizing, making connections, clarifying, and visualizing. And, you'll notice which ones return easily to the text to provide evidence for their answers.

talking: "What surprised you?" (For more on the power of this question see Part II.) This simple question pushes kids into a text—which is a good thing—while it simultaneously allows each student to have a personal response to the text.

We had the students return to the text and look back through it to mark the parts that surprised them. After a few minutes, we started again: "What surprised you about this article?" Hands did not fly into the air, but several (three) students did raise their hands slightly off their desks. We called on one: "I was surprised that doctors thought bad odors would drive out the disease. So they, like, put urine on things. That's gross." His comment on the use of urine as one of the many attempts to eradicate the disease started others talking. We had to keep reminding them to do something we learned from a teacher in Canada: to BIBB it (Bring It Back to the Book). But that simple reminder pushed students into the text repeatedly. Eventually, they did begin raising their own questions:

- ▶ When did they start using microscopes to see germs?

- ▶ I don't get how they thought Jews did this to kill Christians. Does this mean Jews didn't get the Black Plague?

- ▶ So, this makes it sound like if there hadn't been a bad food shortage making everyone crowd into cities, then the disease wouldn't have spread. So, staying in the country was a way to not get sick. Is that right?

Notice the length of the students' questions and the speculative nature of those questions. No one asked, "When did the Black Plague occur?" even though this was the first question that accompanied the teaching notes for this article. Eventually, someone did ask that question, but only when that information was pertinent to the discussion. When someone wondered, "Why didn't doctors just prescribe antibiotics?" another immediately asked, "Well, when did this happen?"

As you look at the questions they asked, most could not be answered directly from this text. These questions required that students turn to another text—something that almost always happens when we're engaged with a text. These kids had moved beyond the content of one single text. We find that when students are engaged with the content, they often do generate questions that send them to other texts.

And it all started with "What surprised you?"

Is There Ever a Time for Monologic Questions?

Absolutely. Monologic questions—those questions you ask when you expect the students to have already comprehended the material and you just want to confirm that assumption—are exactly what we ask for end-of-lesson reviews: Who sought funding from Isabella and Ferdinand? Why did Isabella and Ferdinand eventually agree to fund Columbus's voyage? When did Columbus set sail? These questions are perfect for the last minutes of class as review or for the beginning of the next day's class as a reminder.

> **FROM KYLENE:** After walking up to four boys in a high school biology class as they were discussing—between fits of laughter—the disadvantages of asexual reproduction, I found I was a friend of monologic teacher-directed questions for a long time.

Shifting to Talk That Creates Understanding

This kind of talk in a classroom is time-consuming, noisy, and at times a bit scary, as we hand over learning to students. And it might seem impossible to achieve with all the pacing guides, state standards, district guidelines, and high-stakes tests that must be addressed. Do we really have time to let students create meaning? Wouldn't it be more efficient to simply tell them what they need to know?

Certainly it would be. But telling students what they need to know is a bit like eating dinner *for* a toddler. It would be more efficient and much neater if toddlers would let us eat their dinner for them. The problem is, that wouldn't be too nutritious for the child (well, not nutritious at all). Messy and slow as it is, if the toddler is to grow, even to survive, we have to let him eat. Likewise, the nutritional value of the educational experience is diminished if we do all the thinking and simply tell kids what they need to know.

In the Classroom Close-Up on pages 64–65 we illustrate this type of talk in a classroom. Another example is found by following this QR code. As you consider both, use the "Rigor and Talk" checklist (see Figure 16). We know it's ridiculous to reduce rigor to a checklist. But we did it—twice—once in *Notice and Note* and now here. This checklist is slightly modified to focus on nonfiction. As you talk with others about the conversations offered in the Classroom Close-Up, be sure to consider the indicators of rigor provided in this checklist. Perhaps you will see some of the rigor we thought was evident.

http://hein.pub/readnf1

Rigor and Talk: Nonfiction

Students and Dispositions

☐ Students are curious, as shown by comments such as "Tell me more . . ." and "Show me how . . ." and "What if we did this. . . ."

☐ Students are reflective, as shown by comments such as "To me, this means . . ." and "As I understand what you're saying . . ." and "After thinking about this some more . . ." and "When I reconsider. . . ."

☐ Students tolerate ambiguity, letting multiple ideas or positions exist side by side while evidence is being presented or sorted.

☐ Students are patient, giving ideas and others a chance to grow.

☐ Students are tentative, meaning they *offer* rather than *assert*, are open-minded rather than narrow-minded, are more interested in questions that are to be explored than in questions that are to be answered.

☐ Students show a willingness to rethink ideas, sometimes changing their minds, as shown by comments such as, "After reading this, I now think. . ." and "This section caused me to rethink. . . ."

Students and Texts

☐ Students use texts to expand, deepen, clarify, challenge, and change their own knowledge.

☐ Students avoid the assumption that a nonfiction text is true and accurate.

☐ Students use evidence from one or more texts to back up or refute author's claims.

☐ Students use evidence from one or more texts to back up their claims.

☐ Students refer to and quote from texts when appropriate.

☐ Students make connections within and across texts.

☐ Students refer to what was learned in previously read texts.

Students and Ideas

☐ Students change their minds about ideas when warranted.

☐ Students hypothesize.

☐ Students are able to consider alternative positions and are willing to ask "What if?"

☐ Students identify topics that they need to know more about before reaching conclusions.

Students and Reasoning and Evidence

☐ Students provide evidence for their statements and opinions, and they respect and are willing to be persuaded by substantial evidence and reasoning a text or another reader presents.

☐ Students present information in some sort of logical order—causes and effects, sequential, lists of reasons or examples.

☐ Students avoid "just because" statements and similar expressions that indicate disregard for reason and evidence.

☐ Students recognize faulty assumptions and encourage each other to examine those assumptions.

☐ Students recognize persuasive techniques.

☐ Students question the author's motives/claims/biases/assumptions when appropriate to do so.

Students and Vocabulary

☐ Students use language that shows they understand the vocabulary specific to the topic under discussion.

☐ Students ask for clarification of words they do not understand.

Figure 16 As you listen to small group conversations, keep a copy of this with you. Notice what they do well and which areas need more practice.

On pages 65–65, we present a transcript of a discussion in a seventh-grade science class. These students are using talk to create understanding. We share it so you'll have a chance to "see" what this type of talk looks like in extended conversation. If you truly want to "see" such talk, use this code and watch eighth graders in a language arts class.

TALKING WITH COLLEAGUES

▶ Come together as a grade level, or department, or perhaps a school and share your responses on the "Let's Talk About It" survey. Pay special attention to the three questions at the end.

▶ What makes a great conversation for you and your colleagues? Do those same characteristics show up in your classroom?

▶ Do students in your classroom approach the discussions you encourage with the thought that this conversation will help them learn more, or do they approach it with the thought that this is the time for them to show what they have already learned (or hide what they have not learned)?

Talk to Create Understanding

It was the first day of school in a large, urban middle school. The students filed in to their seventh-grade science class and waited for the teacher to take roll, distribute textbooks, and do other typical first-day housekeeping details. No one seemed excited to be in this classroom because everyone knew this was the science class you took if you were struggling in school. This was basic science.

The teacher skipped right over the class rules and launched directly into a lesson. She distributed a short article about simple machines and asked students to read it. It was very short (one page), and since this was the first day of the new school year, most students were willing to comply. When they finished, she told students to push their desks (which had been in rows) into small groups of three or four and discuss one question: "Which simple machine is most important for us to keep, because I've decided that we're going to get rid of all the rest."

The seventh-grade students moved desks (which took far longer than reading the article) and then began talking. Here's an account of what one group of four students said:

STUDENT 1: Where's the part about which simple machine is most important?

STUDENT 2: I didn't see anything about that.

STUDENT 3: I think we're supposed to decide. [Silence for about twenty seconds as they all stared at the article.]

STUDENT 4: You have to have a wheel and axle because look, that's what makes cars and trains and bikes move. If you don't have that, then we wouldn't have cars.

STUDENT 2: So, is the axle the part . . . what is the axle?

STUDENT 3: It's like the stick that goes from one wheel to the other, you know, that connects the two wheels together, like on the front of the car.

STUDENT 2: I think it's the screw, you know, that you have to keep. Because if you don't have that, then whatever you make you can't keep together. [Pause]

STUDENT 1: Are you sure it isn't in here about which one is the most important to keep? [He keeps rereading the article.]

STUDENT 4: No, you could use nails. You know, instead of screws. [Pause]

STUDENT 2: Maybe we have to look at this part where it says, "A simple machine is a device for altering the direction or magnitude of force." I have no idea what that means. [Pause]

STUDENT 3: Like altering. Like altering your clothes. You know like if you alter your clothes you hem them, like fix them. Fixing the direction. [Pause] That doesn't make sense.

STUDENT 1: And I don't know what the magnitude thing is.

STUDENT 4: Isn't magnitude like, you know, like great, like magnificent?

STUDENT 3: Wait. It's not fixing, it's *altering*, like on that movie, what was the name, well, you know they were on the submarine and the captain said to alter the course. You know, change the course. So this is changing the direction.

STUDENT 3: So, it's like this is a . . . like how would a screw change the direction of something.

STUDENT 1: This is hard.

It was hard work. And it was noisy. But it was also exciting. As the teacher circulated, she noted that most groups could now label levers and pulleys as "simple machines," but they didn't understand the definition the article provided. But students liked trying to decide which one simple machine should be kept, so no groups just shrugged and gave up. Additionally, groups continued to return to the text to read aloud specific sentences to one another.

Toward the end of class, the teacher asked if any group had reached consensus. None had. "Why not?" the teacher asked. One boy said, "We need them all." Another replied, "It seems like you have to have these to have bigger machines." Another replied, "I think we could get rid of inclined planes and do OK." And then another said, "But inclined planes are like ramps. And if you had to carry something really heavy up some stairs, then that would be too hard. The inclined plane means you could push it and it would be easier." And with that, Student 3 from the above conversation spoke up:

STUDENT 3: Hey, that's what it means. It changes the magnitude of force. You know, like how much force you have to use. It means it makes it easier. That's it!

Other students still were confused by the phrase "changes the magnitude of force." Several kept looking at the teacher, asking her to "just tell us what it means." One student (so a small sample size, we realize) said, "Don't do that. I want to figure it out."

****

When class ended, one student said to another as they were leaving "Do you think we're going to have to think that hard every day? I thought this was going to be the easy science class."

If "easy" means copying what the teacher puts up on a PowerPoint, then yes, it would have been easier for the teacher to do the explaining. But it wouldn't have been as satisfying for the students—or at least that one student who had protested that he wanted to figure it out himself. Learning has a chance at being more meaningful when students do the hard, but ultimately satisfying, work of figuring something out. Which they will have to do once they leave school, unless they're going to turn the responsibility over to one of the major news channels.

Disciplinary Literacy

FROM BOB: Kylene went on to write about her journey in becoming a reading teacher in *When Kids Can't Read: What Teachers Can Do* (Beers 2002). She explains in that book that if she had wanted to become a reading teacher, she would have studied elementary education. By the end of that text, it's evident that she not only embraced the call to be a reading teacher but also enjoyed the journey.

If you are a secondary teacher, you have probably been told "we're all teachers of reading." That was news to us when we began hearing that admonition in the mid-1980s because we were both sure we had studied literature and composition. We had been licensed to teach English (or as it was later called, English/Language Arts) for grades 6–12. We had not studied the science of teaching reading, so when confronted with being told we were expected to be reading teachers, we politely said, "No."

Of course, that was an unacceptable answer, but we contend that the pronouncement that we should now "be reading teachers" was wrong. We would have been far more inclined to nod our heads "yes" if we had been told, "Teach your students how to read literature better." Now that would make sense to us. We knew about teaching literature. That would mean helping students notice unreliable narrators, look for implied theme, detect symbolism, understand recurring images. We could show students how to make inferences from Tough Questions or Words of the Wiser. We could teach them how to follow the development of a character through Aha Moments and Contrasts and Contradictions. We could even show them how to use the context to define unknown words. *That* we could do.

Over the past decade, we've seen that most middle and high school teachers echo our sentiments. Biology teachers might not see themselves as reading teachers, but they are quite agreeable to helping their students read biology texts with deeper understanding. History teachers feel the same. Those of us at the middle and secondary level who have studied a specific content and are prepared to teach that content recognize that teaching the mechanics of reading—decoding and fluency—requires preparation that wasn't covered in teaching students how to dissect a frog, understand rate and velocity, trace the economic development of a country, look at the proof of a theorem, or determine which of those two trains traveling in opposite directions will get to point X first.

So, let's make sure we all understand what this book is about, or first, isn't about. This book isn't about teaching you how to help students with decoding or fluency. We don't take up teaching important prefixes. We don't focus on reading with expression. We think those are important skills; in fact, we believe they are so critical that if kids in middle and high school struggle with word recognition or fluency, we want them to be in a special class with a teacher trained to help in those specific areas. We hold in highest regard those teachers who help our most disabled readers, and we suspect you do, too. In your class, we want you to help your students read your texts better.

And that leads us to something called disciplinary literacy.

Understanding Disciplinary Literacy

In *Content Matters* (2010) McConachie defines disciplinary literacy as "the use of reading, reasoning, investigating, speaking, and writing required to learn and form complex content knowledge appropriate to a particular *discipline*" (p. 15). Unlike content area literacy skills— which are literacy skills that can be applied across a variety of subjects—disciplinary literacy "emphasizes the unique tools that experts in a discipline use to engage in that discipline" (Shanahan and Shanahan 2012, p. 8). So, the summarizing strategy called Somebody Wanted But So (see page 201) might be called a "content reading strategy" or a "content area literacy strategy" because it can be used in many contents. Reading to understand the author's bias, however, is more a disciplinary skill that historians develop than (we are told) mathematicians develop. Skimming and scanning are content skills. Understanding how to read the specific symbols of calculus is a disciplinary skill.

We often teach vocabulary using content literacy skills. For instance, in teacher education courses, it's common to find that pre-service teachers are taught that when teaching vocabulary they should have students rate their knowledge of words (see Figure 17) or teach them to use semantic maps (see Figure 18). They are encouraged to have students develop mnemonics, draw pictures that represent the words, determine antonyms, and use them in sentences.

Janet Allen's vocabulary book titled *Words, Words, Words* (1999) is a classic and a must-read. She offers detailed information on rating word knowledge.

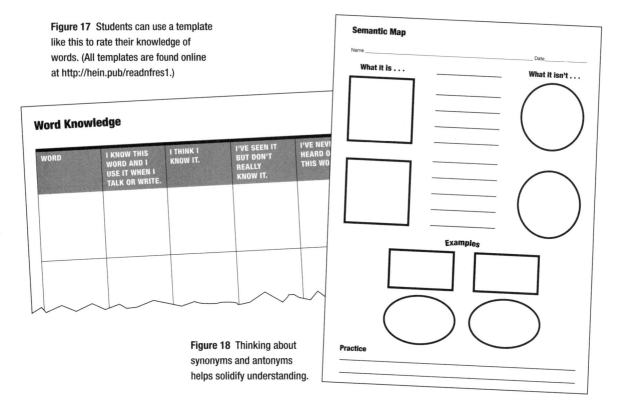

Figure 17 Students can use a template like this to rate their knowledge of words. (All templates are found online at http://hein.pub/readnfres1.)

Word Knowledge

WORD	I KNOW THIS WORD AND I USE IT WHEN I TALK OR WRITE.	I THINK I KNOW IT.	I'VE SEEN IT BUT DON'T REALLY KNOW IT.	I'VE NEVE HEARD O THIS WO

Semantic Map

Name _____ Date_____

What it is . . .

What it isn't . . .

Examples

Practice

Figure 18 Thinking about synonyms and antonyms helps solidify understanding.

Those activities are helpful in a generic way, but they don't help students in specific content. What's more helpful, when in high school biology, is a study of Greek and Latin roots and prefixes that will show students similarities across words. In literature class the teacher might tell the students to put the definition in their own words, but students need to realize that in geometry class, the teacher wants the definition to be precise and exact. A line isn't "something you draw that's straight" but is "a straight path that is endless in both directions." And in history class, students need to realize that specific terms are usually used to describe groups (*sects*, *agitators*) or events (the Dark Ages or the Gilded Age) (Shanahan and Shanahan 2012).

When in Rome

In other words, when in history class, we should read as a historian, and when in science class we should read as a scientist, and when in math class we should read as a mathematician. Let's examine what this looks like in two situations.

Writing a Summary

While we all teach students how to summarize a passage, Shanahan and Shanahan's impressive research (2012) with historians, mathematicians, and scientists reveals that when reading complex subject matter, summarizing looks different depending on the content. In fact, writing a summary of a chapter, say in high school chemistry, isn't as helpful, chemists would say, as using a "structured summary chart" in which students list what they have learned about substances, properties, and processes.

And mathematicians don't think writing a summary of the information presented in a chapter of a textbook is helpful. Rather than summarizing a chapter in a few sentences, they instead want students to hold on to the big concepts that were presented and the formulas or problems that illustrate those concepts.

Historians, by contrast, said a summary should focus on the *who, what, when, where,* and *how* of an event. Additionally, those elements should be considered when comparing one historical event to another. For example, when studying the Silk Road, Sand Road, and Sea Road, students should do more than summarize the purpose of each; they should think about who was involved in each and make comparisons among the three.

Thinking About the Author

In their research, Shanahan and Shanahan also examined how historians, scientists, and mathematicians view the author when reading a text about their content. Historians reported that they wouldn't read a history text without considering "Who is the author and what is his background?" Scientists, though, disagreed and said that a continual focus on the author after a quick check of the quality of the author ("Yep, three PhDs in organic chemistry from Amherst, Hopkins, and Duke, along with some post doc work at the University of Texas and The University of Houston seems pretty good.") would interfere with their reading. Their view is that the science should speak for itself. And mathematicians said they gave the author no notice at all. They were focused on the theorem and asking questions such as "What type of theorem is this?" "What methods can be used to solve this problem?" and "What question does this theorem answer?"

Social Studies Notes

Name _____   Topic _____

Date _____

WHAT DID THE TEXT SAY?	WHO IS DISCUSSED?	WHAT IS HAPPENING?	WHERE IS IT TAKING PLACE?	WHEN IS IT TAKING PLACE?	WHAT'S THE PROBLEM OR OUTCOME?

Our Goal

This book is not a disciplinary literacy book that will attempt to tell history teachers what's important about the reading of history or tell science teachers what's important about the reading of science. We are, understandably, comfortable offering comments about the teaching of literature. We think both content literacy skills and disciplinary literacy skills are needed, with a heavier focus on content literacy skills in our elementary and middle schools. Those disciplinary tools are ones we need as we become disciplinary experts—something more apt to happen in upper high school and certainly college.

The image that comes to mind is the youngster learning to throw a ball. Early on, the focus is on aim, follow-through, the force needed to get the ball from here to there. Later, if she's decided to take up softball, she'll learn how to hold that specific ball; she'll adjust force to match that ball's size; but she'll still have to worry about aim and follow-through. Even later, if she's become her team's pitcher, the instruction will become specific: here's how to throw a fastball and here's what you do differently to throw a changeup. After those two are mastered, she'll go on to learn the drop pitch, the curve ball, and eventually the rise ball. No one would ever suggest that what she learned as a six-year-old is sufficient for her work as the starting pitcher on her high school softball team. But it was necessary.

Likewise, we don't suggest that the strategies we offer in this book are sufficient for the exacting disciplinary study of specific contents. But they are necessary for connecting kids to texts, for helping them become the responsible reader that is needed no matter the content, for helping them learn to question the text and their responses to it.

▶ What is the most important skill or strategy you use when reading articles or texts specific to your content?

▶ Think back on your teacher-preparation courses. Do you think you had enough instruction in your discipline that you understand the specific skills needed for reading your content? Did you have a course in disciplinary literacy needed for your content?

▶ With others who teach the same content, discuss the disciplinary skills you want to develop in your students.

▶ We contend that students need first to develop some general skills that will help them read all nonfiction before they look at the discipline-specific skills. Do you agree?

Challenge and Change

Reading nonfiction, we've come to understand, is some of the most important reading we might do. If we are to read it well, we must develop the habits of mind that let us read with a skeptical eye and an open mind. We must be open to challenge and change.

Look for the Challenges

If you're interested in how we help students with difficult vocabulary, take a look at the signpost called Word Gaps, on pp. 168–179.

At times, the challenges our students face when reading nonfiction will be easily identified problems. Students may not understand how to read a graph. They may encounter difficult vocabulary. They may not have the patience to work through a longer or more complicated text.

But there are other challenges, ones that are more subtle and focus on the information or ideas presented in the text, that we think are more problematic. We don't want students to dismiss a text simply because they disagree with it, nor do we want them to accept a text simply because they do agree with it. If they accept faulty reasoning because the content matches their preconceived notions, they are missing an opportunity to learn. They need to learn to make judgments about what to accept and what to question and perhaps reject.

We find that the nonfiction signposts help students do just this. If you want to jump to those, go to page 112.

So we need to teach them to notice those moments when they grow dubious about what they are being offered, when they grow suspicious that something is not quite right, when the author seems perhaps to be overstating his case or making an unjustifiable claim, and again to pause and consider. Those moments may indicate that they are learning something new, that they are being presented uncomfortable but valid information, or those moments may indicate that they are being offered insubstantial, perhaps fraudulent or inaccurate notions.

If democracy functions best when there is a free and open exchange of thoughts so that the best thinking may rise to the top, habits of mind that lead to insularity are a threat. So the moment when we find ourselves agreeing most enthusiastically may be the very moment when we most need to pause and consider the possibility that the author's convictions, sustained and strengthened by our own strong beliefs, may not have helped us investigate an issue but may instead have simply made our previously held ideas more rigid and intransigent. Teaching students to read with that skeptic's eye means considering both the author's biases and their own.

Be Open to Change

When ideas challenge us, we might need to change our preconceived notions. Change is, of course, most difficult when it affects strongly held beliefs or important social or political bonds. If a student belongs to a family with strong fundamentalist views, it might be difficult for him to deal with the scientific evidence for evolution. If one has worked his entire life in the oil and gas industry, it may be hard to cope with evidence regarding fossil fuel's effect upon the climate. Some cattleman dismiss flatly evidence that red meat may not be good for your health, and some in the dairy industry struggle with the evidence linking increased consumption of dairy milk to osteoporosis.

If democracy functions best when there is a free and open exchange of thoughts so that the best thinking may rise to the top, habits of mind that lead to insularity are a threat.

Closer to home, some teachers find it hard to give up the teaching of grammar in isolation to improve writing, even though research over the last sixty years has confirmed that such instruction does little or nothing to improve students' writing (see Braddock et al. 1963; Hillocks 1986; and particularly, Chin 2000 for a list of pertinent research studies). Principals read reports about the importance of choice when it comes to creating lifetime readers and make no changes. (See "Reading for Pleasure: A Research Overview" from the National Literacy Trust foundation [Clark and Rumbold 2006] for a thorough review of this topic.) As one principal responded, "That's all well and good, but we don't have the time or the money for that."

Studies have shown us the importance of fine arts in schools, and yet they are cut (see "10 Salient Studies on the Arts in Education"); pediatricians warn of the dangers of eliminating recess, and yet it is eliminated (see the American Academy of Pediatrics policy statement, "The Crucial Role of Recess in School"). We—the two of us—read the research on the benefits of exercise and wonder if buying a stair master (Kylene) or exercise bike (Bob) counts as "change."

Perhaps we must teach students that changing one's mind isn't bad. Politics labels people who change their minds "flip-floppers," suggesting that once a position is determined there is no good reason for reversing one's thinking. But of course there is. We learn. We learn more. We discover. And thus, unless our goal is to discount what we learn, we must be open to change.

We write more about this important question beginning on page 100.

When we first began asking students to notice if something in the text had caused them to change their thinking about the topic at hand, many of them just stared at us. One fifth grader commented, "I don't really think while reading. I just read it." We continued to ask students, "How has your thinking changed as a result of reading this text?" and slowly we began to hear some interesting answers. After reading an article about child labor issues and Apple, one student reported, "I'm going to have to think about whether or not I want to support Apple by buying their products." After reading about child labor along the Ivory Coast of Africa, one group of middle-schoolers in Georgia started a campaign to change people's minds about eating chocolate from companies dependent on child labor.

We turn to nonfiction when we have questions we need to answer and answers we need to question.

More importantly, these students all told us that thinking about change affected the way they read the articles. "It was like they [the articles] meant more to me because I was thinking about how they were going to change me," LaTonya, a seventh grader in New York City explained.

Beyond the Four Corners of the Text

But it will be hard to accept that nonfiction should challenge us and change us if we accept what the architect of the Common Core State Standards, David Coleman, has said. In the Publishers Criteria for the Common Core State Standards, Coleman and his colleague Pimentel (2012) assert that as students read, they should "focus on what lies within the four corners of the text" (p. 4). They suggest students have a better reading experience when they focus only on what they find on the page. Publishers of textbooks (and other materials for students) have been told to avoid asking students questions that do not require answers from the text (p. 6). We should, we infer, turn first to questions that can be answered solely from the text.

Let us be clear: we have little patience with a curriculum that diminishes the critical importance of intertextual links and all but omits personal connections. Such a curriculum denies the referential nature of words—words refer to something out there in the world—and denies a primary reason for reading nonfiction—to learn something about our world, our place in the world, our understanding of the world. Such a curriculum leaves out the most important person in the education process: the student. And while it might prepare a student to answer questions on a multiple-choice test, we fear it would ignore the very question that makes a text relevant to a reader: "Why does this matter to me?"

We are required to read beyond the four corners; we are required to let nonfiction intrude; we are required to wonder what it means on the page, in our lives, and in the world.

We want to move students beyond what's in the text. We want them thinking carefully about what's beyond the text. We think such reading makes the reading of nonfiction rigorous, relevant, and radical.

FROM KYLENE: In 2015 Bob tweeted (yes, we can identify his tweets by the year in which they appeared), "We turn to nonfiction when we have questions we need to answer and answers we need to question." If this is true, we are required to read beyond the four corners of the text; we are required to let nonfiction intrude; we are required to wonder what it means on the page, in our lives, and in the world.

TALKING WITH COLLEAGUES

▶ How do you and your colleagues encourage students to think about how a text has changed their understanding or view about a topic?

▶ Education can be criticized for embracing too many changes. Is this a concern in your school? Why is it that some ideas are quickly adopted while others are ignored?

▶ Thinking back over all you've read in this section, what challenged your thinking? What changes would you like to put into place as a result of your reading?

PART II

The Importance of Stance

Fiction invites us to take one stance. The novel invites us to explore the imagined world the writer has created for us. We enter it willingly, and if we don't enjoy it, we put the novel down, acknowledge we just don't like this author or this genre, and move on. If we do enjoy it, we stay there until the end, maybe so immersed in it that we might describe ourelves as "lost in the book." Nonfiction, on the other hand, should come with a cautionary note that reminds us that getting lost in the text might be dangerous. The reader needs to remember that a work of nonfiction will try to assert something about his world, and he needs to take those assertions with a grain of skepticism. They may be perfectly true, they may be somewhat slanted or biased, or they may be flat-out lies. The slightly skeptical stance implies three questions . . .

Creating the Questioning Stance

We began to experiment with asking students to read with these questions in mind:

- What surprised me?
- What did the author think I already knew?
- What changed, challenged, or confirmed what I already knew?

These questions were easy enough that kids could remember them and yet robust enough that they yielded the closer, more attentive reading we wanted. And before long, we began hearing kids say, "When I was looking at my skateboarding magazine, I was surprised that . . ." or "My brother, he has Down's syndrome, and so I was reading about it and I found this part where I didn't understand, and I just asked myself, 'Well, what did the author think I already knew?' and then I figured out what was the problem and I knew what to do next. It was cool."

Reading with these Big Questions (see Figure 20) in mind encourages a critical, attentive stance and develops habits of mind that—if we can instill them in our students—may help them deal more attentively and intelligently with the nonfiction texts they will encounter throughout

> **If nonfiction is going to come knocking on the door of our lives, then once it has intruded, something ought to happen. Something we know should be challenged, changed, or confirmed.**

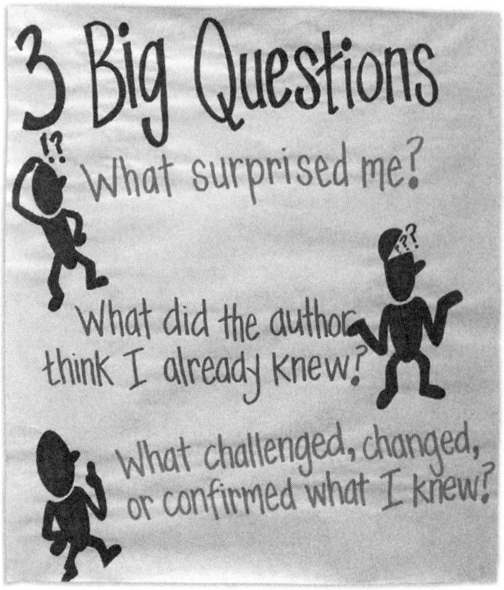

Figure 20 Thanks to Lindsey Jones, from the Desoto County Schools, Mississippi, for sharing the anchor charts she made for teaching the Big Questions. Here is the chart showing all three questions. Throughout this section, you'll see the charts used to teach each question.

their lives. These questions encourage a stance that reminds students that nonfiction is intruding into their lives and their job is to decide if that intrusion is welcome or not.

What Surprised Me?

First, we want students to adopt a stance that suggests they expect the text to offer *something* that's surprising. We're not fond of pop psychology, but we must admit there is something behind the statement, "When you change the way you look at things, the things you look at change" (Dwyer 2009). When students approach a text with a closed mindset, saying to themselves that "this will be boring" or "there's nothing here for me," they are more likely to finish the text with those same thoughts. But if, for a moment, they are willing to read looking for something surprising, then sometimes they will find it.

But if students learn to read searching for the new—the information they didn't know before that moment, the line of reasoning they hadn't thought of that reconfirms an idea they already held, or the evidence that requires them to reconsider and possibly reject a belief that they had, until this moment, strongly held—then they will be able to learn from the nonfiction they read. This stance is critical, and therefore "What surprised you?" is the first question we encourage students to ask as they read.

What Did the Author Think I Already Knew?

Second, we want students to read expecting that when they find themselves confused, *they* can solve the problem. Too often, at the first moment of confusion, kids look at us and declare, "I don't get it," and we—being the fixers we all are—rush to explain what it is they don't get. That solves the problem for that paragraph, but it doesn't help the student with the next confusion. Instead, we want to empower students to identify the confusion and then set about solving it.

So we tell students when they are confused to pinpoint the confusion and ask themselves, "What does the author think I already know?"

> We want to empower students to identify the confusion and then set about solving it.

When we ask students to figure out what the author thought they already knew, they can define the prior knowledge they need to acquire. We no longer have to guess and provide information before students read. Instead, we can let students identify what's missing, as they will have to do once they leave our classrooms and our schools. "What did the author think I already knew?" helps students clarify confusions.

What Challenged, Changed, or Confirmed What I Already Knew?

Third, we want students to expect that something in the text will challenge, change, or confirm what they already knew. If nonfiction is going to come knocking on the door to our lives, then once it has intruded, something ought to happen. Something we know should be challenged, changed, or confirmed.

> These three questions, if we can instill them in our students, may help them deal more intelligently with the nonfiction texts they will encounter throughout their lives.

Most often, the text won't completely confirm or drastically change your thinking; it will merely modify it somewhat, sharpening or refining your understanding. You may be already convinced that climate change is an important issue and, reading about it, discover that emissions from the burning of fossil fuels, though of tremendous importance, may not be as damaging as the methane gas produced in the raising of livestock for food. If so, you won't have abandoned your concern for the environment, but you will have refined and sharpened your understanding. Yours fears may have been confirmed, but the focus of those fears may have changed slightly. In that case, your understanding of the problem should be somewhat sharper than it had been.

These three questions, if we can instill them in our students, may help them deal more intelligently with the nonfiction texts they will encounter throughout their lives.

How Do These Big Questions Fit with the Signposts and Strategies?

If you're looking for an order in which to *teach* the questions, signposts, and strategies, we suggest that almost immediately you teach the Big Questions. Those questions don't take long to teach, and kids should start thinking about them now as they read nonfiction.

We know, though, that for some kids, these three questions won't be a powerful enough scaffold to push them into closer, more attentive reading. Those students need to learn the nonfiction signposts. When you begin reading about the signposts, you'll discover that as students recognize Extreme or Absolute Language or Numbers and Stats, for example, they'll be surprised or discover that something they knew is being challenged. Some kids only need to read with these questions in mind, but others will need the signposts to help them get to those questions (see Figure 21). Finally, others will need some of the strategies to help them clarify confusions as they are reading.

Now let's turn to a closer look at our first big question: What surprised you?

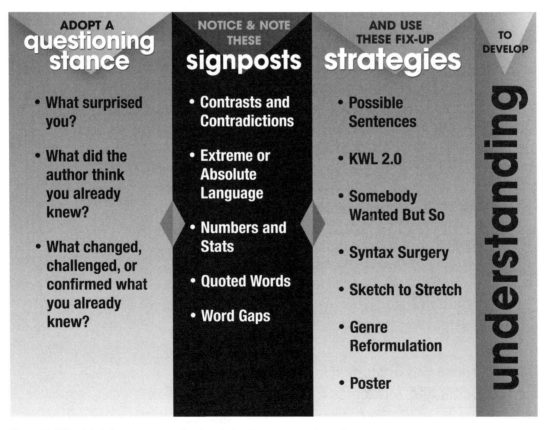

ADOPT A questioning stance

- What surprised you?
- What did the author think you already knew?
- What changed, challenged, or confirmed what you already knew?

NOTICE & NOTE THESE signposts

- Contrasts and Contradictions
- Extreme or Absolute Language
- Numbers and Stats
- Quoted Words
- Word Gaps

AND USE THESE FIX-UP strategies

- Possible Sentences
- KWL 2.0
- Somebody Wanted But So
- Syntax Surgery
- Sketch to Stretch
- Genre Reformulation
- Poster

TO DEVELOP understanding

Figure 21 This might help you conceptualize the relationship among questions, signposts, and strategies.

Question *1*

What Surprised Me?

Of our three questions, this is the one we teach first; furthermore, if we could teach students only one question to keep in mind as they read, this would be it. It takes little time to teach ("Kids, as you read, ask yourselves, 'What surprised me?' and mark those parts."), it works across grade levels, and it is appropriate for all types of nonfiction texts.

TEACHING TEXTS

We use "Vampires Prey on Panama" found on page 261 of the Appendix and online at http://hein.pub /readnfres2.

Understanding the Question

"What did you learn?" we asked a group of eighth graders after they finished reading an article we had given to them. We were hopeful that their comments would reveal insight into their thinking. Most shrugged and responded, "Nothing." Those students with more meta-cognitive awareness (but little patience for complete sentences) offered "IDK." As we visited other classes in other schools, we discovered that "nothing," "not much," and "IDK" were top contenders, though one ninth grader who was particularly frustrated with an article on biodiversity did have a question for the author: "Why did he write such a boring article?" We tried asking, "What did you find interesting?" That question yielded virtually the same responses.

And then, one day, without serious thought, we told one group of sixth-grade students in Orlando, Florida, "As you read this, keep looking for what surprises you."

"Like what?" one boy asked.

"We aren't sure," was our honest response. "We don't know what will surprise you as you read. So just be on the lookout for the things that make you say 'Really?' almost as if you can't believe what you just read."

This anchor chart, from Lindsey Jones, contains only the first question. She'll add the other two questions as she teaches them.

What Surprised Me? **81**

This article, "Hard at Work," by Ritu Upadhyay, was published by *Time for Kids* and is reproduced in the Appendix on page 261. It also appears online at http://hein.pub/readnfres2. You can read the conversation that occurred after students read with this question in mind on pages 89–90.

Students responded with more questions: "How many things do we have to mark?" "Like how big a surprise?" "What if it's not a surprise to *you*?" "So if it makes us say 'Really?' then it can be a surprise?" We had not had this much response from this group with any of the previous work we had done with them and therefore felt encouraged. We distributed the text, titled "Hard at Work." We spent no time introducing it other than to tell students to mark what surprised them.

Soon we saw students actually marking sentences or paragraphs, and then they wanted to explain why the passages they had marked were surprising to them. Students were talking about the text, talking about their understanding of the text, and addressing many of the points we would have made about the article had we been doing the talking.

****

As we've listened to many students discuss what has surprised them, we've found four categories of surprise:

1. New information ("I didn't know that!")

2. Suspicious information ("Really? Is that true?")

3. Clarifying information ("Oh! Now I get it!")

4. A different perspective ("I hadn't thought of it that way" or "How could anyone think that way?" or "This surprises me. Is there another way to see this?")

Teaching the Question

While we almost always simply ask students to identify what surprised them, it's sometimes helpful to ask them to read a particular text looking for a certain type of surprise.

We have often taught this question with only a few comments: "As you read this text, put an exclamation point in the margin of the sections that surprised you. Jot a few notes in the margin that explain why you were surprised." Figure 22 shows one student's mark-up of a text after this quick introduction. Many teachers who tried this question with their students reported that simply telling kids to keep this question in mind as they read was enough of a lesson. Since there is never enough time for all we want to do, if those instructions are enough for your students, then don't bother with giving them something more elaborate.

If, on the other hand, your students are very distanced from thinking about a text as they read, you'll want to present this question with more detail, as in the lesson that follows.

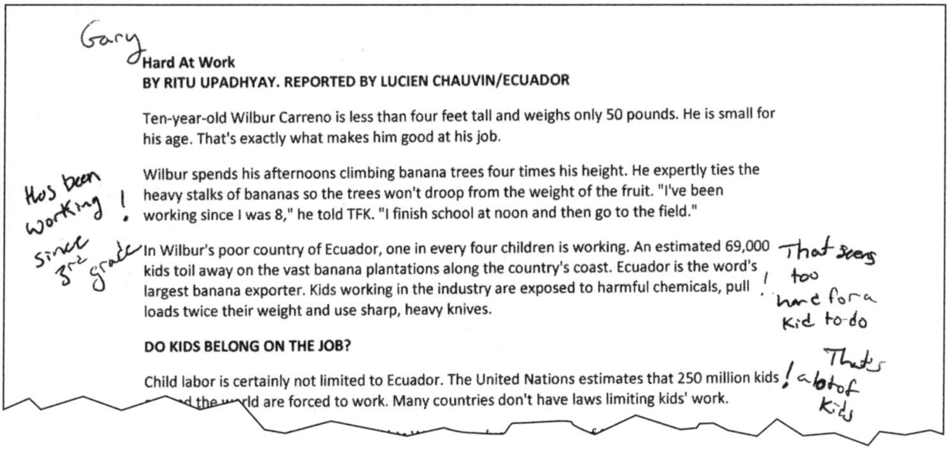

We Explain

We've entered a seventh-grade classroom in New York City. The twenty-one students in this classroom were mostly African American and Latino students, all from homes that struggle with finances, and all adore their language arts teacher. They were excited to have us in their classroom, though they were somewhat less impressed when they discovered that even though we write books we don't know J. K. Rowling. To teach this question, we used an article titled "Vampires Prey on Panama" by Chris Kraul, which we've found works well with students in fourth grade and up. Each student needs a copy. You can find the article on page 261 of the Appendix.

We began the lesson . . .

> We suspect that at some point you've talked with a friend and heard that friend say something that you just can't believe is true. The comment was so surprising that you find yourself saying "Really?" and you want to know more. [Lots of interruptions as students wanted to share the time a friend said something that did indeed make them say "Really!?"] Or you've been riding in a car and something catches your attention and makes you say to others, "Wow! Look at that!" [Now the interruption was about pointing out that in NYC one doesn't ride in cars too often. But these kids did know about busses and subways. Again, we tried to continue.] "You notice—from the subway or bus—surprises that are meaningful *to you*. And once you notice what you found to be surprising information, that's probably what you most want to discuss with others. And if you found nothing surprising, you'd probably consider it a dull conversation or a boring ride. In a similar way, an entire ball game with

Figure 22 You might be "surprised" by how your own students respond to this simple question.

We began the lesson by situating the question in a real-life context. We want students to recognize that they already look for things that surprise them—when talking with friends, when watching sports, when looking out the window while riding in a bus. Life is filled with surprises.

nothing surprising would probably leave you complaining about how dull it had been.

The same is true of the nonfiction we read. If we finish the text and nothing has caught our attention, nothing has made us say, "Really?" or "I didn't know that!" then we probably think what we've just read was dull. If, though, as we read we notice some fact that surprises us—maybe just a little or perhaps a great deal—what we're reading will be more meaningful.

So when you read nonfiction, you should read with that expectation for surprise. A stance that says, "I will be surprised" will help you see information as more than facts; you will see it as information that is new to you. Remember—if you want to find a surprise, you actually must look for one. If you decide you will be alert for those passages that make you say, "Really?" we suspect you will be pleased with what you discover.

We Model

It might seem that we didn't need to model looking for something that is surprising. But, we've discovered that our disengaged students often think that something surprising must be huge. So when we model something for kids, we try to show them that the surprising information is simply something we had not known or had not considered.

Begin by putting two or three sentences from a text up where all can see them.

“ For instance, take a look at these two sentences from a book titled *The Life and Times of the Honeybee*:

> Pilgrims brought the first honeybees to America. By the 1850s, honeybees had flown to California.

When I read those two sentences with "What surprised me?" in mind, I found I actually was surprised. I thought to myself: "Really? I don't think I've ever thought about whether or not honeybees had been in America before the Pilgrims landed. Does this mean that the Native Americans who were already here didn't have honey? How did the Pilgrims get the bees over here? Why weren't they already here? Did the Pilgrims intend to bring them, or did some bees just end up on board?'" Now I realize I'm actually interested in this.

A Florida teacher used our comments about "really" to create the Really worksheet. Sadly, we did not keep her name when she gave us this to use. If she is identified, we would love to give her credit. Read how a teacher used it on p. 109, and find it online at http:hein.pub/readnfres1.

These two sentences are from the children's picture book *The Life and Times of the Honeybee*, by Charles Micucci.

That second sentence also has some information that is surprising. "By the 1850s, honeybees had flown to California." Really?! Since the Pilgrims landed in Massachusetts, this means those honeybees flew thousands of miles to California. How does one bee fly all that distance?

Look at all these questions. They emerged because I let myself be surprised by something the author said.

Students Try

❝ Now let's have you try reading something with this question in mind. You have on your desk an article about vampire bats. As you read it, please mark those passages you find surprising. Perhaps you want to put an exclamation point beside those statements, or you might want to underline them. Then, think about what surprised you and jot that down in the margin. You may find you are writing questions, or you might write an explanation of what's surprising.

When you finish reading, take another look at the article to make sure you've marked at least three or four parts that surprised you. Once the person next to you is finished, turn and talk with that person. The two of you should share what you found surprising and discuss why those passages were surprising to you. [Notice that we've told students that we expect them to have spotted three or four surprising statements. We do that because our most disengaged readers will often say, "Nothing surprised me." By giving them a number, we are at least trying to get them to meet that minimum.]

Most students need about ten minutes to read and mark surprising passages for this article. As students read, you'll want to circulate, looking for those who aren't marking anything. If someone hasn't marked something in that first paragraph of this article, we generally interrupt the reading and redirect the student to that opening paragraph. Then we point out something *we* found surprising: that vampire bats attack cattle or that the cattleman tries to catch them with a big net. In other words, with your most resistant students you'll need to do some over-the-shoulder modeling.

Once students have had some time to share with one partner (five minutes is usually adequate), bring them back to the full group to discuss what they found surprising. You might decide to make a list of all their comments. Or you might simply let the conversation unfold.

> The question "What surprised me?" usually raises more questions. When students point out what surprised them, be sure to ask "Why is that?"

> We also, you'll notice, haven't spent time showing kids where Panama is, talking about any of the tough vocabulary they will encounter, or even showing them a picture of a vampire bat. We've come to realize that often our prereading conversations have taken away the surprises students ought to experience as they read the text.

One smart reader asked if the author of the article meant badminton racket instead of badminton net.

As you listen to what they marked as surprising, you'll discover that students often ask a question: "I marked that the cattleman catches bats with a badminton net. I've never heard of that. How does he do it?" As often as possible, let other students provide answers. This article doesn't describe a badminton net, so unless another student has seen one and can offer an opinion, we won't use valuable class time looking this up; instead, we'll explain what a badminton net looks like and move on.

Other times, the comments will lead to questions that can be answered in the text. When that happens, point students back to the text and let them work together to figure out the answer. That's what happened here:

STUDENT 1: I was surprised that a little bat could kill a big cow. [Many concurred.] But how? I don't get it.

Most agreed that it didn't make sense that a bat would be able to "suck a cow dry" as one student put it. They asked us how this could happen. We responded by telling students that they could figure it out by reading this text closely. We told them to look specifically for the paragraph that explained what caused the cattle to die. We purposefully stressed the word *caused* because that word appears in the text. Students began rereading, and after about three minutes, a conversation began:

STUDENT 2: Here it is—it says that "He lost ten calves to anemia caused by successive bloodlettings," so it tells you that anemia caused the bloodlettings.

[pause]

STUDENT 3: No, anemia doesn't cause the bloodlettings. Bats caused the bloodlettings.

[pause]

STUDENT 4: The anemia was caused by successive bloodlettings.

STUDENT 1: So, what's a bloodletting?

STUDENT 3: That's the, like, that's what the bats are doing when they suck the blood. Like letting it out I guess.

STUDENT 2: And successive, that's like successful. So maybe sometimes they suck blood but it's not successful? Like they don't get it all?

STUDENT 5: No, It's not that kind of successful. I think it's something else. Does anyone know this word?

This conversation—talk to create understanding—took some time, and it certainly would have been faster if we had simply told the kids how the nightly bat attacks ended up causing anemia. But, as we mentioned in Part I, faster isn't better. Better is students figuring it out on their own.

One student pulled out her smart phone and asked us if she could look it up on her phone. Being guests and not knowing the rules about phone usage, we said sure (deciding we could ask for forgiveness faster than we could ask for permission). She looked it up and announced, "No, it's not successful. It's like in a sequence. [pause] Like maybe it means like every night. So it's every night that the bats are sucking their blood."

Students Reflect

We conclude lessons by asking kids to reflect on how this question (or signpost or strategy) affected their thinking. That's because this isn't a lesson about vampire bats in Panama and the problems they offer cattlemen. Instead, it's a lesson to show students how reading with the question "What surprised me?" can shape their response to the text.

In this case, after we asked students to tell us how reading with this question in mind affected their thinking, we found that most students recognize that looking for surprising information does indeed change the way they read. Some note that it slows them down as they reflect on what's surprising; others mention that it makes the text more interesting. In this class, one student told us, "When I was thinking about what's surprising, the article was suddenly filled with things I had never thought about."

LaTonya responded "I didn't notice anything with the question. I mean, what was there to notice? I read it." When we pushed LaTonya to explain what she meant, she shrugged and said, "I don't know. I don't get what you mean by 'What did I notice?' The author, he was just saying what he wanted to be saying. I didn't see him saying any surprises."

We returned to that classroom in late October. Before we started a new lesson, we asked if students were still reading with that question in mind. Most nodded yes. One said, "We have to." We asked if this one question had changed their reading and if so, how. LaTonya's hand went up first:

> "So, when I started reading with 'What surprised me?' then I had to start thinking all the time. At first, I was like not liking that because it is easier to just let the teacher explain something. But then, I don't know, the more I started thinking about what surprises me, it's like now, almost everything I read is like 'Hey, this is surprising!' Now I can't hardly read without thinking about that question."

We thought LaTonya's honesty was refreshing. It is easier to let the teacher just point out what you need to know. But if we can shift that responsibility to students, it is ultimately more satisfying for them.

Listening to Student Talk

We want to share two classroom conversations that reveal the thinking that emerges when we step back and let students identify what's surprising and then talk about it.

Conversation #1

TEACHING TEXTS

The article, titled "Scientists Say Jupiter Muscled Its Way Through Solar System to Form Earth," was adapted by the staff of Newsela.com, and can be found at https://newsela.com/articles/jupiter-earth/id/8747/.

This conversation took place in a ninth-grade science class as the students were reading an article about the formation of the solar system.

STUDENT 1: I was surprised that it said Mars was formed from smaller pieces of another planet. I had never heard that.

STUDENT 2: Yeah. I didn't mark that, but yeah. I had never heard that either.

STUDENT 1: So, Mars wasn't here at first?

[Both students return to reading the article.]

STUDENT 1: Not from what this says. Look, Jupiter smashed into planets as it was moving around, and leftover pieces of those planets formed Mercury, Venus, Earth, and Mars.

Student 1 has identified a surprise that is new knowledge, and it seems to have left him a bit confused or skeptical—we aren't sure which. Even as the boys find some explanation of how Mars came about, Student 1 still seems unsure of this information, and now he's wondering who wrote the article. We like that he doesn't merely accept what he has read, nor does he just dismiss it.

STUDENT 2: Hey, look, that next sentence that says this is why those planets are so much smaller than the big ones. So, that makes sense.

STUDENT 1: But is this right? I mean how do they know this? Maybe some of them were just, you know, from the beginning of the Big Bang, smaller. Who wrote this?

Conversation #2

Now we're in a sixth-grade language arts class that is reading "Hard at Work." The students have finished the article and are talking with a partner about what surprised them.

STUDENT 1: I marked that 250 million kids around the world are forced to work. That shocked me.

STUDENT 2: Why?

STUDENT 1: You know, like why would they be forced to do that? And what does it mean they are forced? And what if they don't want to?

STUDENT 2: OK. I marked that banana workers earn $6 a day. That doesn't seem like much, so that kind of surprised me. You know, why they don't just quit and get a different job.

This code will direct you to a video of middleschoolers discussing what surprised them. http://hein.pub/readnf2

STUDENT 1: Yeah. I marked that, and that it said they had to work twelve hours a day. So, that's like, you know, not even a dollar an hour.

STUDENTS 2: Do you think these bananas they are picking are the ones we eat? I don't think I want to buy any more if these are ones these kids are forced to pick.

STUDENT 1: It doesn't say. [Pause, as both look at the text] Oh. Wait. Maybe here. This part here about Ecuador's big banana companies. See here [pointing to the text] it says they won't hire kids under fifteen.

STUDENT 2: Yeah, but look, see this part, that's only on big plantations. How are we supposed to know if the bananas in our stores are from big or little plantations?

Early on, Student 2 dismisses Student 1's surprise with a simple "OK." The questions that Student 1 raised were certainly worth discussing. But Student 2 wanted to move on to what he had marked, and that led to a critical question: Are these the bananas we eat? While we could have raised this question before kids began reading or when they finished, it is a far more relevant question when students raise it.

Questions You Might Have

1. *Is this a good question to ask all grades?*

   When we visited a first-grade classroom and asked the students to tell us what surprised them as we read aloud Gail Gibbons's *New Road* (1983), we never anticipated not getting past the first page. Every sentence surprised the children. Every detail in the illustrations surprised them. Our favorite, "Miss! Miss! I'm surprised that the road is black because here they are more grayer than black." We knew then we were in trouble. It's possible that this question isn't necessary for our youngest students because everything surprises them! We decided to read the book and at the end ask them what was *most* surprising.

2. *What if my students need more structure than just telling them to mark "What surprised you?"*

   We saw students who certainly needed more structure and sure appreciate the smart teacher in Orange County, Florida, who picked up on our telling kids, "Look for parts that make you say 'Really!' and mark them," and created the "Really?" worksheet for us. Figure 23 shows you how this looks when completed. In the first column, students mark what made them think to themselves, "Really?" In the second they explain why they were surprised. And in the final column, they talk about what this suggests to them.

Really?? Template

Name _____ Date _____ Period _____

Title of Book or Article _____ Chapter (if needed) _____

Directions: As you read, look for things that surprise you. When you find something, ask yourself these questions:
1. Why did this surprise me?
2. What does this suggest?

Strategy: Really???

SOMETHING I FOUND INTERESTING OR SURPRISING	PG. ##	WHY DOES THIS SURPRISE ME?	WHAT DOES THIS SUGGEST??

Figure 23 You can use a worksheet like this for kids who benefit from more structure.

3. *How does this question change across the school years?*

It's not a function of the question changing over the years; it's more about how the question might change as students use it more and more. In one school, in sixth grade, the students began the year thinking generally, "What surprised me?" and by the end of the year they were instead asking:

▶ "What's new?"

▶ "What's odd?"

▶ "What seems wrong?"

▶ "What makes me want to know more?"

These variations occurred as students became more attentive readers, and we thought they were great. We encourage you to start the year with "What surprised you?" and then recognize that as students use this question repeatedly they will reshape it.

4. *With all the focus on disciplinary literacy, should I be asking this generic question?*

We believe these three questions are a critical first step. We offer them knowing—expecting—that as students move deeper into your specific content, you'll offer them additional questions that help them read through the lens of your discipline.

For instance, history teachers tell us that they always want their students to ask "Who wrote this text?" because history is in the eyes of the beholder. And science teachers explain that they want students to ask of an article, "Is this based on the most recent information?" because what was "true" changes as the scientific process discovers more and corrects past errors. Mathematicians tell us they want students to read asking "Does the outcome seem logical?" or "Is this accurate?" But getting students to ask those discipline-specific questions will be easier if we all start kids with these three questions that travel across content, across grades, and across the many types of nonfiction we read.

What Did the Author Think I Already Knew?

We teach this question second, though once kids learn it, we find they often turn to it first. This question requires students to consider confusing parts in the text through a new lens. Rather than simply looking at something in a text and stating, "I don't get it," we now push kids to ask themselves, "What did the author think I already knew?" When they look at confusing passages with that question in mind, they almost always identify what it is they need to do to clear it up. We've found that as students talk about what the author thinks they already know, they begin to identify solutions. When that happens, we can say, "Well, if the author thinks you know the meaning of a term, and you don't, perhaps you need to look it up." Or "If the author thinks you know how to find the area of a circle and you don't, maybe you should turn back a page in your math text to find the formula."

Understanding the Question

Our struggling readers often lack knowledge in two areas: how reading works and how the content works. They don't know the signposts authors use to give us hints about what they are doing, and they often don't know much about the content they are reading (ancient Greece or electromagnetic waves). So when they become confused, they are reduced to "I don't get it."

We wanted to give students enough knowledge that when they were confused, they might be able to solve the problem on their own, or

TEACHING TEXTS

We use an article titled "4-year-old finds 94-million-year-old fossil of an armored dinosaur" found at https://newsela.com /articles/dinosaur-find /id/8643/.

You'll want an anchor chart with this question on it.

they at least could talk intelligently about that problem with another reader. Our first step was to get kids to identify the "it" in their comment "I don't get it." And that's when we realized that we needed them to think, for a moment, less about what they didn't know and more about what it seemed the author expected them to know. So we began "blaming the author" by asking them, "What did the author think you already knew?"

Two things happened, especially for our older struggling readers. First, the cause of the problem was now the author. "The *author* thought I already knew what *anti-coagulant* means" or "The *author* thinks I know how to find the area of circle." We watched our middle-schoolers and high school students relax a bit when they could identify the author as the source of the problem. Second, as students talked about what the author thought they already knew, we realized they were identifying solutions. When students identify solutions, they are becoming that independent reader we all want them to be. Early on, they may only identify problems, but soon you'll hear them offer solutions. And if you don't, you might ask "So, if the author thought you'd know this, what should you do?"

As we listened to many students identify what the author thought they already knew, we began to hear four types of problems:

What we didn't hear were problems that we thought were most troublesome—problems about author's intent or author's biases. This makes sense, because often authors go to great lengths to "hide" their intent or biases. We found that the Nonfiction Signposts were powerful in awakening students to the reflection demanded by texts, especially those that are persuasive in nature.

1. "The author thought I'd know what this word means." (Vocabulary)

2. "The author thought I could picture this." (Visualizing)

3. "The author thought I'd know something about this." (Prior knowledge)

4. "The author thought I'd get how this happens." (Sequencing or causal relationships)

Once students have identified what the author thought they already knew, we can show them what they need to do to clear up their confusion. This is a critical step toward creating independent readers. Now you're not telling students what they need to know; you're helping them recognize what they need to do on their own.

▶   If the problem is vocabulary, they might need to look up the word or phrase if the author doesn't define it in context.

▶   If the problem is visualizing, students might need to use a strategy called Sketch to Stretch (see page 221).

- ▶ If the problem is prior knowledge, at least in math and science the topic almost always will have been covered in a previous section of the book. Start by sending kids back to the appropriate section. Perhaps they'll need to visit another text to fill in some background knowledge.

- ▶ If the problem is sequencing or causal issues, they might need to focus on signal words that can help identify text structure. We have them try Syntax Surgery (see page 209) or Sketch to Stretch if those strategies seem useful with the passage, and we might need to review signal words with them (see page 279). Students may need to reread, looking for the signal words that help them think about sequencing or causal relations.

Teaching the Question

Introducing this question requires more instruction than "What surprised you?" so set aside about twenty to thirty minutes for the lesson. This lesson took place in a ninth-grade reading class that was designed for students who had scored a 1 or 2 (out of 4) on the reading portion of their state exam. The class was small, with only fourteen students. We chose an article from a Texas newspaper about a young boy who found a dinosaur fossil.

We began the lesson . . .

We Explain

" We bet that at some point you've heard something on a sports channel and thought to yourself, "What's he talking about?" For us, that happens when we watch the snowboarding events during winter sports. The commentator announces that the next snowboarder up is known for nailing the McTwist. We have no idea what that is. We realize that the commentators expect us to know something we don't—after all, we've turned to the channel that is talking about snowboarding.

The same thing can happen as we're reading. We can find ourselves confused because the author expects us to bring some knowledge to the text that we just don't have. We find that usually an author expects that we can understand his vocabulary, visualize what he's describing, apply prior knowledge, follow his reasoning.

We use this text with upper-elementary students or older students who have limited vocabulary and limited reading skills. https://newsela.com/articles/dinosaur-find/id/8643/.

When one of those things doesn't happen, we might say to our-selves "I don't get it." And when we realize we're confused, we then should ask, "What does the author think I already know?" [Show the anchor chart.] Trying to identify exactly what it is the author thinks we already know can help us figure out what to do next. Today you're going to read a text looking for places where the author thinks you know something that you don't. Then, we're going to discuss how that question changed your reading.

We Model

" Let's look at what happens when we use the question "What did the author think I already knew?" when we are confused. In a book about teaching American history, the author writes, "Americans who lived through the rise of fascism in Europe and militarism in Japan in the 1920s and 1930s wanted to know about the strengths of American democracy." If we don't know what fascism and militarism are, and say simply "I don't get it," that's not helpful. But, if I say, "I think the author thinks I know about fascism and militarism" then I know it's these two concepts that I need to understand in order to have this sentence make sense. I need to find out information on these topics.

Here's a slightly more complicated example. [Put the paragraph below on your whiteboard so all can see it.] This paragraph comes from a website that is describing something called the Dyson bladeless fan. The first time I read it, I was confused even though I understood all the words:

> The air flows through a channel in the pedestal up to the tube, which is hollow. The interior of the tube acts like a ramp. Air flows along the ramp, which curves around and ends in slits in the back of the fan. Then, the air flows along the surface of the inside of the tube and out toward the front of the fan.

Well, this time my confusion isn't about not understanding a specific word. In this case I know what all the words mean. Now when I ask myself, "What does the author think I already know?" I realize he thinks I can visualize what he's described. I can't! So what I need to try to do is create that visual image I'm lacking.

The most common confusion for kids comes from lacking the vocabulary the author uses. So they will most likely answer this second question with "He thinks I know this word and I don't." The second most common confusion, though, comes from the inability to visualize the author's description. We talk more about this on page 221, where we discuss Sketch to Stretch.

When I give that a try, this is what I end up with: I don't know if this is the way it actually looks, but now I at least have an idea about how it *might* work. I will keep on reading, and as I learn more, I can adjust my own drawing.

Students Try

" Now you give it a try. Let's look at this article about a young boy who found an important dinosaur fossil. As you read, when you notice yourself getting confused, circle the confusing part and ask yourself, "What does the author think I already know?" Jot your thoughts in the margin.

FROM BOB: My drawing, made as I reread the passage aloud to students.

Students will need about five to seven minutes to read and jot responses. Next, let them talk with one partner about what they marked and why they marked those passages. We set aside about five minutes for these paired discussions. Finally, pull students together for a large-group discussion.

An interesting exchange came from the following paragraph:

> Nodosaurs were kind of the armadillos of the dinosaur world—short, squat and covered in armored plates with a soft underbelly. The reptiles, which are not related to today's armadillos, were vegetarians and about the size of a small horse . . .

STUDENT 1: I marked *armadillo.* I think the author thinks I know what it is.

BOB: Did you see anything in the text that would help you?

STUDENT 1: No. [pause] Maybe this part here where it says short and squat?

BOB: Yes. Do you see that dash? Often when authors are going to define or describe a term, they put a dash between the term and the description. That dash means "Here's something that might help you." So, actually, maybe the author didn't expect you to know what an armadillo is.

STUDENT 2: Yeah, but he expected we would know what the dash means.

[Class laughs.]

STUDENT 3: So, in that same place, I circled *reptile*. I don't get why he called them reptiles. Is he saying this was a reptile? Aren't reptiles snakes?

KYLENE: Where do you think you need to look to decide if he's calling the Nodosaurus a reptile?

[Class starts looking at article.]

STUDENT 4: Hey, look, up here in this part [points to a previous paragraph] it says "reptile." We should look here.

These students, in a very short exchange, figured out where to look in the text to decide if the Nodosaurus was a reptile. Once they realized that a previous paragraph answered the question, they decided that they could create a guideline or a tip: "If the author uses a word that confuses you, look back in the text to see if he has used it before. Reread that part. That might help you understand the confusing part." This might seem an obvious tip to you, but it was an important aha moment for our less-skilled readers.

Students Reflect

" We've spent today's class focusing on how we can clear up confusion that might occur as we read. The first important step is to identify where the confusion is and then to ask ourselves, "What does the author think I already know.?" You might discover that it's a vocabulary problem—that the author is using a word or term that you don't know. If that's the case, you might need to look it up. Or you might discover that you can't visualize what she's describing. If that's the situation, you might need to try to draw what's happening in each sentence.

There will, of course, be other reasons you might be confused. But until you ask, "What did the author think I already knew?" it will be hard for you to decide how to fix your confusion. Now, take a moment and think about how asking this one question changed your reading of the article.

Our student who had asked the question about reptiles offered this reflection.

> Don't forget to teach basic punctuation signposts: dashes, italics, colons, parentheses. Math teachers need to focus on how these symbols have special functions in math problems.

"It sometimes is like the smart kids, they just know the answers. I think it's just that they know where to look. In this other part where it talks first about reptiles, I wasn't confused. But then here when he talks about them again, I didn't make the connection. Now I know to look back and see what he said there. Now it makes sense.

Listening to Student Talk

As you read these conversations, focus on how students take charge of fixing up confusion when they read with this question in mind.

Conversation #1

This exchange came from two students in a high school world history class who were reading *Outbreak: Plagues that Changed History*, by Bryn Barnard. The teacher gave students about twenty minutes to read a few pages about smallpox and then discuss with a partner the parts where the author thought they already knew something that they did not. Here we have two girls:

STUDENT 1: So I marked this sentence: "The epochal year in smallpox prevention, however, was 1796, when British doctor Edward Jenner proved that inoculation with the harmless *vaccina* (cowpox) prevented infection with smallpox" (p. 15).

STUDENT 2: Yeah, I circled *epochal* because I think the author thinks I know what it means.

STUDENT 1: I thought that too. [pause] Look, you can tell here he didn't think we would know what *vaccina* is because that's in italics, and right there it says the definition, cowpox.

STUDENT 2: Yeah, so he does think we know what *epochal* is. Maybe we don't need to know it, since he doesn't tell us.

STUDENT 1: Well, look, it says that the epochal year was 1796. So, I think it's important because, because, well, look in 1796, that's when the Jenner guy did something with cowpox that prevented infection.

STUDENTS 2: So, it's like a good year or important year. Like "the important year in smallpox prevention was 1796."

This code will take you to a conversation directed by this Big Question.

http://hein.pub/readnf3

This conversation springs from them marking what the author thought they already knew. Later, one told us "I would normally just say that this is hard. Now I know what to do." And they did. They used context clues to come up with synonyms.

Conversation #2

Now we are in a sixth-grade classroom and students are discussing a societal issue. These students have read the vampire bat article that we have previously mentioned. In addition to marking what surprised them, they have also now marked what the author thought they already knew. This conversation is from a group of three students:

STUDENT 1: I marked that I was surprised that vampire bats were real. I didn't think they were. I thought they were like in movies only.

STUDENT 2: I said I was surprised that anyone would think bats are cuddly. I think they are gross.

STUDENT 3: I marked *anti-coagulant*. I think the author thinks I know what that word means. I don't.

STUDENT 1: Me neither.

STUDENT 2: OK. What's next?

> Well, these kids got half the lesson! Identifying what knowledge is missing is step one. Deciding what to do is step two. When we pointed out to them that they needed to figure out if they needed to understand this word, they happily said, "No, it's OK" and kept on talking about why anyone would think bats are cuddly.

Questions You Might Have

1. *This question seems to be about getting to students' prior knowledge. Isn't it my job to make sure students have the background knowledge they need to successfully read something?*

   Yes, and no. This is one of those areas where our own understanding of prior knowledge has changed. For years, we erred on the side of providing as much background knowledge as we possibly could. We probably presumed all sorts of things about what kids did and did not know. And, basically, that means in all likelihood we shortchanged our students. *They* needed to identify what they did and did not know. Now we are much more likely to tell students that as they read, they may notice places where they are confused. When they do, they should stop and ask themselves, "What did the author think I already know?" We think that's a step toward independence and self-reliance.

2. *So, what exactly is it that kids do once they notice what they didn't know?*

   When students recognize that they don't know what words mean, they can turn to the context or turn to a dictionary.

When students recognize that they are having a hard time visualizing something, we encourage them to use a strategy called Sketch to Stretch. You can read about this on page 221. If students tell you, "The author thinks I know something about this war" (for instance), then they must decide if they need that background knowledge. If you hear students say something like "The author thinks I understand what caused this," then you want to help them see the cause-and-effect relationships in that text. If students say, "He thinks I understand how _____ is like _____," then you want to ask them to think about how those two things are alike.

In other words, use what they tell you to help pinpoint what they need to do next to figure out their confusion.

3. *Wouldn't it be faster for me just to provide the information?*

Faster? Yes. Better? No.

4. *My kids are marking everything. Isn't this defeating?*

Absolutely. We're not fans of giving kids texts that they can't read. That's frustrating, not instructive. Take a look again at the section on pages 47–55 about text complexity. It might be that the text that's too hard now won't be later in the unit.

5. *This just seems as if it will take a lot of time. Is it worth it?*

This does take time. If your goal is to impart content and that's it, then this probably isn't worth your time. If your goal is to create independent learners, then this is a critical step. Remember that what takes more time early in the school year takes less time as the year progresses. Also, we've found that when entire buildings adopt practices, students progress much faster.

What Challenged, Changed, or Confirmed What I Already Knew?

TEACHING TEXTS

We use "The Dung Beetle as a Weapon Against Global Warming" found in the Appendix on p. 263 or online at http://hein.pub. readnfres2.

This question is neither difficult to teach nor hard to understand, though it is one that makes some students uncomfortable by demanding that they think rather than extract information. And it is important for the messages it conveys. This question doesn't emphasize memorizing data from the text. It doesn't characterize student responses as *right* or *wrong*. It tells the students, in a slightly subtle way, that changing your mind is perfectly respectable and that, in fact, it ought to happen occasionally, perhaps even often. It respects the students' responses to the text by asking them to consider how the text has shaped *their* thinking. And it equips them with observations that should sustain their subsequent talk.

Understanding the Question

We were in a meeting with the associate superintendent of a very large school district. We had a year-long contract with the district, and every time we met with this person, her question was the same: "Will you guarantee that test scores will improve?" Every time we answered her the same way: "No."

At this particular meeting, we shared several research studies showing that as volume of reading goes up, reading skills improve. She responded, "I don't care what that research says. I know that doing drills in skills will improve kids' test scores. My mind is made up."

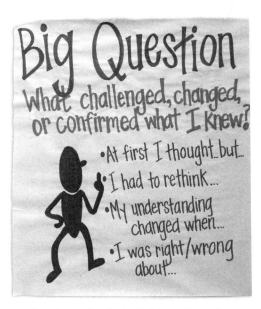

You'll want an anchor chart with this question on it.

That comment, that her mind was made up, struck us as short-sighted for her district. What about the compelling research that reveals a better way to reach an outcome? What about new understandings that ought to cause us all to rethink old practices? What could we say or do that might help her change her mind about the critical role she has decided to give to test scores?

It was that encounter that cemented our commitment to creating readers who approach nonfiction with a willingness to change their minds.

Teaching the Question

Teaching this question is almost as simple as teaching the first of our questions, "What surprised you?" It involves roughly three points.

1. We read nonfiction to learn something.

2. Learning is more than memorizing; it involves changing the way we think about an issue or an idea.

3. We can change in several ways. We can:

    ▶ Confirm what we already thought

    ▶ Modify our thinking

    ▶ Change our minds completely

We Explain

We've entered a tenth-grade science class. Most of the thirty-one students seem ready to learn—backpacks off desks, heads off desks, pencils nearby. The teacher had explained that this is a "basic" science class, one for kids not in AP biology or AP physics but who still need a science credit to graduate. Most students speak English as their home language, although several are bilingual in Spanish or Mandarin. We began the lesson . . .

❝ Your teacher has shared with you two questions we've been teaching kids to keep in mind as you read nonfiction: **What surprised me?** and **What did the author think I already knew?** Today we want to add a third question. [We showed them an anchor chart like the one shown in the opener.] **Although this is the final question we're teaching, in many ways it seems the most important one.**

One student spoke up and said, "I thought I was going to hate mushrooms until I ate some and now I love, love, love mushrooms, especially on pizza." The conversation quickly took a turn to favorite pizza. We were beginning to regret our commitment to contextualizing lessons in real-world examples.

To get started, we'd like you to answer this question: "Have you ever thought you weren't going to like a food and then you tried it and discovered that you did?" [They agreed that, yes, they had experienced this.] "So, what would have happened if you had not been willing to try that new food?" [All said that they wouldn't have known they liked it.]

So, being open to changing your mind was important. That willingness to have an open mind about things is true of much in life, including the things we learn about as we read. In fact, when you read nonfiction wondering "What has challenged, changed, or confirmed what I already knew?" you'll discover that you're reading that nonfiction more carefully and attentively.

We Model

" For instance, we were reading an article about how our brains learn. We came upon this statement . . ." [Put this statement on your whiteboard so all can read it.]

> Any athlete will tell you this: If you're competent at something and you start thinking about it, especially at a detailed level, you're just dead in the water.

This line is from "A Little Disconnect Goes a Long Way to Learn Motor Tasks, Brain Study Says." You can find it at https://newsela.com /articles/brain-learning /id/8508/.

We both marked that sentence as one that confirmed something we already knew, and when we got together to talk about that article, we mentioned that we do some things better if we don't think about them—such as typing or swinging a baseball bat. If we try to think about where every letter on the keyboard is as we type, our speed goes down. And if we try to think about every single thing we do as we swing a bat, we'll never hit the ball. So this sentence really confirmed something we already had come to think.

We let students talk about those things they do so automatically that if they stop to think about them, they will slow down. They mentioned playing a piece of music from memory, reciting words to a poem, doing some skateboarding tricks. One student even mentioned reading and said, "If I start thinking about everything my brain is doing when I read, I just stop!"

" **FROM KYLENE:** In another article, this one about climate change, I read this sentence: "The report warned that climate impacts are already 'severe, pervasive, and irreversible.' Now, that was challenging what I understood about climate change. I had understood that if we didn't start doing some things here in the U.S. and around the world, then eventually, climate impacts might become "severe, pervasive, and irreversible," but this sentence was suggesting this had already happened, that it was too late.

This challenged my understanding, so I couldn't just accept it without checking further, nor could I just forget it. I decided I'd have to do more reading to see if my understanding was right or if this author was right.

FROM BOB: Another time we were reading about air pollution in China. We've both read about this and understand that not only is the pollution a health problem, but that often the government in China does not give its citizens accurate information about the problem. But then we read an article from the *Washington Tribune* that explained that Chinese President Xi Jinping agreed to cap emissions of carbon dioxide and improve its use of renewable fuels. The article also explained that the Chinese were going to more accurately report air pollution. It also said that China has decided to build sixty new nuclear energy plants to provide clean energy. As we read all that China is beginning to do, we realized we had to change our thinking about China's commitment to improving air quality. It appears that the leadership there might be committed to addressing this critical problem.

> The article that offered us new information about China's air pollution can be found at https://newsela .com/articles/china -pollutionapp/id/6833/.

When we read those articles asking ourselves "What challenged, changed, or confirmed what I already knew?" we thought more deeply about what we'd read. Perhaps that's because we weren't just reading facts on a page. We were thinking about how information fit with what we already knew. That helped make the reading more relevant.

Students Try

" Now it's your turn. You have an article in front of you that's about global warming. We want you to read it, and as you do, look for information that changed your thinking or perhaps confirmed some thoughts you already have. Mark those places, perhaps jot some notes in the margin, and when you are ready, turn to your partner and share your thinking.

Students need about ten minutes to read, and then we usually give them another ten minutes to discuss with one another what they've marked. Then we pull the groups back together and ask, "Was there something you read that caused you to rethink what you had believed or perhaps even change your mind?"

> The students are reading an article titled "The Dung Beetle as a Weapon Against Global Warming," by Jennifer S. Holland. You will find this in the Appendix on page 263 and online at http://hein.pub/readnfres2.

STUDENT 1: This line here, about the cows. I marked it because it made me change my thinking. I always thought that cars and trucks were causing all the pollution and global warming. I didn't know that cows were such a big problem.

STUDENT 2: I didn't either. Do you believe it?

STUDENT 3: I guess so. It says that the United Nations said this.

STUDENT 4: So, I'm going to change my mind about all those gas-guzzlers out on the highway. They aren't really the problem, and all those people wanting you to buy a small car or a hybrid probably just want you to buy their cars. They are just scaring you.

STUDENT 5: No. Cows and cars are *both* part of the problem.

It is just that sort of exchange that we want to watch for in assessing our students' thinking. In essence, here's what happened in this conversation:

1. The students noticed a point in the text to which they had responded with surprise or agreement or doubt.

2. One student reported that his thinking had been drastically changed.

3. Another disputed the validity of his reversal, arguing instead that the article supported a *broader* understanding of the factors in global warming, rather than a completely *different* understanding.

> Though the teacher said this was a "basic" class, we saw kids thinking deeply. Test scores pigeonhole kids unfairly.

Well, Student 3 didn't actually say she was arguing for a broader understanding of global warming, but we recognized her efforts as doing so. That, we think, is fairly sophisticated thinking. These students could, of course, go further, but to have achieved even this much with little intervention other than our teaching of this third question, seems a respectable day's work. The students had identified the moment in the text that had caused a change in their thinking, had then moved—with very little urging from the teacher—to conversation about that moment, and ultimately had reached a refined understanding of the problem.

Students Reflect

Keeping this question in mind does slow down reading, but we hope the benefit is worth the extra time needed. As we finish this lesson, we remind students that when they find something that surprised them, they want to ask themselves if this surprise challenges, changes, or confirms what they already know.

We asked students how reading with this question in mind had changed their understanding of the article. Most said something like "It was good" or "It made me think" or "It showed me where my mind had changed." One student gave us more:

> "So, I think if I had just read this without thinking about how has my thinking changed, I would have just read it like, facts, you know? I would have just thought 'OK. OK. OK.' And that would be it. But if I'm thinking, 'How does this change what I think?' then I have to be thinking about what it says and what I already think. This is harder, but it is also, like it is also making it more meaningful to me."

> We all need kids who occasionally make these wonderful statements. They help offset all the ones who say, "What question?"

Listening to Student Talk

We encourage you not only to read this transcript of a portion of classroom conversation, but to go online and watch their longer conversation, too. The QR code will take you to the video clip.

http://hein.pub/readnf4

These are middle school kids who have read an article about Apple's discovery that some of the factories they had contracted with in India were employing children.

STUDENT 1: These two paragraphs definitely changed my thinking on Apple and its products. It changed my thinking a couple of ways. My first thinking was, I kinda used to think Apple made all their products, but now I know they get part of their products from factories, from foreign countries. Like they partner with other countries that make a part of the phone.

STUDENT 2: So Apple [unintelligible] gets all the parts and puts them together. It's not like they're making all of it at all, actually. They're just there to get the pieces and put them together.

STUDENT 3: What changed my thinking was that I thought that Apple was like kind of professionally and that each like factory

Notice how Student 3 mentions what surprised her. You'll hear that often, because there is overlap between change and surprise.

there were like different managers that oversaw everything and they knew what was about going into the different phones. And they knew about the companies that were giving them different materials, and so I was surprised that it took them so long to figure out about the child labor.

These students were asked only to identify something in the text that confirmed or changed how they thought. As the video reveals, doing nothing more than that gave them the raw material for conversation that led to insights into Apple's manufacturing policies, to speculation about how their factories were run, to consideration of the ethics of child labor, and ultimately to their obligations as consumers. Again, nonfiction had entered their world.

It's important to note, though, that these students were manipulating the text, rather than the other way around. They were addressing it responsibly, questioning it, exploring its implication for their own thinking and behavior. They weren't simply allowing it to shape their thinking; rather, they used what it offered them to take control of and shape their own thinking.

They could have gone further, of course. None of them raised the possibility that a competitor of Apple had shaped the article to cast a shadow over the company. At some point, we'd hope that students would begin to question the motives of the authors of nonfiction texts. But they had done significant and respectable thinking in this class session.

Questions You Might Have

1. *Surely not all texts will lead to challenging, changing, or confirming our thinking—aren't some just interesting?*

   Yes, of course. We read the box scores because we want to know if our team won. We read the article about tides and currents and find it interesting but don't worry too much about whether or not it has changed our mind about something. On the other hand, if we fished for a living, that same article might be crucial for the day's work.

   But let's not belabor the point. We'll happily grant that there are some texts we read just because we're mildly interested in the topic. And some we read—the back of the cereal box when we're eating breakfast, for instance—just because they're there.

2. *Some of my students are so determined to be right that the thought of changing their minds is anathema to them. How do I address that problem?*

We created that problem. Too many quizzes, too many yes-or-no questions, too many frowns when a kid said something not quite right and too ecstatic a smile when he said something we thought great. If we could eliminate *right* and *wrong* from the classroom vocabulary we'd be better off. But, to answer the question, you probably can help them overcome this stubbornness if you:

▸ Avoid yes-or-no questions.

▸ Find a way to value the students' observations and questions as much as—and preferably more than—their correct responses.

▸ Help students see that many questions are more valuable explored than answered.

▸ Demonstrate changing your mind. Students need to hear you say, "Oh, I had thought that car pollution was the number one factor in global warming, but now I see that methane from cattle is also a big problem."

3. *Won't some parents say it isn't my job to teach students to question a text?*

Yes. We've experienced this firsthand. We distributed two articles to eighth graders about fracking—a hydraulic drilling practice that uses water, chemicals, and sand to drill deep into the ground and break up rock to release natural gas. We probably should have thought twice about distributing this article in Wyoming. The first presented environmental concerns about the practice. Though the second article offered fracking as an environmentally sound practice, we had students who immediately said, of the first article, "This is stupid," "This is wrong," and "I'm not reading this." We told them we did expect them to read both articles and then to find text-based reasons to support or refute one of the articles. We heard from parents who told us that they would tell their children what to believe about fracking and that they would not be reading "pseudo-science" for any reason.

> . . . teaching our children to think logically and independently and behave ethically and empathetically is critical to our democracy.

This moment was uncomfortable for us but sad for their children. Those students had learned a questionable lesson from their parents: if something might upset your vision of the world—or your community—don't read it; call it names; dismiss it without considering it. As this world grows more complex, we stand firm in believing that *knowing more* is better than *knowing less*; that an open mind is more helpful than a closed mind; that finding the things we have in common is a better starting place than discussing things that divide us; that teaching our children to think logically and independently and behave ethically and empathetically is critical to our democracy.

4. *Do these three questions (What surprised you? What did the author think you already knew? What challenged, changed, or confirmed what you already knew?) have to be taught separately?*

Not at all. We've stretched them out here to show how we have taught them separately—something *we* needed to do to confirm the value of each. For some students, there might be value in doing it this way. With other kids, just show them the anchor chart that has all three questions and send them off to read.

CLASSROOM CLOSE-UP

Experimenting with the Three Questions in a Sixth-Grade Classroom

We're taking you into Tara Smith's sixth-grade classroom via her blog entry that was posted December 5, 2014, at https://ateachinglifedotcom.wordpress.com/2014/12/03/experimenting-with-a-really-stance-in-reading-nonfiction/. Tara's blog post shows you how she took all three questions, presented them to her students as adopting a particular stance toward reading nonfiction, and used the "Really?" worksheet that the Florida teacher created. We were struck by two things: the power of Tara's blog as she shared her reflections with teachers in such a transparent way and the great thinking her kids offered. Thanks, Tara, for sharing. Comments by the figures are ours.

****

Experimenting with a "Really??" Stance in Reading Nonfiction

December 5

Last April, Kylene had shared this post about nonfiction work in which she wrote: "We want students aware of what they are discovering as they read. We want them to enjoy that feeling of surprise, amazement, and even skepticism. We want them to say, *Really*?"

Yes! This is exactly the kind of stance I hope my students take when presented with nonfiction options . . . I would rather that than the unenthusiastic groans I usually hear when I announce that we will be beginning our nonfiction genre study, or begin to pass out our Social Studies textbooks! I was particularly intrigued by this note-taking template that was included in the post:

Name: _____ Date: _____ Period: _____

Title of Book or Article: _____

Directions: As you read, look for things that surprise you. When you find something, ask yourself these questions:

   1. Why did this surprise me?

   2. What does this suggest?

Strategy: Really???

SOMETHING I FOUND INTERESTING OR SURPRISING	PG. #	WHY DOES THIS SURPRISE ME?	WHAT DOES THIS SUGGEST?

Figure 24 This worksheet makes the process of noting surprise concrete.

With our nonfiction genre study just launched, I can finally begin experimenting with these ideas and trying them out with my sixth graders. We began by sorting through the questions that drive new thinking in nonfiction, and how to work with the template as we read our social studies texts:

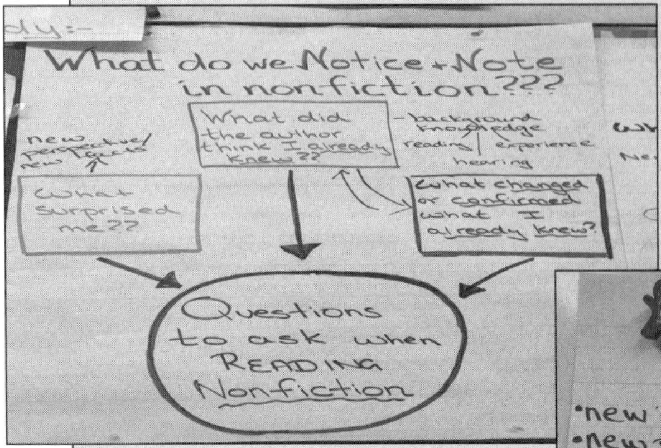

Figure 25 Tara's charts give kids information about the three questions and the "Really?" worksheet.

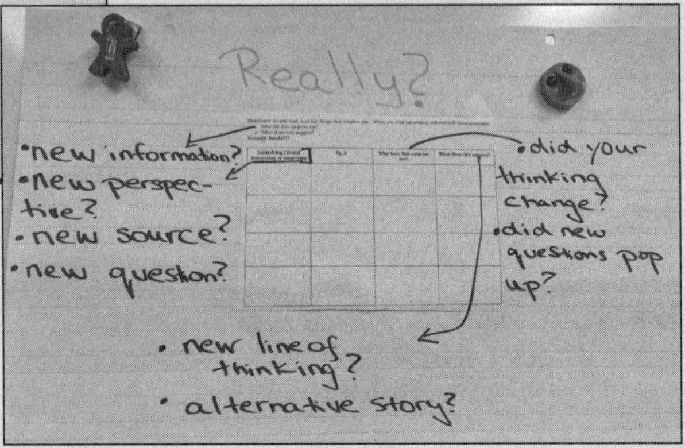

I chose to begin with these texts (Joy Hakim's wonderful series: *A History of Us*) because, quite frankly, I was just as tired of the guided questions we were using as my kids were. I wanted to see if this new way would open up a more thoughtful reading of this text, whether my kids would "enjoy that feeling of surprise, amazement, and even skepticism" as they read about the early days of our nation's history.

Here's one student's take-away:

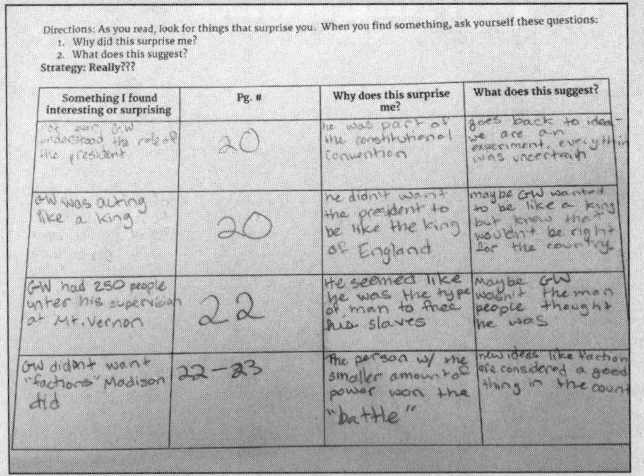

Figure 26 We think column 4 is the most important part of this worksheet.

And another:

He had a lot of responsibility to take care of our country.	Washington was a like a prototype k did a bad job we might never have another president.
As the First President wouldn't you want to do everything by yourself.	Washington is a good leader and was the best man for the job.
We work trying to build a notion of equality.	As a nation we were still working out the way to run our country.

Figure 27 A close up of another student's take-aways.

We had wonderful discussions based on these notes, and I was so pleased to see that this format seemed to allow my kids to engage in a much more meaningful way with the text. Here's what they shared about the process:

- "I think I understood the chapter better this way, I could focus on reading not hunting for the right answers."
- "I felt I just got better information from the chapter."
- "When I took bulleted notes or answered questions, I felt like I was just copying stuff, not thinking about stuff."
- "I felt like I extended my thinking—like it was more than trying to find the answers, before it was like in one ear and out the other."
- "This kind of makes you look for interesting stuff and then figure out more about it."
- "I think we need to practice in class more to get a feel for it—that last column was kinda confusing."

Interestingly, once we began sharing notes from this column, we began to see that this last column was where we were able to do our best "thinking about reading." Here is where my kids began to extrapolate and draw conclusions, make connections, ask deeper questions that would drive further learning. "What does this suggest?" became a way to frame what was discovered through our chapter reading, and to extend our thinking. Through practice and class discussion, we realized that this was, in a way, where our ah-ha moments most often took place.

We will continue to experiment with this template and this new stance in reading nonfiction in the weeks and months ahead. After all, what could be better than a classroom full of amazed sixth graders reading fabulous nonfiction and going "Really??"

What Challenged, Changed, or Confirmed What I Already Knew? **111**

PART III

The Power of Signposts

Two boys who weren't impressed that we were visiting their social studies classroom and didn't much care for the signpost lesson we had just taught, Numbers and Stats, reluctantly agreed to reread a passage and look for the numbers and stats the author used and then to think about why the author used those numbers. We had previously taught them Extreme or Absolute Language, and at this point these two boys had only asked us one question: "Just how many of these signpost things are there?" They were relieved when we said, "Only five."

Slowly, they began, marking very little as they reread. When they turned to talk with one another, supposedly sharing what they had noticed and what thinking had followed, we saw a lot of conversation between the two, but regrettably didn't have audio recorders set up with small groups. Perhaps they were discussing Friday night's football game. When we pulled kids back together for a full-group report on how reading with Numbers and Stats in mind affected their thinking about the text, these two boys eventually spoke up.

> **BOY 1:** So, like, I didn't see all those numbers everyone has been pointing out. I didn't know we could mark word numbers. But I saw an Extreme or Absolute. It was right here when it said "set me free." [Lots of interruptions as students pointed out that wasn't a Numbers and Stats or that they weren't supposed to find Extreme or Absolute language examples. Some decided to argue that "set me free" is not an example of Extreme or Absolute Language. Finally, we got students quiet again and D'Sean continued.] Like I was saying, this was Extreme or Absolute to me, and it made me start thinking

"IF NONFICTION INTRUDES INTO OUR LIVES,

THESE SIGNPOSTS HELP US

EXAMINE THAT INTRUSION."

Initially, D'Sean said he didn't notice any numbers (p. 112). The numbers were written as words (*two* not 2), so he didn't recognize those as numbers. That pointed out to us that when we teach Numbers and Stats we need to specifically explain that 2 and *two* or one-half and ½ are all numbers.

Look at all the questions these boys have asked. This is the type of thinking we want students doing when they read nonfiction.

about how poor people seem to always have to do harder work. This was, well, if you just read the words, then it's about working in mills, but it's really more than that because it was like she was a slave. Man, she was a slave. That's really extreme. Because this was after slavery times and this was still happening, and with kids. At first I didn't even see it, but when I read it again, I don't know, it just jumped out at me as Extreme or Absolute.

BOY 2: Yeah. D'Sean marked something I didn't even mark with the "set me free," and at first I didn't see it. But when we started talking about it I could see it was extreme, and then it was like we, well, now we want to know why there weren't rules about going to school and why did the poor people have to do this, and didn't anyone care that this was just kids? I mean, just little kids. We want to know if this was done because they were disrespecting kids, or is this to just keep some people poor, you know because you can't go to school.

And that conversation is why we wrote this book. It's why we know, with certainty, that teaching students to be alert to signposts is important.

These two boys were in a history class that wasn't for AP students. They were not in the honors class. These kids had not been identified as gifted and talented. They weren't even called the bluebirds. As another student in that classroom told us, "This is the dumb class." We never saw those teens in that light, but something made them see themselves that way. Yet when we taught them to be alert to particular signposts, their thinking was rich and rewarding—certainly to us, but more importantly to *them*. When we put the comments from students on the board and showed them all the smart thinking they had done, one student said, "Hey, we look smart." Another asked, "Can you make a copy of that? I want to show my mom what I said today." That's what scaffolds do. They give us—any of us—the boost we need, until we don't need it. The kids in this classroom are smart; they simply needed a scaffold—a way to see deeply into texts—so that their smart thinking could emerge.

We are sure that someone in all their years of school had explained to them that they should think carefully, reread, weigh word choices, make inferences. We are positive that had happened. We've said such things, too. What we didn't realize soon enough is that struggling readers need concrete clues in the text to help them make those sophisticated moves that more skilled readers seem to make easily, almost intuitively. Remember, anyone can be a struggling reader. Usually, when we struggle, the text is one to which we bring little background knowledge. Then, signposts are critical.

The kids in this classroom are smart; they simply needed a scaffold—a way to see deeply into texts—so that their smart thinking could emerge.

****

In *Notice and Note* we discussed six signposts—markers that alert the reader to important moments in fiction. These appeared in every chapter book or young adult novel we read, so we were confident that they would show up in all, or almost all, of the chapter books or novels that might find their way into your hands and thus into the hands of your students.

Of course, while writing that book, we were already thinking ahead to this book. We wondered if the same signposts would be appropriate for nonfiction. Would different ones emerge as we studied nonfiction? Once the *Notice and Note* manuscript was submitted and we could surface from our deep immersion in novels, we began collecting the nonfiction we would read for this project—meaning the texts you have your students read.

We visited an eighth-grade history class and asked the teacher to show us the texts that his students would read for the unit they were about to begin: The Civil War. From his cabinet, he removed a large plastic tub marked "Civil War." Inside, neatly arranged in folders, were articles, speeches, and primary source documents including letters, diaries, newspaper reproductions, maps, and Lincoln's "Emancipation Proclamation" and "Gettysburg Address." He handed us the textbook and showed us the four chapters devoted to this time period, and he shared copies of many encyclopedia entries. He displayed reproductions of photographs of slaves, soldiers, and plantations. He shared the multiple copies of trade books that included *The Underground Railroad, Fields of Fury; Eyewitness Civil War, I Survived the Battle of Gettysburg 1863* (historical fiction), and *The Civil War for Kids: A History with 21 Activities*. We asked him to stop.

That array of nonfiction—from letters to speeches to textbooks and trade books—reminded us how vast nonfiction is. How could we ever begin to read enough nonfiction to make any claims about signposts? So we turned to you, and in a national survey asked you to tell us which specific nonfiction texts you most often ask your students to read. Surely, we thought, that would generate for us a manageable list, and from it we'd choose the fifty or so most mentioned titles. Well, that was one of the

The literary signposts discussed in *Notice and Note* are Contrasts and Contradictions, Aha Moments, Tough Questions, Again and Again, Words of the Wiser, and Memory Moments.

least helpful questions we have ever included in a survey. The most commonly cited *type* of book was the district-adopted textbook. The only two titles of *specific* texts that were mentioned multiple times (and across multiple grade levels) were King's "I Have a Dream" speech and Lincoln's "Gettysburg Address." After that, most teachers wrote that they did not rely upon a single title, but they could point us to the magazines and websites they most frequently used. See Appendix C for these lists.

So We Began There

We began reading the articles in the magazines you said you used; we opened accounts on the websites you said you frequented. We borrowed textbooks from your classrooms, and we bought the books that were mentioned by anyone! We turned to the folks we find most helpful when it comes to connecting us to books—school librarians—and we asked colleagues Teri Lesesne, Penny Kittle, Donalyn Miller, Jeff Williams, Jen Ochoa, and Franki Sibberson which nonfiction texts they recommended. We watched online for anything you mentioned on social media. Often our text messages to one another would say, "Paul Hankins just recommended *The Great Showdowns*" on Facebook or, "Tara Smith blogged about *I Will Always Write Back: How One Letter Changed Two Lives*."

But because nonfiction is such a sprawling collection of types and kinds, working in so many different ways, we didn't find a unique set of signposts that appeared in all types of nonfiction. History texts, scientific reports, newspaper articles, editorials, repair manuals, Supreme Court decisions: each type had its own patterns and customs and ways of presenting the information or argument.

And so, we can't make the claim that one set of signposts will show up in *all* nonfiction texts. Even considering such a claim seems ludicrous. What we can do, however, is share with you those signposts that alert us to some significant moments in most nonfiction, those moments in which we need to think critically about claims an author makes.

The signposts are:

▶ Contrasts and Contradictions

▶ Extreme or Absolute Language

▶ Numbers and Stats

▶ Quoted Words

▶ Word Gaps

We've included Teri Lesesne's list of her favorite nonfiction picture books for older readers and Franki Sibberson and Mary Lee Hahn's list of great nonfiction for elementary school students on pages 276–278 of the Appendix.

Of course, when we read longer works of nonfiction—*The Boys Who Challenged Hitler* by Phillip Moose, or *Fatal Fever: Tracking Down Typhoid Mary* by Gail Jarrow—there is a greater chance of seeing all five in one text. Shorter articles found on Newsela.com or short sections of a chapter in a textbook are far less likely to use all signposts.

Definitions of Signposts

The following five chapters provide detailed information on each signpost. Here, we provide information that you need to know about all the signposts. We begin with some definitions. In Figure 28 (page 119), we connect each signpost to reading skills.

- ▶ **Contrasts and Contradictions:** The author presents something that contrasts with or contradicts what the reader is likely to know, think, or have experienced, or shows a difference between two or more situations, events, or perspectives.

- ▶ **Extreme or Absolute Language:** The author uses language that leaves no doubt about a situation or event, that perhaps exaggerates or overstates a case.

- ▶ **Numbers and Stats:** The author uses numbers (*2* or *two*) or words (*several, a lot, few*) that show amounts or statistical information to show comparisons in order to prove a point or help create an image.

- ▶ **Quoted Words:** The author quotes others, directly, with what we call a Voice of Authority or a Personal Perspective. The author might also list others in citations.

- ▶ **Word Gaps:** The author uses words or phrases that students recognize they don't know.

> All the signpost lessons use what we call generalizable lessons. You teach the lesson—"Authors use numbers to help you create a picture and make an inference"—and then show them how to apply it to a specific text. Then kids generalize it to other texts. The generalizability is what makes the signpost lessons so powerful.

Anchor Questions

An anchor question is the question we want students to ask themselves when they notice a particular signpost. In other words, we're trying to encourage students to do more than notice a signpost, circle it, and then move on. This is not a hunt, and it's certainly not a way to gain reading points. One teacher told us that she's giving her kids two points for every signpost they circle while reading. We'd rather students notice one or two signposts and think deeply about what the author is revealing through those signposts than circle ten and just keep on reading.

So, the anchor questions are there to slow down the reading, to say to the kids, "OK, you've noticed something the author is doing here, and now it's up to you to think about what that means." Anchor questions help kids do that thinking.

In Figure 29 (page 121), you'll find the individual anchor questions we attach to each signpost. Elementary teachers gave us some feedback on the literary signpost anchor questions and told us that some of their students couldn't remember all the anchor questions, so they made it simple and told students that they could ask the same question for any signpost: "How will this change things?" We've borrowed from their smart thinking and now suggest that elementary grade teachers might want to use a single anchor question with the nonfiction signposts: "What does this make me wonder?"

Middle school teachers, you might want to use the signpost-specific anchor questions. High school teachers, you'll probably want to use discipline-specific questions (see Figure 29).

Signposts and the Big Questions

The Nonfiction Signposts help students think about the Big Questions with more specificity. For instance, we had a group of seventh graders read a text about the fishing industry. One sentence said that most of the fish that people eat in restaurants are not the type of fish they believed they had ordered. Several students marked that line as something that surprised them. When we asked why, one said, "That just seems, like, really surprising," while another reported, "I just, well, I don't know, it's just surprising." We pointed out that sometimes authors use numbers or words that indicate amounts to create a picture and help readers make inferences. Then we asked them to look back at the sentence with that information in mind to see if they could figure out what had surprised them. All went back to the text and quickly identified the word "majority" as the word that created the surprise. We asked them again to explain what surprised them. Now their answers had specificity:

▶ "When the author said 'majority,' that surprised me. I would think that sometime fish might be misidentified, but majority means more than half. This makes me wonder if this is done on purpose."

▶ "This surprised me because I wondered how it could be a 'majority.' That could be almost all. How could that be? If you order one type of fish and one time you don't get what you ordered, that's a mistake. But a majority? Does this mean the restaurants are all telling people that the fish on the menu aren't really what they are serving? Or are the fishermen lying about what kind of fish they are catching?"

THE NONFICTION SIGNPOSTS AND DEFINITIONS	THE LANGUAGE OR OTHER TEXT CLUES TO THE SIGNPOST	READING SKILLS
Contrasts and Contradictions A sharp contrast between what we would expect and what we observe happening. A difference between two or more elements in the text.	Phrases such as *on the other hand, by contrast, however,* and *another viewpoint* provide direct signals of a contrast. Other times, the contrast or contradiction is internal as the reader thinks *we don't live like this* or *our government isn't that way* or *this isn't what I've thought.*	Compare and contrast Generalize Identify main idea Infer See cause-and-effect relationships See details Understand author's purpose or bias
Extreme or Absolute Language Language that leaves no doubt about a situation or an event, allows no compromise, or seems to exaggerate or overstate a case.	Phrases or words that indicate certainty or completeness, like: *all, none, everyone, no one, always, never, totally.* Phrases that express an uncompromising position, such as: *We must all agree . . .* Statements that appear overly certain or exaggerated, like: *Everyone on earth . . .* or *Nothing in the universe . . .*	Draw conclusions Generalize Identify author's point of view Identify main idea Infer Recognize hyperbole See cause-and-effect relationships Understand author's purpose or bias
Numbers and Stats Specific quantities or comparisons to depict the amount, size, or scale. Or, the writer is vague and imprecise about numbers when we would expect more precision.	Numerals such as *90%* or *3,400* or *2* or *ninety percent, three thousand four hundred,* or *two.* Stats and numerals in comparison: 1 out of every 10; four times as many. Also, indefinite quantities should be seen as Numbers and Stats: *many, most, some, taller than, older than.*	Draw conclusions Find facts Generalize Identify details Infer Make comparisons Recognize evidence Understand author's purpose or bias
Quoted Words Opinions or conclusions of someone who is an expert on the subject (Voice of Authority), or someone who might be a participant in or a witness to an event (Personal Perspective). Other times the author might simply cite others (Others' Words) to provide support for a point.	The person may be quoted or his ideas may simply be referred to. If an expert, credentials are likely to be offered.	Compare and contrast Draw a conclusion Identify the author's point of view Infer See cause-and-effect relationships Separate facts from opinions Understand the author's purpose or bias
Word Gaps Vocabulary that is unfamiliar to the reader. This might be because it is a word with multiple meanings, a rare or technical word, a discipline-specific word, or one with a far-removed antecedent.	Some clues are obvious—the word is in italics, bold-faced font, or highlighted. Other times, the author follows a less-known word or concept with the phrase *is like.* For instance, she might write, "Plucking the cotton from the boll *is like* pulling stickers from your socks." Many times, though, the clue is simply that the reader has become confused.	Generalize Identify details Infer Make comparisons Understand author's purpose or bias Use context clues

Figure 28 We've included the information in column 3 to show you how noticing the signposts helps kids with reading skills we suspect you've always taught.

- ▶ "This is really surprising because it says 'majority,' and that surprised me. That means this happens almost all the time. That means something is really wrong."

- ▶ "The author used the word *majority*, and that's a vague amount. I mean, you know it is more than half, because it says majority, but you don't know if that is a lot more than half or just one more. It surprises me that it's a majority, but since he wasn't more specific, I have to wonder if he really knows this. I really think this is challenging me to think about this more than surprising me."

In another class, students were reading about the role of the dung beetle in fighting global warming. Four students marked a part of the text as challenging what they knew (Big Question 3). When we asked why, one responded, "It just seems weird." We asked why it seemed weird. "Because it does," was the reply. We reminded this student (and the others) that he had learned a lesson from us that said students ought to be alert for contrasts and contradictions as they read. (This lesson had happened about five minutes before this conversation. We are obviously impressive teachers.)

He nodded as if he had some vague recollection of that lesson. We sent all the students back to the text and asked them to see if anyone could identify a contrast or contradiction that might challenge what someone had previously thought. Students began rereading, and one called us over almost immediately. "This is it! It's right here. It says that the *dung beetle* [emphasis added by the student] is a weapon in the fight against *global warming* [same emphasis added]. That's the contrast. The dung beetle is tiny. Global warming is huge." He grinned. We asked him to give us a couple of sentences that explained why he found this to be a challenging thought and to include a comment about the signpost. After a moment he began:

> "When the author said that the tiny dung beetle is a weapon in the war against global warming, then I saw that as a Contrast and Contradiction because a beetle is small and global warming is huge. This contrast of something little attacking something so big made me wonder if the author is right. This is challenging me to think about what I know about how little things can have a big effect."

THE NONFICTION SIGNPOST GENERALIZABLE LESSONS	THE SIGNPOST ANCHOR QUESTIONS FOR ELEMENTARY AND MIDDLE SCHOOL	DISCIPLINE SPECIFIC (HIGH SCHOOL)
Contrasts and Contradictions When the author shows you how things/people/ideas contrast or contradict one another, or shows you something that contrasts or contradicts what you already know, you need to stop and ask yourself . . .	**Elementary:** What does this make me wonder about? **Middle School:** What is the difference and why does it matter?	**History:** Why did the author point out this contrast/contradiction? Does this reveal a bias or just new knowledge? **Science:** How does this differ from previously held beliefs or understandings? **Math:** Under what conditions is this true?
Extreme or Absolute Language When the author uses language that is extreme or absolute, you need to stop and ask yourself . . .	**Elementary:** What does this make me wonder about? **Middle School:** Why did the author use this language?	**History:** What does this reveal about the author's biases or purpose? **Science:** Is this science or pseudo-science? Why would this author use this language? **Math:** Is this language appropriate at all?
Numbers and Stats When the author uses specific numbers or provides statistical information, you need to stop and ask yourself . . .	**Elementary:** What does this make me wonder about? **Middle School:** Why did the author use these numbers or amounts?	**History:** How do these numbers help me see patterns occurring across time, regions, and cultures? What do these numbers help me see? **Science:** What purpose do these numbers serve in this context? Do these numbers help prove a point? **Math** (in a word problem): What question is the author asking me, and how do those numbers help?
Quoted Words When the author chooses to quote someone, you need to ask yourself . . .	**Elementary:** What does this make me wonder about? **Middle School:** Why was this person quoted or cited and what did this add?	**History:** What is this person's perspective? **Science:** What are the qualifications of this person? **Math:** Why was a quote needed? What does it add to the thinking?
Word Gaps When the author chooses to use a word or phrase that you don't know, you need to ask yourself . . .	**Across all grades:** Do I know this word from someplace else? Does it seem like technical talk for this topic? Can I find clues in the sentence to help me understand the word?	**History:** Is this term describing a period? What does the term imply? **Science:** Is this a word describing a concept? What do I know about the concept? **Math:** Is it a word important in solving the problem?

Figure 29 This chart connects signposts to anchor questions. Our suggestions of when to use certain anchor questions are only suggestions. You use the anchor questions that best suit your students.

Signal Words, Text Features, and Punctuation

Are signal words (*beforehand, lastly, by contrast*), text features (headers, graphics, bullets, bold-faced fonts, italics), and punctuation (dashes, colons, parentheses) signposts? They are, and these are the ones you've probably been teaching. We think signal words are particularly important for helping students understand text structure. We've included a lengthy list of signal words and their functions in the Appendix on pages 279–280.

Why Not Use the Same Literary Signposts with Nonfiction?

The literary signposts discussed in *Notice and Note* reveal the thinking of characters or patterns in their experiences. With those signposts in mind, readers, for example, notice the Aha Moments a character experiences. Readers could read nonfiction texts with these same six literary signposts in mind if they are able to be alert to how these signposts affect their own thinking. They would ask themselves, "How does this information contrast with what I know?" "What aha moments does this information provide for me?" "What tough questions has this raised for me?" "What words of advice might I form from reading this?" "What lessons/rules do I keep noticing again and again?" "What does this remind me of?"

But, to think deeply about the author's purpose or author's bias, we discovered we needed additional signposts, ones that focused students' attention on what the author was doing. We like it best when students use both sets of signposts as they read nonfiction.

Contrasts and Contradictions

The Contrasts and Contradictions Signpost alerts readers to opposing ideas. That opposition might be seen within the text, especially if it is an argumentative essay, or it might be seen between the reader and the text, especially in historical texts. Recognizing contrasts and contradictions helps students with several reading skills, especially making comparisons, noting cause-and-effect relationships, identifying supporting details, finding the main idea, and reflecting upon the author's purpose.

When we teach this signpost, we use an anchor chart similar to this one. All the signpost anchor charts were created by Jennifer Ochoa, a middle school teacher in New York City. Notice this one has an anchor question most appropriate for middle grades. In the sidebar, we show other questions that could be used with younger and older students.

ANCHOR QUESTION PROGRESSIONS

ELEMENTARY: What does this make me wonder about?

MIDDLE: What is the contrast or contradiction and why does it matter?

HIGH SCHOOL: Discipline-specific questions such as . . .

History: Why did the author point out this contrast/contradiction? Does this reveal a bias or new knowledge?

Science: How does this differ from previously held beliefs or understandings?

Math: Under what conditions is this true?

TEACHING TEXTS

We use "Garana's Story" or "Hard at Work" both found in Appendix B and online at https://hein.pub /readnfres2.

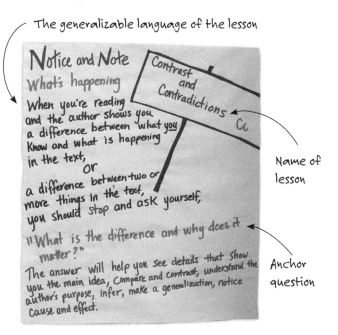

The generalizable language of the lesson

Notice and Note
What's happening
When you're reading and the author shows you a difference between what you know and what is happening in the text,
  or
a difference between two or more things in the text, you should stop and ask yourself,

Contrast and Contradictions · Cc

Name of lesson

"What is the difference and why does it matter?"
The answer will help you see details that show you the main idea, compare and contrast, understand the author's purpose, infer, make a generalization, notice cause and effect.

Anchor question

Understanding the Signpost

We were in a first-period, seventh-grade language arts classroom teaching students about the Contrasts and Contradictions signposts they might see in *fiction*. The bell rang to signify class was over, and kids got up to head out. In this school, the kids rotated as a cohort from class to class. So, the kids who came to us had just finished social studies, and now our students were headed to that class. When second period ended, we had a break, as did the social studies teacher. We know because he came to see us in the language arts classroom. He came in, shut the door, and asked, "What the hell have you folks been teaching down here?" He had our attention, to say the least.

> His comment was not said unkindly. He was perplexed, and his slightly colorful language pointed out his confusion.

"Why?" we asked.

"Because when I put an article about a girl living in Pakistan up on the screen we couldn't get past the first paragraph without the kids interrupting and saying 'There's a contrast!' or 'That's a contradiction.' They all wanted to know why the government over there would act this way.

"They pointed out that the article says loudspeakers call people to prayer early in the morning and over the loudspeaker they hear that it is better to pray than to sleep. One boy interrupted and said that was a huge contradiction because his dad wouldn't say that. Another girl said that it was a contradiction because in this country we have loudspeakers only for football games, not to wake everyone in a city up. Another kid said that it looked as if they don't have rules about keeping government and church apart as we do. I've taught this article for a couple of years and never had that type of interest or conversation from the first paragraph. They said it was because of what you taught them. What *are* you teaching?"

We were positive, at that moment, that no matter what other nonfiction signposts we discussed, Contrasts and Contradictions would be in the list.

****

In literary texts, we tell students to look for places in which the character acts in a way that is a departure from previous actions. We also tell them to look for places in which the character acts in a way they, themselves, wouldn't act. Similarly, we want readers looking for two types of contrasts and contradictions in nonfiction texts—those that are discussed in the text and those that arise as the reader thinks about how his life or knowledge contrasts with what's described in the text.

Contrasts and Contradictions within the text are often directly signaled with words such as *but, yet, unlike, however, opposed to, on the contrary, instead,* and *although.* These signal words (and the others shown in the Appendix on page 279–280) can help students navigate complex texts. Contrasts and Contradictions between the text and the reader's understandings require that the reader be thinking about how the text matches what he knows. We've found that if we teach students to read with the question "What surprised me?" in mind before teaching this signpost, they see far more Contrasts and Contradictions than we would have imagined.

The Anchor Question

Once students see a contrast or contradiction within the text, we want them to ask, "What is the contrast or contradiction and why does it matter?" Again, elementary teachers might simply ask "What does this make you wonder about?" and high school teachers might consider the discipline specific question listed on page 123.

Teaching the Signpost

If students have previously learned Contrasts and Contradictions for literary texts, then we offer little introduction but just point out that this signpost is as appropriate for nonfiction as it was for fiction. On the other hand, if students have not been taught this signpost, we spend a little more time with an introduction.

We Explain

" **FROM KYLENE:** When my son was young, his favorite question to his grandpa was "How were things when you were little?" His grandpa would tell him about growing up listening to the radio rather than watching television; about waiting weeks for a letter to be delivered from a relative across the ocean; about never seeing a restaurant that the family would "drive through" to pick up food; about the one telephone that his home eventually had, that was secured to a post in the kitchen by a coiled cord. Once, after another list of examples of how life then contrasted with life now, I remember my son asking, "Do you think things are better now?"

FROM BOB: I've got similar memories of my sons asking our elderly neighbors—folks who were their stand-in grandparents—what life was like when they were young. As did Kylene's son, my sons would stop and ask if all the advancements have been good. What Kylene and I both like is that when our sons heard the contrasts between what was and what is, they asked questions about the differences, about the contrasts between now and then.

That's what ought to happen when we see something that contrasts with what we know or something that contradicts our understanding of the world. This is especially true when we're reading. When the author presents something that contrasts with or contradicts what we are likely to know, think, or have experienced we really ought to pause and ask ourselves "What's the contrast or contradiction and why does it matter?"

We Model

" Let's look at how contrasts or contradictions can show up in a printed text. Sometimes it is very obvious, as in this short passage: [We always write passages on the whiteboard, no matter how short they are. Our visual learners need this cue.]

> Sparta was content to keep to itself and provided army assistance when necessary. Athens, on the other hand, wanted to control more and more of the land around them.

"On the other hand" is the author's signal that he's going to show how Athens differed from Sparta. [You might start a list of contrast signal words on an anchor chart at this point. Take a look at Figure 30 for some examples you might include.]

Here's another example:

> Even though the temperature dipped below 32 degrees, the water did not freeze.

You are tipped off by the phrase "even though" that something you would expect to happen isn't going to happen. You know that water freezes below 32°, but the phrase has warned you that something unusual is going to happen, so you're prepared for the contradiction when the sentence tells you that the water did not freeze.

When you notice contrasts like the one between Sparta and Athens or contradictions like water that's colder than 32° not freezing, you ought to ask yourself, "What is the contrast or contradiction, and why does it matter?" [If you haven't shown students the anchor chart for Contrasts and Contradictions, we'd put it up now.] In this case, it matters that we understand what had happened to keep the water from freezing. That seems very strange.

Often authors use signal words to help us notice Contrasts and Contradictions.

At other times the Contrasts and Contradictions are between what we know about a place or a situation and what's in the text. Let's take a look at this opening paragraph from the article "Garana's Story," which appeared in the magazine *National Geographic Explorer* a few years ago. You follow along while I read the opening paragraphs aloud: [You can show this via your document camera, though we think it's better when students have their own copy before them.]

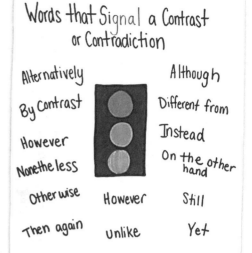

Figure 30 One eighth-grade teacher's Contrasts and Contradictions signal words chart.

> The sun has not yet risen over the rocky hills outside the city of Peshawar, in Pakistan. Loudspeakers from the top of the mosque or Muslim house of worship, call out to the people, "God is great! It is better to pray than sleep! Come to prayers."
>
> Ten-year-old Garana rises from a mat on the dirt floor of her family's house. She puts on her black robe and covers her head with an old shawl. Then she walks to the mosque to pray.

Your grade level and specific content will dictate the text you use. We encourage you to study a text your students will read in your content area and use that one to teach this signpost.

I'll stop here because I see several contrasts between the city in this text and where I live. A voice over a loudspeaker tells these people in Peshawar when to wake up? Really? Alarm clocks—or moms—wake people here in the U.S. And these people are being *told* to go pray. In this country, no one can force someone to pray. Finally, this girl named Garana is only ten years old, but she gets up, puts on a shawl, and seems to take off on her own to go to her mosque while it's still dark. In this country, not too many people send a ten-year-old out walking alone in a city when it's dark.

These contrasts matter because they point out to me not only how different Garana's life is from my own, but how her country is different from the United States of America. I'm wondering why her country would be this way.

Students Try

We want students to identify Contrasts and Contradictions with a few shorter texts on their own, and then we'll practice with a longer one. First, we display a couple of very short sentences that use signal words to indicate a contrast within the text. Because the texts are so short, we don't expect students to be able to speculate on the reason for the contrast. Our focus at this point is to make sure they are checking the signal word chart and thinking about what two things are contrasted.

" Take a look at these two sentences and then tell your partner what signal words you noticed in each.

In the second sentence, one student said, "I'm not sure what a *dignitary* is, but it must be someone out of school since it says instead of being filled with *dignitaries* it was filled with schoolchildren. It must normally be adults who go there."

> 1. Unlike most planes, which run on jet fuel, Solar Impulse 2 doesn't create air pollution. (available online at http://magazines.scholastic.com/news/2015/05/Flying-on-Sunlight)
> 2. On April 23, the General Assembly Hall at the United Nations was packed. But the room wasn't filled with dignitaries. Instead, hundreds of students from schools in the New York City area waited to watch *Selma*. (available online at http://magazines.scholastic.com/kids-press/news/2015/05/The-Long-March-to-Freedom)

We try to find those texts that are accessible to fifth graders who read on grade level but would still be interesting to the high school student. "Hard at Work" is one such text.

Next, we want students to think about the Contrasts and Contradictions they might notice as they compare what they understand about something with what's in the text. We often use the text "Hard at Work," which is reproduced in the Appendix on page 259. We have students read it—or we might read it to them if their lack of fluency is going to obscure the point of this lesson, which is noticing Contrasts and Contradictions. As they read, we ask them to mark contrasts or contradictions in the text that they notice. We remind them that some will be easily spotted by signal words; other contrasts, though, will be between what they know and what's being presented in the text.

We want to share with you in Figure 31 how one student marked up this article, but you should expect that other students will mark different passages. We all read a text somewhat differently, and what stands out to one reader often goes unnoticed by the next. When students begin sharing either in small groups (our preferred arrangement) or a large group, they'll hear what others have marked. A student asked us once, "Is it cheating for me to mark this now?" after hearing a smart comment from a classmate. Somewhere along the way, we've given kids the idea that it's cheating to learn from others. No. In the midst of a conversation—large group or small group—if someone says something that makes sense to another student, why wouldn't we celebrate that moment? That's not cheating. That's learning.

As students are reading their longer text, you'll want to circulate, noticing what they're marking and what they're not. You'll need to remind kids to think about the anchor questions, or they will end up with several circled words and that's all. After students have read and marked the text, we put them in small groups (two or three), or if time is an issue we might pull them back into one big group. Either way, the point is that we discuss what the students saw as a contrast or contradiction and why that matters. Here is a brief exchange from three students, one of whose work is highlighted in Figure 31.

STUDENT 1: I marked "That's exactly what makes him good at his job." Because it says he's short and he doesn't weigh much. That normally wouldn't make someone good at a job. This contrast is important because it makes me wonder what will happen when he gets taller.

> He's noticed an interesting contrast—shorter and thinner aren't usually prerequisites for doing a good job—and he's raised his own great question: What happens when these kids are too big to do this job?

STUDENT 2: That's good. I didn't mark that at first. I marked "working since I was 8" because my brother is 8 and like, he couldn't do a real job like that. And I don't think it is legal here either. So, I was, like, this was really a surprise. I don't get why he doesn't have to go to school.

> This student is seeing interesting contrasts between the United States and Ecuador.

STUDENT 3: I said "pull loads half their weight and use sharp, heavy knives" because I was, like, "This is a huge contrast and contradiction with living here because here, you know, you can't even ride a bicycle without a helmet, and there they trust you enough to give little kids sharp, heavy knives." This matters because it seems like kids there are more mature. It's

> This student's thinking has moved far beyond the text as he raises some questions that several of us helicopter parents might consider.

Figure 31 This student, a slower reader, only read the first six paragraphs before we called students back together. He actively participated in the conversation saying at the end, "It was cool to have marked things I could discuss."

Hard At Work
BY RITU UPADHYAY. REPORTED BY LUCIEN CHAUVIN/ECUADOR

CC
MOST MANUEL LABOR NEED BIG STRONG PEOPLE

Ten-year-old Wilbur Carreno is less than four feet tall and weighs only 50 pounds. He is small for his age. That's exactly what makes him good at his job.

Wilbur spends his afternoons climbing banana trees four times his height. He expertly ties the heavy stalks of bananas so the trees won't droop from the weight of the fruit. "I've been working since I was 8," he told TFK. "I finish school at noon and then go to the field."

CC I DON'T KNOW ANY 8 YEAR OLDS WHO WORK

In Wilbur's poor country of Ecuador, one in every four children is working. An estimated 69,000 kids toil away on the vast banana plantations along the country's coast. Ecuador is the word's largest banana exporter. Kids working in the industry are exposed to harmful chemicals, pull loads twice their weight and use sharp, heavy knives.

WE NEVER HAVE TO DO THIS AS KIDS
CC

DO KIDS BELONG ON THE JOB?

Child labor is certainly not limited to Ecuador. The United Nations estimates that 250 million kids around the world are forced to work. Many countries don't have laws limiting kids' work.

CC MOST ADULTS IN THIS COUNTRY ONLY WORK 8 OR 9 HOURS A DAY

A concerned group called Human Rights Watch conducted a study of Ecuador's banana plantations last April. They found that most children begin working on plantations around age 10. Their average workday lasts 12 hours! By age 14, 6 out of 10 no longer attend school. Many families face the difficult choice of either putting food on their tables or sending their kids to school.

The family of Alejandro, 12, struggles with that choice. Alejandro has had to work beside his father, Eduardo Sinchi, on a plantation. "I don't want my kids to work," says Sinchi. "I want them in school, but we have few options." Sinchi has nine children and earns as little as $27 a week. "It isn't even enough for food, let alone school, clothes, transportation."

HARD WORK FOR LITTLE PAY

Sinchi's pay is typical in Ecuador. The average banana worker earns just $6 a day. One reason pay is so low is that Ecuadorians are not allowed to form work groups called unions. In countries like Costa Rica, where laws allow unions, some banana workers earn $11 a day. Such countries have fewer child workers because better pay means parents can afford to keep their kids in school.

Ecuador's big banana companies have begun to do something about child labor. Last year, they signed an agreement not to hire kids younger than 15 and to protect young workers from chemicals. "We need to eliminate child labor," says Jorge Illingworth, of Ecuador's Banana Exporters Association. But small plantations did not sign the agreement, and, he says, they employ 70% of the kids.

Banning child labor is a start, but it doesn't really help families like the Sinchis. Now that Alejandro can't work, his family suffers more. The answer, most believe, is better pay for Ecuador's adult workers. For that to happen, U.S. shoppers would have to put up with higher banana prices or stop buying Ecuador's bananas to make their point. Guillermo Touma fights to help Ecuador's workers. "If we could raise awareness," he says, "we could raise wages and invest in education for our children."

From *Time for Kids* January 24, 2003 Vol.8 No.14

just like they really trust kids with more responsibilities.

The students kept sharing as they moved through the text. Before they concluded, Student 3 said,

> "I wonder, you know, all the way through this, it was never about how the kids whined or said anything bad. They just did the hard work. That made me think that the author, he was, like, showing that kids can do the work, but they just shouldn't have to do the work. He doesn't say that these kids are tough, but they sure seem tough, like in a good way. I wonder if kids doing, like, this child labor work, well, it's like they don't have school that's teaching them, but they are still learning."

Students Reflect

When we asked the students in this class how staying alert for Contrasts and Contradictions affected their reading, one student responded

> "Most of the time, when I read, I just think about what's there. You know, I read it and I'm, like, I got it or I was confused. When I think about Contrasts and Contradictions and then ask myself, 'Why does this matter?' then I have to think about what I know. It's like pushing my thinking."

Because this class had learned the Big Questions, we were happy when several students mentioned that they noticed that the Contrasts and Contradictions were the things that surprised them. One student said, "If you read looking for what surprised you, often what you find are the Contrasts and Contradictions" and another followed up, "And the Contrasts and Contradictions are what surprise you. They go together."

They do "go together." Remember, the signposts are an extra scaffold for students who need help with those Big Questions.

Listening to Student Talk

We find that students easily learn to read keeping this signpost in mind. Your job will be to listen to their comments and decide how noticing the signpost and thinking about the anchor question is affecting their understanding of the text. This is the part of teaching we like best—listening to students' thinking. We share some additional conversations here—from other texts—to show you what we're listening for when we eavesdrop on conversations, or, put more professionally, take anecdotal notes.

After high school students read an article about "black boxes" for cars (much like the black boxes on a plane), they immediately pointed out several Contrasts and Contradictions:

This link will take you to a small group of sixth graders discussing the contrasts and contradictions they noticed in an article about the clothing industry. http://hein.pub/readnf5

STUDENT 1: This said that these parents did it [had "black boxes" that record how fast and where cars have been driven installed in the cars] to show their child how much they loved him. I think this is showing how much they *didn't* trust him. And look, this part, it says that all these teens whose parents brought home a black box said the same, and that contrasts with all these parents who said it was for safety.

STUDENT 2: Yeah. This is like a big contrast between safety and trust. You see that all the way through it.

STUDENT 1: See here, it says "But others said."

STUDENT 2: And this part, "Although some believe."

STUDENT 1: Is *however* a signal thing? So, look, here, "They said they would; however, their son said . . ."

STUDENT 2: So, this is like the main idea—what kids want and what parents want aren't the same. You see the main idea so easy when you think about all the contrasts, and it's the whole article. This is about finding the main idea.

After some elementary school students read an article about a chimp in a zoo who used a branch to swat down a camera drone being used to capture video for a TV show, they got in small groups to talk about Contrasts and Contradictions:

STUDENT 1: It was a big contradiction that this chimp would do this because I didn't know that chimps would be smart enough to do this.

STUDENT 2: I've never seen a chimp do this.

STUDENT 3: Look! Here's a signal word. *But.* We can mark that.

STUDENT 1: That's not a contrast or contradiction. [pause]

STUDENT 3: But, no. You have to read the whole thing. See, "Tushi's behavior might look like an act of aggression, *but* [student emphasis added] primatologist Susana Carvalho says the chimp was probably just curious about the object."

STUDENT 2: I don't get it. What's the contrast?

STUDENT 3: It's . . . It's . . . See, it looked like the chimp was being mean. But then this woman says she was just curious. It's, like, is the chimp being mean or curious?

STUDENT 1: Yeah, but that is only, like, for her opinion. She [the primatologist] doesn't know if she [the chimp] was curious. The chimp could have been angry. See, the beginning. "Most folks wouldn't be thrilled." She could be like most folks.

STUDENT 3: Yeah, but, this is—what's a *primatologist*? Maybe she knows how chimps think. And that's why she said that.

STUDENT 2: Miss [calling out to Kylene] we need to know what a primatologist is. We think the author thinks we know.

Questions You Might Have

1. *Is it important that students spend time correctly labeling something a contrast rather than a contradiction?*

   We don't think so. One of us often calls something a contrast and the other sees it as a contradiction. We like it when students have the conversation about why something seems more a contrast than a contradiction, but we don't worry if talk like that doesn't emerge.

2. *How do I know if this is helping kids understand the text?*

   You will probably hear it in their conversations. If all they can say is "This contrasts with that," then they probably are not thinking more deeply about the text. If, on the other hand, they get into a conversation about why the contrast matters, then you'll hear deeper thinking.

   And, of course, the other way to find out if this is helping kids is to ask them directly: "You noticed a few contrasts or contradictions in this article and talked about them. Did that help you think more deeply about the article? If it did, how?"

3. *Many articles—especially the short ones we find online—seem simply to present an issue from two perspectives, without giving the reader much assistance in making a decision about where he ought to stand. This can be frustrating and difficult for the kids. How should we deal with that problem?*

   Journalists seem to seek both balance and opposition. We suspect they like the opposition because it leads to debate, to conflict, to heat. If one side can be pitted against the other, then we have the excitement of a good football game. And they probably like the balance because they don't want to be accused of taking sides, of failing to be objective and fair.

   That approach has the virtue of leaving the responsibility for making some final decision about good and bad, right and wrong, in the hands of the reader. But it can also lead to misrepresentation of the actual situation. For instance, those articles that seem to give equal weight to a politician who, possibly in the effort to defend the economic well-being of his state, denies anthropogenic climate change and to the 97% of scientists who have concluded that humans are catastrophically damaging the climate may suggest to the casual reader that there is some equivalency between these two positions. A fairer and more balanced article might devote 97% of its space to the scientists and 3% to the politician.

But in any case, it's the responsibility of readers to decide where they stand on issues. This is just one of the frustrations and joys of living in a democracy: You have the freedom to do your own thinking.

4. *My entire elementary school is reading this book. How do we teach this differently across the grades?*

Though this question came from an elementary teacher, we suspect it could just as easily be asked by middle school and high school teachers. It's a great question, and we've given this a lot of thought.

First, a text for students that's appropriate for third grade won't be appropriate for eighth grade and most certainly won't be appropriate for twelfth grade without readers making some adjustments. That's why we're offering so many examples throughout this book. We worried that if we offered only one text for each lesson, it would be seen as the only text to use. We hope this suggests to you that with your colleagues you should look for texts that best fit your students as you teach these signposts. Mostly, though, we trust you. Make the changes needed for your students and your content.

Second, we've watched some differences appear across grades as we've been testing these lessons. In primary grades, we keep all the anchor questions the same: "What does this make me wonder about?" By middle school—or upper elementary— we begin moving to the specific anchor questions for specific signposts. In middle school, we expect kids to be more precise in their language as they discuss "how something contradicts" or "how this contrasts," and we expect to see them using their knowledge of Contrasts and Contradictions to help them in their writing. By high school, we would hope that students are considering the Contrasts and Contradictions through the lens of each discipline. For instance, when we shared the vampire bat article in a high school chemistry class, that chemistry teacher immediately changed the anchor question to "What would a scientist say about this?" As students read the article, they still marked Contrasts and Contradictions, but their comments shifted to reflect thinking like a scientist:

STUDENT 1: I marked this sentence: "'I certainly defend vampire bats' right to a place in the ecosystem,' said Klose, a young German zoologist." A scientist would say that all living things have a place in the ecosystem. I wonder if there isn't another solution. Maybe a chemical could repel bats.

STUDENT 2: I don't know if bats have a sense of smell. I didn't mark anything because I wasn't sure what to mark, but I think scientists would wonder why bats need radar to find a cow. Cows are huge. I thought they used radar to find tiny things like mosquitoes. Why do they use radar to find cows?

We asked some of these same students to read this again, this time thinking about it as a historian. We changed the anchor question to "What would a historian say?" Our same two students responded:

STUDENT 1: When I looked at it, like, it was for history, my teacher is always saying, "Who wrote the history?" So I was thinking, it seems like the author is more on the side of the zoologist. Look at this. When he's talking about Oliva, he uses words like *swarm*, *blood-slurping*, *dive-bomb*, *exterminate*. When he's talking about Klose they are *cuddly*, and *boons to humanity*. Not just to research but to humanity.

STUDENT 2: I think the Contrasts and Contradictions stick out more if you're in history class because history is more about people and what happens to people over time. Science is more, you know, detached. But this article, it's really about how the bats are hurting this cattleman's livelihood and are killing cattle. Which I guess were going to get killed anyway. But it's like the Contrasts and Contradictions are bigger in history for this article.

Signpost *2*

Extreme or Absolute Language

Extreme or Absolute Language makes an exaggerated, overblown, and probably untrue claim. It admits of no exceptions, and it seems to forbid doubt or questions. Clues such as *every, all, always*, *indisputably*, and *unarguably* should raise questions for readers. When readers spot this language, they will be alerted either to the strength of the author's feelings or to the possibility that the writer is exaggerating and may even be deceiving or misleading the reader.

When we teach this signpost, we use an anchor chart similar to this one. You might also want a second anchor chart of words that signal extreme or absolute language. In addition to the examples above, perhaps include *never, none, totally, unquestionably, hardest, meanest, hungriest, perfectly, completely, absolutely, unconditionally, entirely*, and *exclusively*.

ANCHOR QUESTION PROGRESSION

ELEMENTARY: What does this make me wonder about?

MIDDLE: Why did the author use this language?

HIGH SCHOOL: Discipline-specific questions such as . . .

> *History:* What does this reveal about the author's biases or purpose?
>
> *Science:* Is this science or pseudo-science? Why would the author use this language?
>
> *Math:* Is this language appropriate at all?

TEACHING TEXTS

We use "Vampires Prey on Panama" (page 261 in the Appendix or online at http://hein.pub /readnfres2) with our less skilled readers and "Evidence of Acceleration of Anthropogenic Climate Disruption on All Fronts" (found online at http:// truth-out.org/news/item/22999-evidence-of -acceleration-on-all-fronts-of-anthropogenic -climate-disruption) with our more skilled readers.

The generalizable language of the lesson

Notice & Note
What's happening

Extreme -E- or absolute language

When you're reading and you notice the author uses language that leaves no doubt, exaggerates, or pushes to the limit, you should stop, and ask yourself, "Why did the author say it like that?"

The answers will tell you something about the author's point-of-view and purpose. Or, you might realize the author is exaggerating to make you think a certain way.

Name of lesson

Anchor question

Understanding the Signpost

We debated (um, argued) including this signpost because we think that many of you probably teach it already. You might call it hyperbole; you might call it a propaganda technique. You might call it a test-taking skill: "Items that ask you if *no one* or *everyone* does something are probably false." We think we all (oops!) teach kids about Extreme or Absolute Language.

Just when we were leaning toward not including this signpost, we taught this lesson in Jen Ochoa's classroom at MS 324 in New York City. We gave the kids an article that had several examples of Extreme or Absolute Language using terms such as *no doubt, unquestionably, every single voter,* and *worst ever.* The kids identified the language, said it made them wonder if the author was exaggerating, and that was about it. We were back to wondering if the signpost was worth teaching.

This was a double-block class, so we moved on to the next signpost lesson. We gave the kids the vampire bat article ("Vampires Prey on Panama" found on page 261) and said we wanted them to read looking for Quoted Words (another signpost lesson we taught after Extreme or Absolute Language). They were to ask themselves if the person quoted was a Voice of Authority or a Personal Perspective and then they were to think about what the quote added. The kids marked the quotes, and we had a good conversation when we came back together as a big group. Then a couple of boys spoke up:

BOY 1: So, I saw the quotes, but I also noticed the extreme language. I marked "blood-slurping creatures."

BOY 2: Yeah, me too, so I marked "dive-bombed." That was like, so, you know, *dive-bombed.* That made me think of a fighter plane dive-bombing. That was really extreme.

BOY 1: Yeah, and then later, here [pointing to paragraph nine] it says "continual battle." "Wage a continual battle." Really? Continual? And battle? Like a war?

BOB: And you recognized this as extreme?

BOY 1: Yeah. You said that it's language that doesn't leave any room for doubt. Well, going to battle, wanting to exterminate them, putting poison on them, saying they dive-bomb and are blood-slurping. There's no doubt he hates them. That's extreme.

> For those of you wondering which of us obviously won the argument, we switched sides so often, we aren't sure. That's nice. We both think we won.

We discuss Quoted Words, Voice of Authority, and Personal Perspective beginning on page 158.

And he was right. The author had set up an extreme situation via his word choice. And once those boys saw it, they asked, "So, were these the author's words or the farmer's [cattleman's] words?" When we asked why they asked that question, they said, "Maybe the farmer doesn't really hate them that much, but the author just made it sound that way to, like, make his story better."

We considered the boys' comments and realized these more novice readers (more novice than we are) had shown us something about this signpost that we had not considered. Since we first noticed the obvious examples—*all, none, never, always, completely, irrevocably*—we had wondered why the obvious would need to be taught. Surely kids had noticed those words, too? But these boys showed us that they were thinking far beyond the obvious. They took us at our word, and when we told them that Extreme or Absolute Language meant the author used language that left no uncertainties in mind, they began reading looking for phrases or words that did just that. We had to reconsider just who the novice readers were.

A few weeks later, we taught this signpost in a workshop. About a week after that workshop a teacher who was there told us that he told his tenth graders that Extreme or Absolute Language was language the author uses to eliminate all doubt or to suggest a condition that has nowhere further to go—*undisputable, fastest, worst, total.* He said his students were reading about cyber-terrorism as a part of a unit on first-world problems. He also said his students saw far more than the obvious words (*all, none, everyone*), and their class discussion was more rigorous than he had expected as they pointed out extreme language:

> **STUDENT 1:** This says that cyber-terrorism will destroy the civilization as we know it. That's extreme.
>
> **STUDENT 2:** Yeah. And it said that people who think that anti-malware protection is protecting them are fools. Not *maybe* are fools. Just *are* fools.
>
> **STUDENT 3:** And did you see that part that said that no computer is safe? Really? No computer? Not one?
>
> **STUDENT 4:** Is this true? I mean if it's true, this is bad.
>
> **STUDENT 5:** Or is he [the author] just, like, really trying to scare people? That part about hacking into electricity grids, that was scary if it's true.

STUDENT 6: So how do we know if it's true? I mean, look, he's quoting people that seem really smart. You know, they have important-sounding jobs.

STUDENT 5: But, I don't know. How do we know if it's true?

That teacher encouraged us to keep this signpost, telling us that his kids were reading closely, looking for far more than those obvious words. We agreed, stopped arguing, and have found repeatedly that this is the signpost that encourages kids to think about word choice, which often leads to conversations about author's purpose and occasionally author's bias.

Extreme Language: Innocent or Deceptive?

We all use extreme language. (See?)

Sometimes Extreme or Absolute Language is merely an innocent attempt to grab the reader's attention, an effort on the part of the writer to let his reader know how important he thinks an issue is, or perhaps to jar the reader out of complacency or indifference. Kids say, "I'm freezing" when the temperature plummets to 60 degrees for the first time in the fall. They tell us, "Everyone else gets to go to the party" when they know only five others are going. "It was the worst movie ever" is what we say when we are frustrated that we have just spent $14.00 on a movie worth less than that. A lot less. This is hyperbole, a rhetorical device the speaker has used, and it's not meant to be seen as literally accurate. No one is trying to deceive anyone.

Other times, though, the absolute language is less innocent. When a former administration member told the American public, "Simply stated, there is no doubt that Saddam Hussein now has weapons of mass destruction" (Cheney, August 26, 2002), he was attempting to win our approval for a war that would ultimately cost thousands of lives, justifying it by the claim that Iraq possessed weapons of mass destruction. The extreme nature of his language lies in the first words: "Simply stated," he begins. And yet the issue was not simple and was being debated—in complex and sometimes convoluted, rather than simple, statements—in the media around the world. And then he made it worse, saying, "there is no doubt." Making that claim at a time when there *was* great doubt being expressed almost daily was a flat denial of the reality that most would recognize, which was that there *was* doubt, and plenty of it.

> These students made us start looking at the relationship between Extreme or Absolute Language and Quoted Words. We saw it and students did, too. One student reported, "If the author wants you to believe his extreme language, he often uses Quoted Words to make it like the language isn't really extreme."

This was extreme language intended to deceive, and recognizing that allows the reader to decide if he wants to accept or reject the statement.

The Anchor Question

When students notice Extreme or Absolute Language, they should ask themselves, "Why did the author use this language?" The answer will sometimes be that it was simply part of an expression, a forgivable exaggeration: "Everyone rushed out to see the comet." (Everyone?) Other times, though, students will recognize that the author might be working too hard to convince the reader of a particular position, perhaps because he doesn't have evidence or it's revealing his particular bias. And at still other times, it might be a way for the author to show how dire a situation is.

Teaching the Signpost

We've found this to be an easy signpost to teach, with one caveat: some kids will focus too much on whether language is extreme or absolute. If that's a problem for your students, just call this Extreme Language. Let's look at how we introduced this in a ninth-grade language arts classroom. There were twenty-two students who all still seemed a bit wide-eyed at being in high school. Some were obviously avid readers (we say that because they wouldn't stop reading) and others were quick to report they hated to read (one said, "Well, before you go any further you should know I *hate* to read"). All were curious as to what we would be teaching.

We began. . .

We Explain

❝ Let's take a look at some statements we heard in your school hallway:

> All the teachers and administrators in this school dress very casually.
>
> That was the funniest movie ever.
>
> I can't wait for lunch. I'm starving.

"We heard these comments in the hallway, and they all are examples of what we call Extreme or Absolute Language. In the first sentence, we wonder if *all* teachers dress very casually. Really? *All? Very* casually? Maybe some dress very casually. Maybe more dress

These are comments we heard while visiting this one school, but we could have been anyplace. Stand in the hallway of your school. You'll hear some Extreme or Absolute Language and, sadly, much of it will be put-downs, homophobic slams, or racial slurs. "She is the worst." "Gays are such fags." "Those kids are just trouble." These attitudes must be addressed. If you haven't read Lester Laminack and Reba Wadsworth's book *Bullying Hurts* (2012), we encourage you to do so.

casually. Probably some show up like Mr. Probst—suit, tie, and even socks that usually match. The words *all* and *very* make that statement extreme and absolute.

As two girls talked, one said, "That was the funniest movie ever." We realized we had said similar things: that was the best meal ever; that was the funniest joke ever; that was the best vacation ever. In actuality, when we have made those comments, we didn't stop and pull to mind every movie, meal, joke, or vacation and make a mental comparison. We were just making a point. We suspect that the girl who said that merely wanted her buddy to realize that she laughed a lot during the movie. But is it the *funniest* movie *ever*? *Funniest* is extreme and means no movie can be funnier and *ever* means, well, *ever*. That's an absolute statement that suggests that we might as well stop trying to call to mind another movie from another decade that made us laugh hard because this is the funniest *ever*.

The last statement—"I can't wait for lunch. I'm starving"—is another example of extreme or absolute language. The reality is, though, in all likelihood he will be able to wait for lunch. He might not want to, but he *can* wait, and we suspect he *did* wait.

We do that—we use extreme or absolute language all the time— and I did it just then! Did you notice? I said, "We use extreme or absolute language *all* the time." Once you begin listening for it, we suspect you'll notice it often. Sometimes it doesn't mean too much; it's just how we're describing things right then. But other times, extreme or absolute language should rightly raise some questions about why the author has chosen those words.

Absolute language is simply the most extreme of extreme language. We pay attention to it because it comes with such obvious clues—*always, never, all, none, no one, everyone*, and the like. Other words slip by often, though they too should be noticed: *completely, undoubtedly, no doubt, totally, undisputedly, unquestionably. Tallest, funniest, most, hardest, meanest, hungriest*—all of those suggest an extreme and should be considered carefully.

We Model

" Now let's take a look at what extreme or absolute language looks like in a text. Here are the first two sentences of an article by a man named Dahr Jamail about climate change.

> **FROM KYLENE:** A student heading toward a perfect SAT verbal score turned our extreme statement into a more measured one: "A few teachers dress very casually, and one or two, like Mr. Probst, are sartorial splendors, but most are somewhere in between, neither very casual, nor very formal." Bob and I both laughed as "sartorial splendor" is rarely how we'd categorize his more usual blue jeans and button-downs.

> "No one on this planet will be untouched by climate change," the Intergovernmental Panel on Climate Change announced. The report warned that climate impacts are already 'severe, pervasive, and irreversible.'"

FROM KYLENE: Only one paragraph in, and I'm already struck by some Extreme or Absolute Language. "No one on this planet." That's definitely absolute language. *No one?* How could he know that?

Seeing that language makes me ask myself why the writer chose the words. I wonder, first of all, if it's true. Not one single person on this entire planet will be untouched by climate change? I don't know, but I suppose that if the change affects the whole globe, then it might be true that everyone will be affected. But that still seems absolute—no one will be untouched. Perhaps he's just trying to catch my attention. If so, he's succeeded, because I'm pretty sure I'm one of those who *will* be touched.

But then I get to what seems to me to be most startling claim: "Climate impacts are *already* 'severe, pervasive, and irreversible.'" That is frightening! To say that we have already reached the point at which climate change is irreversible seems extreme. If it's true, it seems to mean that nothing at all can be done about the changing climate. If it's *already irreversible*, we must be doomed. Again, the question is, Why would the writer use this language? And as I think about it, I wonder why others aren't reporting that our problems are irreversible. Shouldn't that be making a lot of news? I have to wonder if I'm seeing some bias from the author.

When I notice Extreme or Absolute Language that is this troubling, I have an obligation to think about it, wonder why the author chose those words, and recognize that I might be seeing clues to the main idea, the author's purpose, or the author's bias.

FROM BOB: When the two of us first read this article, Kylene was sure that "already irreversible" just couldn't be right. I thought it might be true. As we talked about the phrase we decided that for two skilled readers to have such different responses, we had to check to see if the comment is accurate. I downloaded the 1,500-page report, scanned for the phrase, and then saw that he misquoted. He should have said, "If we don't make some changes, then we face irreversible damage."

Students Try

After we've modeled our thinking, we want students to spend some time looking for Extreme or Absolute Language. In some classes (usually our eighth graders through high school) we use the rest of the article on climate change. With our fourth, fifth, sixth, and seventh graders, we use the vampire bat article. Primary grade teachers tell us they use nonfiction picture books that they read aloud and have students listen for examples.

Previously, we discussed what some students saw in the vampire bat article. And, if you'll follow this QR code, you'll see a couple of third graders discussing the extreme language they found in an article about the tornado chasers.

http://hein.pub/readnf6

Here, we'll share what ninth graders said about the remainder of the climate change article.

As students read, we wandered around the room, watching both to see what the readers were marking, and to see if any students seemed lost, marking nothing. Those we helped by directing their attention to paragraphs or sentences in which we'd expect they would notice some extreme language.

Generally, these lines were marked, although we saw other lines catching students' attention as well:

- "massively disruptive impacts"
- "large scale collapse of Antarctic and Greenland ice sheets"
- "mass extinctions"
- "result in a virtually uninhabitable planet"
- "snakes the size of yellow school buses"
- "largest mammal was the size of a shrew"
- "eliminates all or nearly all plankton in the ocean"
- "majority of land plants"
- "already severe, pervasive, and irreversible"
- "humans will not be involved"

After students marked some lines, we had them turn to a partner, share what they had marked, and discuss the anchor question—"Why did the author use this language?" We were pleased that these students not only sustained conversation with a partner for about ten minutes, but they stayed on topic, kept going back into the text, and when we told them time was up, they said they weren't ready to stop.

Students Reflect

We asked students how reading with this signpost in mind affected their reading. Some just shrugged. Most, though, responded with telling comments:

- "It made me slow down and think."
- "I saw things I wouldn't normally see."

> We've found that our least skilled and most skilled readers tend to see the fewest signposts. Our least skilled are unpracticed in reading with this much attention. Our most skilled are often fast readers and, grasping the big meaning, rush right past the details that we want students to notice. You'll have to encourage both readers to be more attentive.

The student who admitted that reading doesn't necessarily mean thinking was probably describing how many kids read. Their eyes travel over words; they turn pages; they *finish*. But they don't necessarily think. This student, now, has discovered that thinking while reading actually makes the topic more interesting. And he's recognized that nonfiction ought to—if it means something to us—raise questions that sometimes send us to other texts.

▶ "I didn't see all those things but then when I thought about extreme language it was like they were just there."

Others reflected by pointing out how this signpost made them think about the issue of climate change:

▶ "I would have just read this and thought this is bad and then just kept on reading. This made me slow down and really wonder if it is right."

▶ "I would have just thought 'It's nonfiction and so it's true and the climate is worse than I thought' but wondering what was extreme made me not just accept so quickly."

▶ "Normally, I just sort of read things. You know? You just read them. That doesn't mean you're thinking about them. But this made me *really* think. So it meant I had to go slower. And at first I didn't like that. But then as I was going slower, it was a lot more interesting. Now I'm really interested in this and wondering what is right about climate change. How do you know when someone is telling you the truth about this?"

Listening to Student Talk

We always think we learn the most by listening to students' conversations. Be sure to take notes as you listen so you can review them later. Take a look at this short exchange and ask yourself what you learn about these kids as thinkers and then read our comments regarding what we noticed. These are the ninth graders who have finished reading the climate change article and now are talking in pairs about what they noticed.

STUDENT 1: I marked "virtually uninhabitable planet."

STUDENT 2: I didn't mark that because doesn't *virtually* make it sound like *nearly*. Nearly uninhabitable.

STUDENT 1: So, some bacteria make it. That's not much better.

STUDENT 2: OK. I marked "humans will not be involved." That's really extreme.

STUDENT 1: This is, like, well, when is this going to happen? I mean if you think, why did he use these words, you get it that he's really worried.

STUDENT 2: And he wants us to be worried, too. So, like the author's purpose. It's to make you worry.

STUDENT 1: What if he's not, well, what if it's not true?

STUDENT 2: But it's nonfiction.

STUDENT 1: Maybe it's nonfiction but not true? Like, well, I don't know. This doesn't seem true. Hey, Mr. Probst, can you come here?

What struck us was that these girls were bothered by their discovery that this article was purporting to tell them something about the world that they didn't want to believe but that perhaps they should believe. One even points out, "But it's nonfiction." They seemed to be trying to reconcile their understanding of the term *nonfiction*—something that's true—with their concern over whether this text was offering accurate information. These students, in high school, are certainly ready for a definition other than "Nonfiction means not false and that means true."

Questions You Might Have

1. *Don't we all use extreme or absolute language from time to time? Isn't it usually just harmless exaggeration?*

   Much of the time it is. No one objects to calling a bright and cheerful morning "the start of a perfect day," even though we know that a bill might show up in the mail and mar what would otherwise be perfection.

   But when it isn't harmless it can be dangerous. When our unnamed politician tells us that "there is no doubt that Saddam Hussein now has weapons of mass destruction," when there was, in fact, a great deal of doubt, the extreme language amounts to a lie. And when that lie becomes the justification for a war that leaves a great many people dead, the extreme language is anything but harmless exaggeration.

   So we think it pays to be alert to Extreme or Absolute Language. When statements are harmless, smile indulgently, note the author's enthusiasm or commitment, and read on; when they seem to be deceptive and misleading, give them the critical assessment they demand.

2. *Why don't you just call this hyperbole?*

Hyperbole is a rhetorical device intended to make the point that something is being exaggerated. We often think of hyperbole as a part of tall tales. Sometimes your students might mark something as Extreme or Absolute Language and then upon reflection recognize that the author didn't really mean "everyone" or "best" but just used exaggeration to make her point. When the language is used purposefully, when it leads us to false conclusions, then it's no longer hyperbole. It's extreme.

3. *I teach my students propaganda techniques such as "bandwagon" and "loaded words." This seems like another term for those terms. Is it?*

We agree, to a point. Many of us have been teaching those terms for a long time (years), and students still read right on over them. We had a teacher tell us that she teaches debate, and she has taught propaganda techniques for years, and her students still didn't seem to catch on. When she started teaching kids to look for extreme language as the signpost, then they were able to attach the terms "loaded words" or "bandwagon technique" to the language they noticed. She said that this was the most efficient and effective way she had ever taught those terms.

4. *Isn't teaching this signpost likely to make my students so skeptical that they become almost cynical?*

Some skepticism is healthy. Gullibility—the willingness to trust or believe when there is little reason to do so—is dangerous. It allows someone else to do our thinking for us and thus puts our fate in someone else's hands. Cynicism—an unwillingness to accept anything or trust anyone—probably leaves us incapable of accepting new or challenging ideas. Healthy skepticism implies a careful scrutiny of ideas, a tentativeness that might end in either rejection or acceptance depending upon the credibility we vest in the writer or his sources and the evidence they provide.

And we're not encouraging that same skepticism with a reading of a book on trucks for six-year-olds. If the author says this dump truck is a dump truck, we want that child to believe that. But we were happy when the eight-year-olds reading a short text about the Iditarod said, "It says it is so cold that your nose will freeze off. That's pretty extreme. The author must really want us to understand how cold it is." These kids are well on their way to becoming the attentive readers we want them to be.

5. *What if my students only look for those obvious clues, words such as* everyone, absolutely not, with no doubt, all, *and* no one.

Many kids will start there; we just don't want them ending there. So if that's what they are noticing in September, October, and November, we wouldn't be disappointed. But if their thinking hasn't sharpened by March, April, and May, we have to ask ourselves if we modeled other types of statements that are extreme and absolute but perhaps didn't use those specific terms. If you want students to recognize that "The choice was perfectly clear" might be an extreme statement and they don't, then ask yourself if you have modeled noticing that type of statement as extreme.

Signpost *3*

Numbers and Stats

Authors use numbers and statistics to provide precision—or to avoid it. It's not "a bunch" of dentists but "9 out of 10." The refugee camp isn't just "large" but holds "50,000" makeshift houses. Some words let authors avoid precision: *many, often, occasionally, impressive amount,* and *few.* This signpost helps students make comparisons, draw conclusions, make inferences or generalizations, differentiate fact and opinion, identify details, recognize evidence, and understand the author's purpose or bias.

When you teach this signpost, you'll want to make an anchor chart similar to this one. Be sure to remind your students that numbers might show up in a text written as "two" or as "2."

ANCHOR QUESTION PROGRESSION

ELEMENTARY: What does this make me wonder about?

MIDDLE: Why did the author use these numbers or amounts?

HIGH SCHOOL: Discipline-specific questions such as . . .

History: How do these numbers help me see patterns occurring across time, regions, and cultures? What do these numbers help me see?

Science: What purpose do these numbers serve in this context? Do these numbers help prove a point?

Math: (in a word problem): What question is the author asking me, and how do those numbers help?

TEACHING TEXTS

As you read this lesson, you'll see several very short passages that you might just write on your whiteboard. We also use two longer texts, which you might have to photocopy for the students. These are "Garana's Story" and an excerpt from *Up Before Daybreak,* both of which are found in the Appendix and online at http://hein.pub.readnfres2.

The generalizable language of the lesson

Notice & Note
What's happening

Numbers
N/S and Stats

When you're reading and you notice specific numbers, number words or amounts, you should stop, and ask yourself,

"Why did the author use those numbers or amounts?"

The answers might help you come to a conclusion, make a comparison, see the details, infer, find facts, or recognize evidence.

Name of lesson

Anchor question

Understanding the Signpost

We began thinking about Numbers and Stats after a comment from a fifth grader. With her class, we were reading the vampire bat article. Our goal was to talk with them about Contrasts and Contradictions. But as is often the case when working with kids, the best laid plans . . .

With our younger kids we tend to refer to this signpost as simply Numbers.

Early on in that article, the reporter explains that a cattleman captured "several dozen" bats, and then applied a poison to the back of each. Those bats, when groomed by "20 other bats," would spread the poison. The reporter explains that the cattleman sees this as necessary to protect his 300-head herd from the bats.

We noticed one student wasn't participating in the class conversation but was instead jotting lots of notes in the margin of the article. When we asked her what she was doing she explained:

> "So, isn't a dozen twelve? So several dozen, would that be like three dozen? So like twelve times three that would be thirty-six. And then those thirty-six get groomed by twenty. Is that twenty different bats for each of the thirty-six? I don't know. But if it is, that's 720 bats. The author should have said that 720 bats lived near his cattle. That's huge. I mean huge. When you think of a bat, you think of this little thing. I haven't ever seen one, but in pictures they aren't so big. So, one little bat against 300 cows doesn't seem like really a problem. Even a couple of dozen against 300 cows. But 720 bats? That's a lot of bats! And that's just the ones he caught in his net. What if there were twice as many out there? Or more than that? The author should have said there were 720 bats. I could have seen how big a problem this was with that."

****

That's what numbers do; they provide readers the details that help them visualize the point the author is trying to make. In this case, the student was explaining that although the numbers the author used were impressive, he could have used numbers to an even bigger advantage. In this article, the numbers helped prove that the problem the cattleman faced was large.

As we began reading nonfiction staying alert to the Numbers and Stats, we realized how often numbers did help us visualize a situation or a problem or a scene. We had to admit that while we always saw the numbers authors used, we didn't always pause to reflect on why the author had been so specific. And then, when we talked with students about the signpost, we realized that students, too, sometimes failed to grasp the importance of numbers. Students told us:

- ▶ "Sometimes I just skip over the numbers."

- ▶ "I just sort of look at the numbers, but that's it."

- ▶ "What do I notice about the numbers? I don't know. Like, they are dates and things. I guess I don't notice them too much."

- ▶ "It's like I see them, but I don't know. I want to get more to what happened, so I just look at them and then keep reading."

Once we began to encourage students to stay alert for numbers and stats, we began to hear different comments from them:

- ▶ "These numbers, they made me see that it's a bigger problem than I thought."

- ▶ "So, some of the numbers here, they were like, just numbers. You know, it said that he was twenty-two years old. But then this next part, it was talking about how much money we spend on tips, and it showed that people give the same percent, like 20%, to a dinner whether that was just a $10 hamburger or a $50 steak even though the waiter giving you the steak might have worked harder. When I asked myself why the author used these numbers, I saw he was showing how unfair it is."

- ▶ "When it said that the bill passed by a margin of 51% to 49% I realized that if the author had written that the bill passed, that wouldn't have shown me how close it really was."

The Anchor Question

We almost skipped having an anchor question for this signpost.

We noticed that *most* students moved so automatically to questioning the authors' use of the numbers once they were encouraged to be alert for Numbers and Stats that we began to wonder if this signpost needed an anchor question. Then we interviewed an eighth grader who had dutifully circled all the numbers in the article he was reading. *All* the numbers, including page numbers. We asked him how any of the numbers had affected his thinking. "Affected my thinking? You didn't say anything about that. You just said to stay alert for numbers. I did."

OK. Back to an anchor question. We've found that the one that works best is "Why did the author use these numbers or amounts?"

Teaching the Signpost

Although this signpost requires little time to teach, it often generates the most conversation and the most questions. Once kids are reminded to be alert for numbers, you'll hear them begin to wonder, for example, if the percentage is accurate, why including the person's age is important, why more people weren't interviewed, why the cost of buying gasoline was included but not the cost of producing gasoline. As one student said, "You hear people say that numbers don't lie, but sometimes when you ask yourself, 'Why did the author include those numbers?' you see that maybe he's trying to convince you of something." Another student said, "Now that I'm looking at numbers, it's like this is the best way to really help me visualize what's happening." Our favorite comment came from the ninth grader who said, "This just proves that numbers do count."

Here we are in a middle school social studies class in a large urban district. We've been working with the teachers in this school for several months and have visited this particular classroom several times. Most of the students knew us by name, though the day we taught this lesson, one did ask, "Hey, have I seen you before?" Yes, dear child. Last week.

We began . . .

We Explain

“ If your teacher says, "Turn in your quiz soon," then you aren't sure if you have one more minute or ten more. "Soon" isn't very helpful. If the physical education teacher says, "Run a few more laps," you might not be sure if that means three or four, and if you're tired, that extra lap could make a difference. Someday when you're working, if your boss tells you she's giving you a raise, you're going to want to know exactly how big a raise.

In each case, specific numbers help you have a clearer understanding of what's going on. That's the main reason all of us use numbers—to give specific details about what we're discussing. And that's the same reason authors use numbers and stats—to help you better understand the topic.

> We begin, as always, by trying first to remind students that this signpost is something we see and pay attention to in our conversations each day.

But too often, numbers are simply skipped over as people read. We see a number and think, "Oh, there's a date," or "That's how many soldiers were in the war," or "That's the ratio of people who live in cities compared to those who live in the country," and then just keep reading. We see the numbers, but many times we don't actually pause and ask ourselves, "Why do I think the author included these numbers or stats?"

When we do think about that question, we will sometimes realize that the reason wasn't critical. The author was just telling you someone's age, or the author was simply saying that it was a two-story house. Other times, though, when you ask yourself, "Why did the author use these numbers or stats?" you'll discover that it was to help you visualize something or make an inference or a comparison or draw a conclusion. Sometimes it helps you figure out what's a fact and what's an opinion. And sometimes it helps you decide if the author is biased about something.

We Model

" Take a look at this short passage:

> Garana and her family have lived in their one-room house for two years. It's one of thousands of mud-brick homes in the Shamshatoo Afghan Refugee Camp. The camp holds about 50,000 Afghan refugees.

I'm going to circle all the numbers I see: *one*-room, *two* years, *one of thousands*, *50,000*. Notice that some of these numbers are written out as words. That's OK. As I ask myself, "Why do I think the author included these numbers," I realize that all of them give me information about where Garana is living. I think the author suspects that most readers have little first-hand knowledge of refugee camps. All the details that the numbers provide help me understand how awful the conditions are.

Let's look at another example, from a different article:

> In fact, nearly half of all bottled water is reprocessed tap water, sold at prices up to 3,000 times higher than consumers pay for tap water.

This is from an article called "Garana's Story" by Page Kent. It's included in the Appendix on page 265 and online at http://hein.pub/readnfres2.

We also use this article to teach Contrasts and Contradictions. In one class, after teaching that lesson, one student asked, "Do you think these terrible places are called camps so people won't think they are bad? Like maybe you'll think it's like summer camp or church camp? Is that why concentration camps were called camps?"

The obvious number is 3,000, but I also need to see that "half of all bottled water" represents an amount, too. I don't know how many bottles of water there are, but I've seen how many are in a single grocery store, so I know that half of all bottled water is a lot. Now I want to ask myself, "Why did the author use this specific number—3,000?" I think he wants me to realize that it's ridiculous that we'd spend 3,000 times more for a bottle of water than what water costs from the tap. This number is so extreme that it does make me wonder if this is right. I might need to see if someone else says the same thing before I accept this. But the number caught my attention, and now I'm rethinking how smart it is to drink bottled water.

Let's look at one more example:

> The singer, 28, joined us for the interview.

This comment tells me the age of the singer. As I read on, I don't see anything that makes his age special. This isn't about singers who are about to turn thirty or how he just became a pop start last week. I think the reporter just gave us a detail about him, but it's not a too important point of the article. Authors do that sometimes—provide a detail that doesn't change our thinking about the point of the article.

Students Try

We're going to share a few examples here that we have used with students, but the best ones will come from your own content. As you choose some, you might look for ones that mirror the examples we're providing here.

Example 1:

Lincoln's Gettysburg Address honored the 50,000 plus soldiers who were killed or wounded during one battle, the Battle of Gettysburg. It was only about 300 words long. Even though it was very short, it reminded us of all that was lost in that battle and must never be lost in our nation.

Example 2:

In 1979, Iranian militants took over the U.S. embassy that was in Tehran. These militants held 52 Americans as hostages for 444 days.

This stat comes from an online article your students might enjoy: www.cbsnews.com/pictures/bottled-water-10-shockers-they-dont-want-you-to-know/2/.

We simply write these examples on the whiteboard so all can see them.

Why did the author use these numbers? One student explained that "he used 50,000 and one" to show us how awful this one battle was. Another said, "Three hundred seems like a lot, but I counted 300 words in my book and it's not long at all. The author wanted me to see just how short this famous speech is."

Students said that using the specific number 52 rather than saying "many" "showed that each person was important." Others pointed out that the author "used 444 because each day counts if you're the hostage."

One student said, "Using *2014* shows that this is happening right now." Another said, "If 20% die each year, and they've been dying for nine years, how many bees are left?"

One student responded, "I circled *one, 22, one, first,* and *one-way.* Look at how many times *one* is used. I think that *one-way* is most important. He's not coming back. And I think this time his age is important, because you need to be young."

Example 3:

The year 2014 marks the ninth year in a row that at least 20% of the bee colonies in the US have died. Because bees are so important to pollination of fruits and vegetables, this is a problem. Any losses more than 10% are considered significant. (Johnson and Corn 2014)

Example 4:

One recent college graduate, age 22, wants to be one of the first people in a manned trip to Mars. Because this is planned to be a one-way trip, he doesn't want to date anyone so that he doesn't worry about leaving someone who loves him here when he takes off.

Students Reflect

When we ask students across all the grades to share how being alert for Numbers and Stats has changed their reading, we generally get responses that are encouraging. Students report that this signpost is "easy to spot" and "shows you details" and "helps me think about what the author thinks is most important." In the class that provided the comments for this lesson, one student remarked:

> "You don't just put in a number unless you really, really want to make a point. I mean, when you use a number, you had to do some research to, like, find that number. If you don't do the research, then you just say 'many' or 'most' or 'a long time ago.' Numbers really help you know what the author thinks is important."

At another time, in another class, a fifth grader shared a similar thought: "Numbers and Stats are like an author is saying 'Ding! Ding! Ding! Pay attention here!' Once you start seeing them and thinking about them, then I'm, like, how did I ever skip over them? They are super important."

Listening to Student Talk

Once you begin listening to what students are saying about the Numbers and Stats they notice, you'll see that this signpost encourages close reading. Here we want to share a portion of a conversation from a middle school social studies class in which students were reading about child labor issues. They read:

> Like most children, Mary turned her pay over to her parents for a long time. "Papa set me free when I was nineteen and after that what I made was mine," she said. After years of work, Mary managed to save $1,400. "Then the bank went busted and I lost my money."
>
> Emma Willis spent a lifetime in mills, from age twelve until seventy-five. "I worked in a cotton mill for sixty-three years, but I never did care for it much," Emma said when she was eighty-one.
>
> In the beginning, Emma worked from six in the morning until seven at night, earning thirty-five cents a day. "Every pay day that come, I brought my money home and laid it in my mother's hand; then after she died, I turned every cent over to my sister who kept house for almost fifty years. I worked steady, too, once while I was at the Cannon Mill I went eleven years without missing a day's pay. Back then if you didn't go, they'd send for you because they didn't have anyone else to do your work." (From *Up Before Daybreak*, by Deborah Hopkinson)

> You might use this passage from *Up Before Daybreak* as another example, perhaps one for kids to try on their own. It is reproduced on page 270 and online at http://hein.pub/readnfres2.

After students read this passage, we had them reread marking the numbers and then talking with a partner about the numbers they saw and why they thought the author used those numbers. Then, we pulled the kids back together and asked them to share what they had discussed with their partner. Several students explained that when they first read it, they only saw one number, $1,400, but then they realized that the other numbers were written out as words and "they should count as numbers."

Others said that as they looked at the numbers, they realized the author included specific ages, specific amounts of time worked, and specific wages earned to "make it be more fact, not just opinion" or "to help me see how little the kids were." And some said, "Because of their young age they probably couldn't say no," or "This helped me realize that children had no rights."

> By noticing the numbers and asking why the author used them, students made inferences, focused on details, visualized, and made causal connections.

One student reported that once she had circled all the numbers and looked at what the author was describing, she saw that the author "wasn't just giving a report about the people who worked in the mills.

He was, like, really making a point about how hard these people worked and how they had to start when they were kids." Another confirmed that observation saying, "I didn't even realize at first how little they were. You could just, like, read it but not really realize what you are reading. But when you looked at the numbers, it changed your understanding of it."

Questions You Might Have

1. *How do we help students decide which Numbers and Stats are important to notice?*

   Well, that's part of the reading experience—looking at a number and asking yourself, "Why did the author include this number?" So we try to avoid telling kids which types of numbers to consider. The problem arises when students see all numbers as equally important. If you hear students say, "The author included this to show me a detail" over and over, then you might tell students that if they're not sure if a number is important, they should replace it in their mind with a less precise word and see how that changes their understanding of the passage.

   For instance, if they read, "He was born in 1902," they could change that to "He was born at the turn of the twentieth century." Did the specific year make a difference, or was the author just trying to show that he lived in a very different time? If the author wrote, "She walked four miles," and the reader isn't sure if "four" is critical, he could think, "She walked several miles." Does that change the point the author was trying to make? When the answer is no, the specific number might not be important to the meaning of the text.

2. *Why do you say "numbers" when technically the correct word should be* numeral?

   We chose to go with the colloquial rather than the formal. We just didn't like the way Numerals and Stats sounded.

3. *Why do you use the word Stats? Most kids don't read real statistics reports for a long time.*

   We discussed using this word until the moment our editors yelled, "Stop! No more revisions." We know that statistics actually refers to averages, means, modes, and medians. But calling "9 out of 10" or "more than 50% of the time" *numbers* didn't work for us. So, numbers that were used in some sort of comparison became a statistic, and that led us to Numbers and Stats.

4. *In math class, it's all about numbers. So how do math teachers use this signpost?*

We got some great advice from math supervisor Will LaRiccia in Solon, Ohio, who reminded us that in word problems, students need to look at what's happening to the numbers. Too often, kids make assumptions based on the order of the numbers. For example, read this problem: "Bob bought some donuts for $8.00; he bought some bananas for $11.00; he also bought several small cartons of milk. He spent $26.00 total. How much did the milk cartons cost?" Kids often see 8, 11, 26, and the word *total* and add all three numbers. What we want them to do instead is to consider what they are supposed to do with those numbers. Will suggested that the anchor question needs to change from "Why did the author include those numbers?" to "What question is the author asking me, and how do those numbers help?"

5. *Sometimes authors use extremely large numbers or extremely small numbers. How do we help students "see" quantities such as one billion or 1/1,000,000?*

We've found that in many instances this is when authors create comparisons that make these huge (or infinitesimal) numbers comprehensible. For instance, to help students understand the enormity of one billion, they are told that if you wanted to count to a billion, you'd be counting for 95 years.

When authors don't use those more concrete examples, you might help students create their own examples. For instance, we can help six-year-olds understand how big one million is by asking them to hop ten times. Then point out that they would have to hop ten times a day for 273 years to have hopped 1,000,000 times.

Young children can learn a lot about big numbers from David Schwartz's picture book *How Much Is a Million?* and David Adler's *Millions, Billions, and Trillions: Understanding Big Numbers.*

When we shared this concept with a six-year-old, he promptly suggested we hop more than ten times a day.

Quoted Words

Asking students to be alert for Quoted Words really means asking them to think about what was quoted and who was quoted. This helps students recognize the author's purpose, make inferences, draw conclusions, and identify point of view. Noticing who is quoted and what is quoted might also help students think about facts and opinions, see cause-and-effect relationships, make comparisons or contrasts, draw conclusions, infer, and think about the author's point of view, purpose, or bias.

Students quickly identify quoted words; what they do less quickly is think about why the author used a quote and what that quote added. When they look closely at what was quoted, they often see it was to offer a Personal Perspective or a Voice of Authority.

ANCHOR QUESTION PROGRESSION

ELEMENTARY: What does this make me wonder about?

MIDDLE: Why was this person quoted or cited and what did it add?

HIGH SCHOOL: Discipline-specific questions such as . . .

> **History:** What is this person's perspective?
>
> **Science:** What are the qualifications of this person?
>
> **Math:** Why was a quote needed? What does it add to the thinking?

TEACHING TEXTS

We use several short passages in this lesson and then we use the vampire bat article which is reproduced on page 261 of the Appendix and online at http://hein.pub/readnfres2.

The generalizable language of the lesson

Notice & Note
What's happening

Quoted
" Words

When you're reading and you notice the author quoted a Voice of Authority, a Personal Perspective, or cited Other's Words, stop, and ask yourself

" Why did the author quote or cite this person? "

The answer will help you think about the author's point-of-view, purpose, bias, or Conclusions. Or these words will give a perspective, facts and opinions, or a generalization.

Name of lesson

Anchor question

Understanding the Signpost

No matter the text we read—save technical reports and how-to manuals—we almost always found Quoted Words. As we looked closely we found that these Quoted Words could be divided into three categories:

- ▶ Personal Perspectives
- ▶ Voices of Authority
- ▶ Others' Words

Personal Perspectives offer students an up-close look at events or ideas. The person being quoted often has no expertise other than having lived through something. For instance, in an article about tornadoes ripping through the small city of Van, Texas, the basketball coach is quoted as he describes rushing people from the school gym to the basement. This isn't an article about basketball, nor is the coach a part-time meteorologist. But he was there, and his personal perspective balanced the Voices of Authority and showed how any person might react in that situation. Often the Personal Perspective is a critical tool for creating an empathetic bond.

Voices of Authority often appear alongside Personal Perspectives, to balance the person-on-the-street view with the more detached, more expert view. So, in that same article, a meteorologist explained why conditions were right in Van for the tornadoes, the local law enforcement officer explained how people were warned, and the city manager explained how the town was prepared for such a disaster.

Others' Words are those citations often used in research papers (or books) when authors want to show that there is strength in numbers. The author doesn't highlight the words of one particular authority; instead, she shows that many others have studied this topic. The Quoted Words signpost in research documents often takes the form of citations rather than quotations, and we find it is more appropriately discussed when students are writing or reading research reports themselves.

The Anchor Question

As students read, we tell them to look for the Quoted Words Signpost—and this one is extremely easy to spot. Then (and this is where the thinking comes in), they must move to the anchor question: "Why was this person quoted (or cited) and what did it add?"

We don't spend a lot of time talking about Other's Words for citations unless kids are writing research papers. A middle-schooler, researching the aftermath of Hurricane Katrina, noted that comments about the causes of levee breaks had many citations. When we asked why the author cited so many people on this topic, she didn't know. Later she said, "No other topic had this many sources. Maybe the author is showing this is the problem most people have focused on."

We were pleased when two ninth graders, reading about the demise of fish in an area around Hawaii, pointed out that the Voice of Authority was an authority on transportation, but not on climate change, pollution, or the fishing industry. "Did the author think we wouldn't notice?" one asked. The other said, "We wouldn't have two months ago."

Of course, answering that question requires making an inference, generalizing, drawing a conclusion. As you listen to students, early on you'll hear, "Because the author wanted to quote that person." In other words, those kids haven't been giving any thought to *why* a person was quoted. So you'll have to do a bit of pushing at first: "Yes, but why did the author want to quote *that* person?"

Of all the anchor questions, we found that this one was the most important to ask. Without it, students would tell us that the author quoted someone because "He wanted to" or "If you copy someone's words, you have to use quotes." Once we had students thinking about quotes as Personal Perspectives or Voices of Authority, and then kept asking, "But why quote this person?" their answers began to show more critical thinking:

  ▶ "The author quoted this person because this Personal Perspective made you feel like you were there." (second grader)

  ▶ "The author quoted the woman because he was showing that just normal people have opinions about this." (fifth grader)

  ▶ "He was a doctor. And this was about smoking not being good for you. So it was good a doctor said how bad it is." (Fourth grader)

  ▶ "They had to say what NASA said, because it's about what it would take to send a person to Mars. So you have to ask NASA. You can't just ask, like, anyone. Like a dentist. Dentists don't know about going to Mars." (Sixth grader)

Over time, you'll hear students incorporate the term "Voice of Authority" if you use it. We have also used the term "expert's words" when sharing this signpost with kids, and we hear them begin to use that quickly, as well: "This author depended on the expert's words to help you realize that the polar ice cap is melting at a faster rate than it has in the past" (tenth grader).

Teaching the Signpost

Introducing this lesson doesn't take long because students quickly grasp the idea to look for quotation marks and then ask themselves why the author used that quote. Be prepared, though, to spend time—as the year moves on—discussing with kids that "why" question. We've discovered that as we look at why this person was quoted, too many times (especially in newspaper articles) there really isn't a great reason. The person was an expert, so the author was trying to establish a Voice of Authority, but the person quoted wasn't really an authority on the topic being discussed. As one high school student pointed out, "Sometimes it's like they needed a quote and this person was good enough."

We'll share how we taught this lesson in a heterogeneously grouped, ninth grade class. The students have learned the other signposts and now we're adding this one. Most of the students were attentive, if not to us, then certainly to the cell phones supposedly put away for the lesson.

We began . . .

We Explain

❝ **We want to share some comments we've heard from kids, and we want you to take a look at them and decide what they all have in common.** [Put comments you've heard your students make up on your whiteboard. Be sure these comments include quoted statements.]

> "Did you hear what she said? She was like, 'It's not my fault' and saying that over and over again, but everyone knew it was."

> "So, then, he went, 'So, let's all go to the game,' but then she said, 'No, let's all go to the mall,' and it was like no one could decide."

> "The teacher said that this wouldn't be on the test. Remember, her exact words were, 'You do not have to study this section because it will not be on the test' and so I didn't."

Choose any quotes you want that kids have said. It's important that you write these so kids can see the quotation marks.

Kids quickly pointed out that all of the comments have quotes in them. We then asked the students why conversational talk often includes quoting someone else. Several students responded and explained that they quote someone:

> "So that you know what someone else said."

> "To show it's not just your opinion."

> "To show what someone else is thinking."

> "Sometimes it's so if your mom is going to get mad, she gets mad at someone else."

We Model

We don't need a lot of modeling with this signpost. We prefer to get students thinking on their own. But they do need to hear our language as we think through why an author quotes someone.

So after students shared why they quote others when talking, we told them . . .

We've used the article "New Citizen Exam is Democracy 101" in middle and high school. You can access it at http://usatoday30.usatoday.com/news/nation/2006-12-01-citizenship_x.htm. Permission costs keep us from reproducing it here.

" Authors do the same thing—quote people to help make the text more interesting or to help prove a point. For instance, let's take a look at this article that appeared in the newspaper *USA Today*. It was titled "New Citizen Exam is Democracy 101." [We accessed this online and displayed it on the whiteboard. Once all could see it, we started reading it aloud to students and stopped after the following sentence:]

"The goal is to make it more meaningful," says Emilio Gonzalez, director of Citizenship and Immigrations Services. . . . "You really ought to know what you're swearing allegiance to," he says.

The first several paragraphs of this focused on how the questions on the immigration test will change, but now the author has quoted someone. When I notice an author using a quote, I want to stop and ask myself why that person was quoted. I obviously don't know Gonzalez, so I notice that the author told me what he does—he's the director of the Citizenship and Immigrations Services. I suspect he's got some real opinions about this new exam. It looks like he thinks these changes are important.

He says this makes the exam more meaningful, and this comment, about knowing what someone is swearing allegiance to, shows me he thinks this test is very important. I think the author is showing me a Voice of Authority who supports this change.

We continued reading the article and pointed out some more quoted material, this time several quotes from some high school students who have taken the new immigration test described in the article. We shared our thinking again.

I see that the author has turned to high school students. Now he's giving me the personal perspective of people who have taken the test. Their comments are interesting, but it makes me wonder, why didn't he talk with immigrants? Then I realize that no immigrants have taken this new test. It's good that the author is sharing the opinions of high school students, because like immigrants who have been studying for their citizenship exam they, too, have been studying U.S. history and U.S. government. This use of personal perspective is a powerful reminder that this test will affect regular people.

We wrapped up our modeling by reminding students that finding Quoted Words is easy. What's important is to think about *why* a person was quoted. Sometimes it will be to give us a personal perspective and other times it might be to show us what an expert thinks. Our job is to speculate on why the author used the Personal Perspective or Voice of Authority and then to think about how this affects our thinking about the topic.

Next, we shared short portions of longer articles from a variety of sources. We generally read one aloud and then have students turn and talk with a classmate about what they noticed. We'll spend only a couple of minutes on each short passage.

You'll want to share short portions of text from the content you teach. Here are some of the passages we've shared with grades 4–10.

> Drought relief did not come this winter—California's wet season—as hoped. Though California is the third-largest state in land mass, nearly all of the state is abnormally dry at best, and in exceptional drought at worst.
>
> "There's been a drought of some extent for multiple years now, and it doesn't look like it's going to be ending anytime soon," Storm Shield meteorologist Jason Meyers said. (Retrieved online from https://newsela.com/articles/drought-jobs/id/8682/. If you want to retrieve the remainder of this article, or other ones from Newsela, you'll need to create an account. We think doing so is well worth your time.)

Students will easily recognize that this is a Voice of Authority. We are happier when they realize that this person did what meteorologists are supposed to do: predict what will happen next. It looks like the author of the article is highlighting that this is an ongoing problem.

At the beginning of a chapter in a book about how children had to work in mills that turned cotton into thread, the author shares this quote:

> "I shall not stay here . . . . Up before day, at the clang of a bell and out of the mill by the clang of a bell—just as though we were so many living machines." (Anonymous Mill Girl, Lowell Massachusetts [*Up Before Daybreak*, by Deborah Hopkinson).

This is a Personal Perspective that is not attributed to one particular girl. One fifth grader pointed out, "Oh, I think the author didn't give us her name because in the mill who she was didn't matter." Yes!

This one is a little longer:

This passage begins with a quote that doesn't have a reference. We're just told that it's the oath of the President of the United States. Then it moves to a Voice of Authority quote from Lincoln that offers a very personal perspective. If students don't understand why this second quote was used, point out that the presidency is a position, but the people who occupy that position are individuals. We try hard in this country to respect both the position and the person.

Every single President has taken this oath: "I do solemnly swear (or affirm) that I will faithfully execute the office of President of the United States, and will to the best of my ability, preserve, protect, and defend the Constitution of the United States."

Only thirty-five words! But it's a big order if you're President of this country. Abraham Lincoln was tops at filling that order. "I know very well that many others might in this matter or as in others, do better than I can," he said. "But . . . I am here. I must do the best I can, and bear the responsibility of taking the course which I feel I ought to take."

That's the bottom line. Tall, short, fat, thin, talkative, quiet, vain, humble, lawyer, teacher, or soldier—this is what most of our Presidents have tried to do, each in his own way. Some succeeded. Some failed. If you want to be President—a good President—pattern yourself after the best. Our best have asked more of themselves than they thought they could give. They have had the courage, spirit, and will to do what they knew was right. Most of all, their first priority has always been the people and the country they served. (*So You Want to Be President*, by Judith St. George)

Students Try

Next, as usual, we gave students a longer text. While we often have let kids work together on the shorter passages, with the longer one we ask students to work alone as they identify quotes and jot down in the margin why the author shared this quote. Then we let them turn to a partner and share their thinking before we have a class-wide discussion.

For a longer text, we often use the text "Vampires Prey on Panama" by Chris Kraul (see page 261 in the Appendix). This article quotes two sources—a cattleman and a biologist. Each is a voice of authority and each also offers a personal perspective. As we listened to these ninth graders, we wanted to see if they recognized that. Many decided that the biologist is the voice of authority and the cattleman is the personal perspective, although one student recognized that even though the cattleman doesn't have a title, he does know a lot about keeping his cattle safe. "He seems like a good authority," the student explained. And the biologist seems to have an affection for bats, so, although he speaks primarily as a scientist, he may also be expressing a personal perspective. Some readers noticed that the language from the cattleman is harsher and one explained that "He seems really angry."

Students Reflect

About a week after students learned this signpost, they wrote comments about how reading with this signpost in mind was changing their thinking:

> ▶ "A lot of times I just skip over the quotes. This made me really think about what was being said."

> ▶ "I didn't know that there could be Personal Perspective or Voice of Authority. Now when I look at quotes it's like I see it all the time. Now when I see that the author uses one and not the other, I wonder what's up with that."

> ▶ "This is my most favorite signpost because it is so easy to spot. Look for the quotation marks and there it is! But then you have to think why, and then you see that sometimes it is, like, all Personal Perspective and that shows you a lot of opinion thinking."

We think this student has shared something that is probably true for many students. If this can slow them down so they will look at the quoted words, they may discover that some quotes are so inconsequential they could have been skipped.

Listening to Student Talk

This exchange is from two eighth graders in a small town. They'd read the vampire bat article, marked quotes, and jotted notes in the margin:

STUDENT 1: I noticed "We have to look for answers because this little animal is very stubborn" from Oliva.

STUDENT 2: Me, too. And I said he [the author] quoted Oliva because the author has been describing Oliva's job. But now you get to hear Oliva's thinking. Oliva is saying that the animal is stubborn.

STUDENT 1: Oh, that's good. That's like opinion. What he was doing—catching them with a net—that's his actions. But this is his thinking. That's good. This shows opinion.

In this language arts classroom, the teacher had taken our lesson and added that authors sometimes use quotes to show people's opinions. These students were picking up on that lesson.

While we liked that these students realized that the Quoted Words provided an opinion, we were more impressed with the following conversation between two eighth graders reading the climate change article we've already mentioned.

STUDENT 1: "So I marked "already severe, pervasive, and irreversible.""

STUDENT 2: I did too except I didn't include "already."

STUDENT 1: Why didn't the writer put *already* in quotes?

STUDENT 2: Because I guess the report didn't say "already." That's what he's adding.

STUDENT 1: Well, that changes everything.

When we asked all the students to share their comments with the class, Student 1 remarked, "This showed me that you really have to look at what's in quotes. Not quoting "already" is so important because now seeing that it's not quoted is making me wonder if that's just his opinion or if the report said that."

This question is exactly the type of critical thinking we want from students as they read.

Questions You Might Have

1. *Should I try to get my elementary school students to think about such a sophisticated issue as the credibility of quoted authorities? That seems beyond them.*

   It probably is, but you might still encourage your young readers to think about why a writer has chosen to quote a certain individual.

   Often, in books for young readers, the authors are likely to use quotes simply to bring the topic to life through a unique personal perspective. They may quote someone who witnessed or participated in an event, for instance. When you encounter those moments in a text, it's surely appropriate to ask students questions like "Why do you think the writer tells us what this person has to say?" to help them realize that the writer's source has a unique perspective on the event. "Because he lived through the tornado, and so he can tell us what it was really like," is a suitable answer. If your students come to realize that witnessing an event establishes some credibility, they will have learned something about assessing the sources a writer relies on.

2. *My students seem to either accept or reject both an author and his sources based solely on their prior beliefs or on the groups (usually*

political or religious) with which they identify, without considering the ideas being offered at all. What do I do about that?

Your students aren't alone in that problem. Too many adults accept the authority and credibility of those who have none and ignore or reject the well-grounded thinking of those who do have something of substance to offer. Think of all the otherwise literate, educated adults who go to politicians for their expert opinion on climate change, or to religious leaders for their expert opinion on evolution, or to movie stars for their expert opinion on, well, on anything. These adults are in the same situation as your students. They either can't, or won't, assess the knowledge, reasoning, and intellectual integrity of those presented to them as experts.

So, what do we do? Keep reminding them of the importance of thinking about the beliefs they hold and espouse. With perseverance, you'll encourage critical thinking by at least some.

3. *Many of these signposts seem to be closely connected with one another. For instance, two experts on different sides of the question will contradict one another. Will that signpost be Quoted Words or Contrasts and Contradictions?*

Yes! The signposts are interrelated. If students see that, great. If not, as long as they notice something, we think that's a great first step. We certainly don't want the students quarreling about what label to attach to this particular text feature. Instead, we want them discussing the content, the ideas that the contradictory quotes and the disagreeing experts have presented.

4. *This seems to focus on quotes; often people are cited and then paraphrased. Why don't you discuss this?*

We didn't like the way Quoted, Paraphrased Statements, and Citations sounded as a signpost name! That said, we did like the way Quotations and Citations sounded, and perhaps in upper grades you can migrate to that. We know you'll point out that authors don't always directly quote sources. We'll start kids on the road to examining why someone was quoted. As they move through the years, you'll help them decide why a citation was all that was needed rather than a direct quote.

Word Gaps

This final signpost turns our attention to the gap between the words authors use and what students know about those words. For many this gap is the critical problem in understanding nonfiction texts. That said, our youngest students can struggle with unknown words, too, as pointed out by a second grader who explained, "Some authors just show off all the hard words they know when easier words would let you have easier understanding."

In this chapter, we share what our research reveals about causes of vocabulary problems and then we share some solutions. We don't follow the same lesson format you've seen in the other chapters, but we do still encourage you to create an anchor chart to remind students what to do when they encounter words they don't know.

ANCHOR QUESTIONS FOR ALL GRADES

Do I know this word from someplace else?

Does it seem like technical talk for this topic?

Can I find clues in the sentence to help me understand the word?

TEACHING TEXTS

Find examples of short passages with the various vocabulary challenges we present in this chapter. Additionally, you might reproduce the "The Dung Beetle as a Weapon Against Global Warming" article found on page 263 of the Appendix or online at http://hein.pub/readnfres2 to use a quick assessment of types of problems students identify as problematic.

The generalizable language of the lesson

Notice & Note
What's happening

Word Gaps

When you're reading and the author uses a word or phrase you don't know, you should stop and ask yourself

"Do I know this word from some place else?"
or
"Does this seem like technical talk for experts of this topic?"
or
"Can I find clues in the sentence to help me understand the word?"
The answers will help you decide if you need to look the word up, or keep reading for more information.

Name of lesson

Anchor question

Understanding the Signpost

If there is anything that unifies teachers across content areas and across grades, it is probably the issue of vocabulary instruction. We all know the difficulties of helping kids learn new words. Collectively, we've felt the dismay of giving that quiz on National Vocabulary Test day (Friday, of course) only to have students stare at us blankly when we use the same words during Monday's lesson. It's not only that they forgot the words; they don't remember having ever learned them.

Many of us have bought special materials to help kids master vocabulary. We've taught roots and prefixes and put up synonym charts. We've even used the words we're teaching: "Oh, what a vibrant verdant field that is!" And still, words confound our students.

Far too often the lesson design that includes identifying words for kids, discussing the meanings of those words, and eventually giving quizzes on the words hasn't turned our students into the wordsmiths we want them to be. Our textbooks have highlighted words, put them in bold-faced font, defined them in the margin and still kids say, "I don't get it." Something needs to change.

Realizing that, we didn't want to offer a chapter on how to teach vocabulary. Others have skillfully done that (Allen 1991; Baumann and Kame'enui 2004; Beck et al. 2002; Blachowicz and Fisher 2004; Graves 2000; Nagy 1990; Stahl 1999). Instead, we focus on tools kids might use when a lack of word knowledge gets in the way of comprehension. So, the format of this signpost lesson doesn't match the others— purposefully. We begin this signpost lesson—one we call Word Gaps— by sharing our own realization about what confounds *us*. Next we discuss what kids identified as problems. Finally we move to steps we teach students so they can close word gaps.

Our Own Confusions

Words, which ought to be the gateway to understanding, too often are barriers. We experienced this firsthand when we overheard one ninth grader explaining something to another during lunch: "No. If you're going to do an Ollie North, you have to heelflip like when you learned kickflips, and then you can move to those and to a nosegrind. See?"

Lacking prior knowledge of skateboarding, we had no schema to activate. We didn't know those technical words, so we were up a creek

> Though this question was directed to his buddy, we looked at each other and mouthed the word, "No."

FROM BOB: That was Kylene. I felt I was up the creek without a canoe, but then, I haven't spent as much time skateboarding as Kylene has.

without a paddle, flying as blind as a bat, or, put most directly, had no idea what he was talking about. We could immediately identify what we didn't know, but identifying the unknown words didn't help. When you don't know anything about what you don't know, then realizing you don't know it doesn't actually help you know it.

We saw this again when we read this passage:

> In mathematics, a **Lie algebra** (/li/ not /lai/) is a vector space together with a non-associative multiplication called "lie bracket" [x,y]. It was introduced to study the concept of infinitesimal transformations. Lie algebras are closely related to Lie groups, which are groups that are also smooth manifolds, with the property that the group operations of multiplication and inversion are smooth maps" (http://en.wikipedia.org/wiki/Lie_algebra).

It did not help that the term *Lie algebra* was bold-faced, that pronunciation was provided, that a definition was offered, or that we were told its origin. We still looked at each other and said, "I don't get it."

Sadly, though, we could answer the following questions:

1. What is a Lie algebra?

2. Why was it introduced?

3. To what are Lie algebras closely related?

4. True or False: Smooth manifold groups include Lie groups.

Well, we aren't positive about question 4, but if this were a test (with each item worth 25 points) and we received credit for the first three we *could* answer correctly, we would have scored 75 points and would proudly display that grade on the refrigerator door. And there's a 50-50 chance we'd get that final one right and be able to brag that we got 100 on the test.

An A+ and we would have no idea what any of it meant.

****

Although noticing what we didn't know was humbling, it didn't offer us a lot of insight other than the fact that we obviously don't know much about skateboarding and even less about algebra. We decided to move on to listening to kids.

Listening to Kids

As we visited classrooms, worked with kids, and asked them to tell us what was happening as they saw words that confused them, we began to see confusion in four distinct areas: descriptive language, multiple meanings, distant references, and rare words and technical talk. Let's look at those four types of confusion now.

Descriptive Language

In a middle school classroom of a very large urban district, we gave a group of eighth graders a one-page handout that a science teacher had given us about photosynthesis. The only technical terms that were in bold-faced font included *photosynthesis, chloroplast, organelle, stroma,* and *chlorophyll.* We asked students to read the page and circle the terms that were confusing.

We told them that as they circled terms, they should make a note of the problem in the margin. We were surprised at what students circled and wrote:

> ▶ *Grab:* "How does chlorophyll 'grab the sunlight?' I don't get that."
>
> ▶ *Combine with light:* "It says, 'Carbon dioxide and water combine with light to create oxygen and glucose.' How does something combine with light? That makes no sense to me."
>
> ▶ *Magic:* "How can chlorophyll be a 'magic compound?' How could it be magic? This is science."

We asked students if they understood the bold-faced words such as *chlorophyll* and *photosynthesis.* Most said they did *not,* but that they thought if they could understand these words and phrases, they would better understand the harder terms, the ones in bold-faced font.

In an elementary school, the students read the article about dung beetles (see Appendix page 263), which included these sentences: "It may seem like an unlikely environmental hero. But the dung beetle, with its sordid habit of laying eggs in and eating cow poo, might just be a weapon in the battle against global warming." Several students identified *weapon* as a problem. That surprised us, but again, we understand the role of descriptive language. When we asked why this word confused them, they all remarked that they didn't "get" how a beetle could be a weapon. One student explained, "It's like, well, I know what a weapon looks like. But how is a beetle a weapon?" Others agreed.

We aren't providing the handout because we didn't have a source for the information it contained, and the science teacher didn't either. She had brought it home from a workshop—something we all do. We do quote short phrases. If someone recognizes this text from the bits we share, we sure would like the source.

We've included this article in the Appendix for two reasons. First, we think if we've read about dung beetles eating cow poo, you should, too. Second, we encourage you to give your students this article—at any grade—and ask them to identify confusing words and discuss why they are problematic. We think you'll gain insight into vocabulary issues from their comments.

It became apparent that although authors use descriptive language, metaphors, and similes to prevent confusion or to make the language more vivid, the result is often the opposite. Perhaps this is because understanding metaphors and similes means holding two competing images in mind. When students have difficulty with the image that is supposed to be helpful, it is most often because they can't see the comparison the author wants them to picture. And that descriptive language—such as chlorophyll *grabbing*—might pull to mind images that just don't make sense in the science context. Possibly this is why science teachers tell us that we should avoid anthropomorphism, or what language arts teachers call personification.

Multiple Meanings

In a middle school, we watched students as they read about tsunamis from a *National Geographic* article:

> A classic aboveground eruption is just one of the ways a volcano can disturb the ocean and generate a tsunami. Waves can also be triggered by submarine events—eruptions, cascades of ash, or the collapse of a volcanic flank. The 1883 volcanic explosion of Krakatau and the collapse of its caldera stirred up 130-foot-high waves and killed some 36,000 people. (*National Geographic*, April, 2005)

Because this was from a magazine article, no words were highlighted, put in bold-faced font, or defined in the margin—all typical textbook "supports." Again, we asked students to circle the words they did not know and then jot down margin notes about the problem. The class had been discussing tsunamis and volcanoes, so we didn't expect those would be circled. One often-circled word was *submarine*, and one student asked, "How does a submarine make eruptions? Like, does it blow up something?" Other comments suggested similar confusion. One student circled *volcanic flank* and wrote in the margin, "horse's flank?" Several circled *triggered,* and one wrote, "Gun = trigger. I don't get it here." One circled *cascade* and wrote "Like for the dishwasher?"

From another class, a student had trouble with the word *aerobic* in the sentence "Animal cells need an aerobic environment (one with oxygen)." The student wrote, "Aerobic? Exercise? Like in PE?"

We saw time and time again that kids know words; they just don't know the multiple meanings of words. This is especially true for our English language learners.

Distant References

Let's move to another class. In Ohio, a middle school student pointed out that he wasn't sure what "rollers" meant in the sentence "Ocean rollers can travel 12,000 miles around the globe to the sixtieth parallel and never bump into anything. The spinning of the earth causes these mighty waves to spiral endlessly to the east building momentum as they go" (from *Shipwreck at the Bottom of the World*, by Jennifer Armstrong). "What's a roller?" he asked. "Do you see anything that might help you figure it out?" we asked. "Nope," he replied after a quick glance. "Where did you look?" we asked. "In the sentence. I read the sentence."

In another district, high school students studying U.S. history read portions of Susan Campbell Bartoletti's award-winning book *Hitler Youth*. One short paragraph from the longer excerpt they read caused some problems. Take a look at this paragraph and mark the words you suspect students identified as problematic:

> But millions of other Germans were simply apathetic about the news of Hitler's appointment. They found it hard to feel excited about the changes he promised. In 1933, Germany had forty different political parties, each one making promises as it struggled for power.

We suspect you marked *apathetic* as a word that students identified. Many did mark that word, and we'll discuss it next. First, though, let's consider another word that was identified as a challenge.

Many students (about ten out of class of nineteen) circled the word *appointment* and asked "What appointment?" One student remarked, "An appointment is like, you know, when you have to show up for something. Why do millions care what his appointment is?" For students to understand *appointment* in this context, they needed to remember one sentence from *seven* pages back: "Earlier that day, Germany's aging president, Paul von Hindenburg, had appointed Hitler chancellor, making him the second-most powerful man in the country." When students returned to that passage, one said, "That's

Three students also marked the word *parties*. These three wanted to know how a party makes a promise. One said, "I don't get why Germany had forty parties. Like, forty parties?" This was a multiple-meanings problem, rather than a distant-reference problem.

not fair. *Appointed* is like being made it, like you get appointed captain of the football team; but *appointment* is like making a doctor's appointment. How are we supposed to know they are the same?" Another complained, "Appointed was too far back there."

Recognizing that the gist of the word, if not the definition, was offered somewhere other than the immediate sentence or in margin notes was a problem. We think that textbook reading has convinced kids that definitions always occur at the point of use. That makes for a considerate text—a term coined a few years ago to point out features that supposedly made a textbook easier to navigate. We think it probably has helped create dependent readers.

Rare Words and Technical Talk

In that same class, many marked *apathetic* and said that they knew this was important because millions of Germans felt that way, but they didn't know what it was. This is an example of what is called a Tier II vocabulary word—words that most people don't use in their everyday oral vocabulary, but not words that are specific to only one discipline.

When we asked students to think about *apathetic* in relationship to the next sentence, only a few recognized that the phrase, "found it hard to feel excited," gave them a clue to the meaning of *apathetic*. When we pointed out that the ones who were apathetic found it hard to feel excited, several complained, "Why does the author think we know that?" or "How are we supposed to know that?" or "Why didn't he just say that?"

Our elementary students reading about the dung beetle marked the word *sordid*. One student quickly spoke up, saying, "I don't know what it is either, but it's not good. I mean, eating cow poo. That's gross. That is, like, so disgusting. But I don't know what it means." When we asked if it might mean "gross" she said, "No. It would be in the side [margin] if that's what it means."

We also found that kids were stumped by what we call "technical talk" or what others would call Tier III vocabulary. We lacked the Tier III vocabulary necessary to understand the comments about skateboarding or the paragraph about Lie algebra. Tier III vocabulary is the precise language of a discipline. It's sometimes called "jargon," but more often—when we're in over our heads—it sounds like gibberish.

One eleventh-grade boy opened his physics textbook, looked at it, dropped his pencil in the hinge of the book, and closed it. We asked why he closed it. He opened it back up to the page his pencil marked, pointed to the text, and said "So, I have no idea what this means, 'The electric field is a vector quantity.' I get field, even though I don't get what an electric field is, and I know quantity; that's like amount. I don't know what vector is, and then when you put it all together it is just nothing. I don't know what any of this is." And he closed the book again.

Rare words and technical talk offer specific challenges. But too often they are seen as the only challenges. They aren't, and if we can help students with other word challenges, they'll have more energy to devote to these words.

What We Came to Understand

From these examples we reached some critical understandings:

1. Students are confused by words with multiple meanings and figurative language as often as they are by rare words and technical talk.

2. Struggling readers have little idea how antecedents can provide meaning for some words.

3. Students don't realize that understanding *something* about the word might enable them to keep reading.

4. Rare words and technical talk can so overwhelm students that reading comes to a halt.

In other words, the breadth of challenges students face when dealing with vocabulary exceeded what we had anticipated. *We* know multiple meanings of words; *we* understand the role of antecedents; *we* expect the context to be a clue to what we don't understand; *we* recognize that sometimes knowing a little is enough to keep on reading. Our problem, as skilled readers, is truly confined to rare words or the technical words of a particular discipline. All too often, however, those words—rare words and technical words—are the only type of words that textbooks identify for kids. But their gaps in word knowledge extend beyond this one type of issue. And once we saw all those gaps, we knew the signpost lesson we needed to teach: Word Gaps.

Anchor Questions

The Word Gaps Signpost lesson tells students that as they are reading, they need to be aware of the words that create gaps in their understanding, much as the "Mind the Gap" signs in British subway stations remind

This student's quick gesture of defeat made it look as if he had put little effort into the reading. But his comments showed he was indeed trying to make sense of the text. He identified what he knew—field and quantity—and tried to make that make sense in the context. The technical words proved to be too much.

FROM KYLENE: Bob is a true wordsmith, and he rarely encounters words that he doesn't know. I, though, find them often. In this case, I ran across the word *pellucid* and when I asked him what it meant, he said, without hesitation, it's one goal for this book. Well, that was helpful. Once I looked it up, I agreed.

subway riders to beware the distance between the platform and the train. Once students notice a word that's a problem, they need to ask themselves:

- **Do I know this word from someplace else?** If yes, this is probably a word with multiple meanings, and they need to think about what they know about the word in the other context to see if that helps. If not, they will need to use a dictionary or context clues to figure out what it means in this situation.

- **Does this seem like technical language just for this topic?** If yes, they might need help from outside the text—a dictionary, an easier text on the same topic, a friend, a teacher.

- **Can I find clues to help me understand the word?** If yes, they need to be reminded that the gist of a meaning is sometimes enough to keep reading. Tell them to look back a few sentences or paragraphs, and remind them that they might need to read on to find those context clues.

When we pointed out to students—elementary through high school—that sometimes the author uses words that make us feel as if there is a huge gap between what she has written and what we understand, they all laughed at that obvious statement. Then we pointed out that often the words that are most confusing are not the words they have never seen before, because authors work hard to explain those. Their job, we tell them, is to do more than announce, "I don't get it" or look to the margin for a definition. Their job is to think about those questions because the answer will help them fix up their confusion.

But If They Need to Do More . . .

The best way for kids to close the word gap is for them to read more (Allington 2002; Beers 2002; Guthrie 2004; Miller 2009). The more kids read, the more words they see. The more words kids see, the more they learn the multiple meanings of common words and the meanings of rare words; they learn how context works to define a word; and, they learn the technical words of a discipline. But that doesn't help them with *this* word today. When students need more help than the above anchor questions provide, we suggest the following steps.

First, Identify the Exact Problem.

It's easy for kids to say, "I don't get it." And it's just as easy for us to presume we know what the "it" is and fix the problem for the kids. Resist that urge and push students to define exactly what the "it" is.

Second, Look for What's Familiar.

Many times students will recognize a part of a word. That might be a prefix or a root word. Other times, they know what a word means in a different context. That information might be helpful. But too often, students decide that a "hard word" is "too hard" and they shut down. Remind them that if they'll study the word and think about all they know about it, they will probably realize they know something, and that something just might be helpful.

This means it's helpful for you to discuss the root words that will most often occur in your discipline, discuss with students what prefixes mean, and talk with students about multiple meanings of words. It's fun to start a class with questions such as:

- What might *volume* mean to a hairdresser? A musician? An encyclopedia company? Do these meanings have something in common?

- What might *cell* mean to a biologist? A prisoner? Do these meanings have something in common?

- What might *line* mean to an artist? A mathematician? A soldier? Do these meanings have something in common?

- What does *staff* mean to a band director? A business man? A doctor? Do these meanings have something in common?

Third, Look for "Like This" Language.

When our students are confounded by technical talk—an issue high school physics and chemistry students tell us they face all the time—we tell them that the problem isn't the *word*. The problem is that they don't understand the concept behind the word. We remind them that you can't really understand the word *hot* until you touch something that is hot. It's hard to grasp the notion of electromagnetic waves or communism because we don't see those things. This is why authors often use concrete examples (often introduced with the words *like this*) to explain complex topics.

If your students point out the technical talk as the problem, ask them to look for illustrations, sidebars, or examples in the text that provide that "like this" example. That concrete example will help them develop an understanding of the word.

Fourth, Try Strategies Such as Syntax Surgery and Sketch to Stretch.

These two fix-up strategies are described in detail in Part IV. Neither of them will give your students a definition of a word, but they will help students understand the gist, and usually that's enough for them to keep reading.

Fifth, Use a Dictionary or Thesaurus.

Sometimes, students simply must decide that the definition they know for a word isn't enough. The students who thought the Germans were throwing forty gala events when they read the term "forty parties" finally recognized, "Party has got to mean something else" and reached for a dictionary. The student who didn't understand that "submarine" might also mean "under the water" and not "a ship that travels under the water" had to eventually look it up. But they all started by recognizing that they knew something about the word, just not enough.

We want students to use glossaries, dictionaries, thesauruses, and even Wikipedia when all else fails. What we don't want them to do is close their books and give up.

Questions You Might Have

1. *Why are technical words so hard?*

   Technical words aren't hard; the concepts behind them are. Too often kids are trying to learn the concept and the term at the same time. They need to, when possible, grasp the concept first and then learn the term.

   We watched a teacher begin to teach kids what photosynthesis is about two weeks before they began reading about it. She brought in two small green plants. She placed both on her desk and then covered one with a small box. Kids immediately said, "It's gonna die." She said, "Let's see what happens." Both got watered, but one was kept in the dark. Two weeks later, they examined both. Sure enough, the covered one looked withered. The kids said to her, "We told you. It's got to have light." Then she asked, "Why?" She pointed out that both had soil; both had water. "What does the sunlight do?" Kids decided that the sunlight had to do something that helped the plant grow. One even said, "The sunlight makes something in the plant do something." Now they were ready for the technical talk in their chapter.

2. *Is it a good idea to give kids a list of words for them to define before reading?*

Absolutely. If the text does not in any way define a word that is critical to the meaning, then you might decide to define it ahead of time. Our concern, though, is that if we're trying to create independent readers, we can't keep pointing out to kids which words they need to know. *The New York Times* won't do that for them. On their own, they have to identify the problematic but important words and figure out how to cope with them.

3. *Should I look for textbooks that define words at the point of use?*

Textbooks are a special type of book written to explain something. For that reason, definitions of technical terms—that Tier III vocabulary—ought always to show up at the point of use, and those definitions should be revealed through direct explanations, examples ("like this" language), figures, illustrations, and comparisons. We're less happy when Tier II words are defined in the margins. Students need to learn to identify which words they need to know. They need to find their own gap in understanding and then work to close that gap. After all, when is the last time you read a newspaper, a novel, or an article with words defined in the margin?

PART IV

The Role of Strategies

From Kylene: Very early in my teaching career I told my class of seventh graders to complete the worksheet I had distributed. It was a worksheet in which students were to read short passages and then underline the causes and draw arrows to the effects. After I distributed the worksheet, and after all the students had inhaled the fumes from the mimeographed paper, I gave them these instructions: "Read the following passages, and for each one, underline the cause and draw an arrow to the effect."

Quite proud of my orderly management of the day thus far (though the kids were probably orderly because they were all stoned from the fumes), I returned to my desk to do something critically important, I'm sure. Most likely I was rewriting the names in my grade book because a new student had arrived and that meant my neatly alphabetized list of names was going to be out of order. But then that new student came and stood at my desk.

"I don't get it," the student said.

"Don't get what?" I asked.

"This. How to do this," he said waving the worksheet in his hand.

I nodded and patiently explained again what I had just said. "Well, you read the passages, then underline the causes, and draw arrows to the effects."

The student stood there and patiently said again, "Yeah, but how do I do this?"

I began to grow confused. "Do what?"

"This," he stated not quite as patiently as the first time.

"This what?" I asked, also not staying as patient as I had been. "You just read the passage and then underline the cause and draw an arrow to the effect." I said it slower and louder. Surely that would help.

The student seemed more puzzled and looked around the room. He finally said, "How does you telling me to underline the cause and draw an arrow to the effect help me do that unless I already know how to do that? How do I know unless I already know?"

"STRATEGIES ARE THOSE SCAFFOLDS
WE SHARE WITH KIDS
TO MAKE THE INVISIBLE
THINKING PROCESS VISIBLE."

I thought about that for a long moment. Then I asked him to return to his desk. His statement haunted me a long time (and I wrote about that student in *When Kids Can't Read: What Teachers Can Do*). I eventually concluded that I had confused two critically important words: *instructions* and *instruction*. I was great at providing instructions; I still had a lot to learn about offering instruction. *Instructions* are giving directions, orders, steps to follow. *Instruction* is providing insight for how to do something.

So in an effort to give kids *less* so they will use those tools *more*, we share only seven strategies in this section.

That year, I kept asking myself, "How can I show kids what a cause is if they can't already identify that cause? How do I show them how to make a comparison if they can't already do that?" *How do you know if you don't already know?* Eventually, I came to understand that the first thing I had to do was make kids' thinking—that invisible process of thinking—visible. I had to be able to listen to their reasoning, their understanding, their tentative attempts to reason through things if I hoped to be able to identify where they needed help. And that meant I needed to show them some strategies.

Our Definition of Strategies

Our definition of strategies differs a little (well, a lot) from other folks you might read. Many people call visualizing, predicting, summarizing, connecting, clarifying, and monitoring *strategies*, or they refer to them collectively as *strategic thinking*. We call them *comprehension processes*. Why? Well, we're going back to some of the earlier research in reading comprehension from the 1960s and 1970s that employed the term "information processing," which was in vogue because educators were picking up on the language of computer programming. During those decades, researchers called the types of thinking we do—visualizing and predicting, for example—*processes*, not strategies.

That resonated with us because these processes are how we think. Our brains form pictures, make predictions, make connections, seek to clarify. These are thinking processes. When we need students (or ourselves) to make these invisible processes visible, we turn to strategies. Strategies are those scaffolds that make the invisible thinking processes visible. For instance, if we need to see how kids are visualizing, we can have them use a strategy called Sketch to Stretch. If we need to see how they are making connections, they can use Genre Reformulation. If we want to help them summarize, we can teach them Somebody Wanted But So (SWBS).

Signposts as Strategies

If strategies are what bring thinking out to the visible level, then aren't the signposts we just discussed in the previous section *strategies?* Yes. They are. And we hope that eventually Notice and Note Signposts (for fiction and nonfiction) will simply take their place among the many other strategies teachers share with students. For now, as we're all learning them, we're still calling them the Notice and Note Signposts or simply signposts.

Strategies versus Activities

Sometimes teachers ask us if an activity is the same as a strategy. If somebody wants to call Possible Sentences an activity, we're not going to tell them that's wrong, even though we do see a critical difference between a strategy and an activity. For us, a strategy is something that lets us look closely at how a student is thinking. So if students do Possible Sentences while we sit at our desks rewriting the names in our grade books, and then we simply take up the worksheet and give kids a completion grade, then we've used it as an activity, something to keep kids busy for a while. But if we're listening to students, noticing who has said, "Well, the sentence could say that the ten-year-old was forced to work, so he could no longer attend school," letting us hear that causal link between being forced to work and not attending school, then we're using it strategically. And when we show the student the causal connection she's just made, and we underline that cause and draw an arrow to the effect, then we're helping her see that she does know how to connect causes and effects.

Strategies and Skills

In that example, the strategy Possible Sentences showed us that the student has the skill of connecting an effect to a cause. So what is a skill? A skill is a behavior that can be isolated and practiced, something that we get better at with repetition and sometimes with instruction. So, we used Possible Sentences and heard a kid making a causal connection. What type of thinking processes did that reveal? It reveals making connections, perhaps making a prediction; plus, there might have been some visualizing. And the skill involved was that of connecting cause and effect.

Let's look at another example. Sequencing is a skill. One strategy we might use to show us if kids can keep events in a sequence is Genre Reformulation. What type of thinking process does that reveal? Probably some connecting, monitoring, inferring, and perhaps even visualizing. We rarely (if ever) use one thinking process in isolation from another. That's why we find it difficult to try to teach these thinking processes as if they are strategies because that encourages teaching them one at a time. "Now, today as you read, we want you to predict." No. "As you read, be alert for Signposts. When you notice one, we suspect you will discover you are making a prediction."

The Strategies We Share

Often, we think we have shared too many strategies with students. Their toolbox of strategies doth overflow, and they have no idea which one to use or when to use it. So in an effort to give kids *less* so they will use those tools *more*, we share only seven strategies in this section. They are:

- ▶ Possible Sentences
- ▶ KWL 2.0
- ▶ Somebody Wanted But So
- ▶ Syntax Surgery
- ▶ Sketch to Stretch
- ▶ Genre Reformulation
- ▶ Poster

These strategies are listed in this order because this moves you from before reading (Possible Sentences and KWL 2.0) to during reading (Somebody Wanted But So, Syntax Surgery, Sketch to Stretch) and then to after reading (Genre Reformulation, Poster). We find it better to give kids fewer tools they can learn to use well than so many tools that they never develop any expertise.

As you read through this section, you'll notice that these strategies have two things in common: they require students to do some rereading of a text, and they encourage students to talk about what they have read. Both practices—rereading and talking—have been shown to be important in improving students' comprehension (Keene 2012; Langer et al. 1990; Stahl and Clark 1987).

Possible Sentences

Understanding This Strategy

Possible Sentences, as we envision it, is a before-reading strategy that helps students think about the content of a text before they begin reading. You choose eight-to-fourteen words (or phrases) from the text, words you believe students know. Students then write five "possible sentences" that might appear in the text, using three to five of the given words in each sentence.

Possible Sentences

Name _____ Date_____

Key Vocabulary

Making Predictions: Write up to 5 sentences using the words above. Be sure to use at least three or four words from the Key Vocabulary list in each sentence. Do not use more than six words from that list in any one sentence.

1.

2.

3.

4.

5.

Modifying Predictions: After reading the selection, review the sentences you wrote. Correct any information that is not accurate.

1.

2.

3.

4.

5.

If you prefer, students can write sentences on their own notebook paper—if you have an extra twenty minutes for students to find one clean sheet!

TO GET STARTED

MATERIALS: Possible Sentence template; We teach this lesson with "Hard at Work"

TEACHER PREP: Choosing words from text

WHEN TO USE: Before kids read the text; return to it after reading

GROUP SIZE: Best in pairs; can work alone

VARIATIONS

Math: Give kids examples of problems and let them write the "possible rules" that guide solutions. For instance, you give $\frac{3}{8} + \frac{1}{4} = \frac{5}{8}$ and $\frac{5}{16} + \frac{3}{16} = \frac{8}{16}$. "Possible rule" might be "Bottom number must stay same and then you add top numbers." They correct "rules" as needed.

When Moore and Moore (1986) presented this strategy, their intention was to give students a list of unknown vocabulary words from a text they were about to read. Students were to use those words to write "possible sentences" that might appear in the text. Moore and Moore were specific in their directions and instructed students to use two vocabulary words in each sentence. So, from an article about the desert, the word list might include terrain, barren, precipitation, and denuded and a student sentence might have been "There was <u>precipitation</u> and it was <u>denuded</u>." Finally, students were to correct their sentences after reading the text and learning definitions. Used as originally intended, we thought that asking students to write sentences with unknown words didn't seem helpful, and it also rarely seemed to raise curiosity about the text.

We have made a slight modification. In our work with this strategy we have found that when unknown words were included in the word list, students made too many errors with their sentences and became too frustrated by the many corrections they had to make. So we encourage teachers not to use many Tier II words and to use no Tier III vocabulary with this strategy. It's just too hard for students to write a possible sentence if they do not know the meaning of the words. Also, we found that when students only included two of the key words in their sentences, too many times the sentences they wrote had little to do with the actual text. As a result, we now ask students to use no fewer than three key words in each sentence they write. We also tell them not to use more than six key words in a sentence, to prevent some students (and you know who they are) from writing just one sentence that contains all the key words.

Teaching the Strategy

This begins with you choosing eight to fourteen words or phrases from the text that students are about to read. Share these words with your students by putting them up on your whiteboard and then reading them aloud. Be sure to tell students whether the words are from a nonfiction or fiction text. Then, working with a partner, students write five sentences that use these key words. We use the Possible Sentence template, but you certainly could just have students write sentences on their own paper. They should use no fewer than three or four key words in a single sentence and no more than five or six.

After students have completed their sentences, they share some with the class. As a class, students then make a prediction about what the text will be about. After reading, students return to their predictions, discuss their original sentences with the class or another student, and correct the sentences as needed.

Sharing the words with students and letting them write five sentences should take about fifteen minutes of class time. If you don't think your students can write five sentences in about fifteen minutes, have them write three or four.

The class we're featuring here is a tenth-grade language arts class. Most of the students are also taking a "reading improvement" class as they read multiple grades below grade level. Several speak Mandarin, Spanish, or Vietnamese as their first language. We are there to model for several teachers how we get kids into a text without telling the kids something about the text.

We began . . .

We Explain

" On the board are several words and phrases from a nonfiction text you're about to read. [On the next page are words and phrases for the text "Hard at Work." We have used this text with students grades 4–12.] All these words and phrases come from the same text. Work with one partner to write five sentences on the Possible Sentences worksheet you each have before you. They are called "possible sentences" because these are sentences that you could *possibly* read in the text. Each sentence should use at least three of these words but no more than six. Be sure to underline each word you use. When you've finished the last sentence, you'll have used all these words and phrases. Remember, these are all from the same text, so when we read your sentences, one after the other, they should give us a good idea of what this text might be about.

Before you begin, I want to remind you that even though you are working with a partner, you each should write on your own worksheet. So if you want to write different sentences, that's fine. Use your partner to help you think about how you might want to combine words into a sentence. Also, remember, these words and phrases all come from a text that is nonfiction. That means no "attack of the killer banana trees as they carry sharp, heavy knives." These words and phrases are from an article that tells us something about the real world. OK. Let me read you the words and then you should get started.

Here are some tips for primary grade teachers. First, use fewer words; second, consider grouping the words for students; finally, let students talk with a partner and then report to you. You can make a list of their sentences on chart paper as shared writing if students lack the fluency to write for themselves.

WORDS/PHRASES TO SHARE

Ecuador	10-year-old	banana trees
sharp heavy knives	poor country	harmful chemicals
250 million kids	child labor laws	12-hour-workdays
as little as $27 a week	no longer attend school	forced to work

Students Try

We don't need a "We Model" section because you're not teaching students a strategy they will need to use on their own. You're giving them directions for something you want them to do: choose some words and write some sentences. Modeling is important when we need students to be able to use a strategy later on their own. They will never use Possible Sentences without you to provide the words and phrases.

As students begin working in pairs, circulate among them and make sure they are including at least three of the key words in each sentence. If students ask what a word or phrase means, we always tell them. If many students ask about the same word, then you've chosen a word that's outside their Tier I vocabulary. Either interrupt the class and explain it to everyone, or just tell all to omit it.

You will see students write sentences that you know are not accurate. For instance, with this set of words, many students will write something like "There are 250 million kids in the poor country of Ecuador who no longer attend school." When they read the text they will discover that there are 250 million children *worldwide* who are forced into labor situations. When you see students make that mistake, don't correct it. You want them to discover the problem, talk about it, and figure out how to correct it.

We find that English language learners benefit a lot from this strategy. We modify it slightly by first having them categorize the words into one of four groups: people, places, problems, and outcomes. Once their words are placed into categories, they write their sentences. See Figure 32.

Also, students with special needs can be more successful if we group the words for them, showing them which words should be used in the first sentence, second sentence, and so on. Later, after some practice, we instead give them six words and tell them to choose three to use in the first sentence and three to use in the second. Once they are comfortable with grouping words this way, we give them more words.

A great change-up for any group is occasionally to give students words and tell them that instead of writing sentences, they are to work with a partner to place them into these four categories. Then, as a class you can compare placement, and students can discuss what it seems the text will be about.

Name Nick   **Date** 10-7

Key Vocabulary Ecuador, sharp heavy knives, 250 million kids, as little as $27 a week, 10 year old, poor country, child labor laws, no longer attend school, banana trees, harmful chemicals, 12 hour work days, forced to work

Making Predictions: Write up to 5 sentences using the words above. You may use more than one word/phrase in a sentence.

1. Ecuador is a poor country with 250 million kids who no longer attend school.

2. Because Ecuador has no child labor laws, kids who no longer attend school can be forced to work 12 hour work days.

3. These kids make as little as $27 a week and work with harmful chemicals and sharp heavy knives

4. A 10 year old can be forced to work 12 hour work days in a banana tree with sharp heavy knives

5. Ecuador is a really dangerous country for kids who no longer attend school because it has no child labor laws

Modifying Predictions: After reading the selection, review the sentences you wrote. If the way you used it fits with the text, simply write, "No change needed." If not, revise your possible sentence to fit the text.

1. Ecuador is a poor country with 69,000 kids who work with banana trees

2. Because Ecuador has few child labor laws kids who no longer attend school can be forced to work 12 hour days

3. Plantation workers can make as little as $27 a week and are exposed to dangerous chemicals and work with sharp heavy knives

4. No change needed.

5. There are 250 million kids worldwide who are forced to work because their countries have few child labor laws.

Figure 32 Two tenth graders said, "This was the best way we've ever gotten into an article. We wanted to figure out if what we thought was right. It was, for some of the sentences."

Remember that Possible Sentences should take no more than about fifteen minutes of class time. Once students have finished writing, pull them together and let them share some of their sentences. Then see if, as a class, they can predict what the text will be about.

After reading the text, students should return to their Possible Sentence worksheet and review the sentences they have written. As they read, they decide if their sentences need correction or not. If a sentence contains information that is accurate, then below, by the corresponding number, they write "No changes needed." If it does not contain accurate information, though, they rewrite it, correcting the misinformation. This is the important part of the strategy as it forces students back into the text to check the accuracy of their sentences.

Students Reflect

When we asked this class what they thought about writing Possible Sentences before reading "Hard at Work," one remarked, "This was way different than a teacher just telling you about the article. That's what they usually do." Another added, "And I liked this better. This was being more creative." A third said, "But it was harder, some, because you had to do the thinking. Usually the teacher does the thinking for you."

All the students laughed at that comment, but as they laughed, they were all nodding their heads in agreement. We were too, though we didn't laugh quite as much. We remembered too many times when our intention was certainly to support students learning, but we were instead probably taking over the learning.

As the reflection continued, a quiet student spoke and explained,

> "I liked thinking about this and it was cool to see that I really had good thoughts. I mean I had to fix some of my sentences because I thought the 250 million kids were in Ecuador [all nodded in agreement and laughed] but I was right that kids were forced to work and couldn't go to school any more. That made me wonder why not and that made the article more interesting."

And that student's comment is why we think this is a great before-reading strategy.

Listening to Student Talk

We used this same strategy with the same text in an eighth-grade social studies class. This short exchange took place after they had written sentences but before they had read the text.

STUDENT 1: So, I wrote, "Ten-year-olds no longer attend school and are forced to work picking bananas from banana trees for 12-hour workdays."

STUDENT 2: Do you think these are the bananas we eat?

STUDENT 3: I was wondering that, too.

STUDENT 4: Yeah, I was wondering if they are, if we should stop buying them.

If you follow this QR code, you'll find a very short video of Kylene listening to one small group from an eighth-grade class as they are revisiting their Possible Sentences and correcting them. As you watch, notice how they go back to the text to confirm their changes. You'll also see, if you look closely, that the worksheet they're using has them writing ten sentences. We tried that for a while and discovered that it took too much time.

http://hein.pub/readnf7

Notice that the students say, "I was wondering." When students give any indication of curiosity, they are headed toward relevance.

STUDENT 5: Or does that make it worse if we stop, like they need that $27 a week.

STUDENT 6: We need to read this to find out. Miss, are we going to read this now?

Also, we often find that talking about the sentences leads students to wanting to read the text. One reason for that is that students are curious about something they've written; another is that they want to discover if their sentences are "right." We're happy anytime kids ask to read a text.

Questions You Might Have

1. *Why should I do this?*

   Too often we try introducing students to a text by telling them something about it. That makes us active agents and students passive. This strategy reverses that dynamic, because students look at a few words to determine what might be happening in the text. Additionally, when students return to the text after reading, they have the chance to do some rereading—a critical part of close reading—as they correct the sentences they wrote.

2. *How do I choose the words?*

   This is actually harder than it seems, so you might want to gather some colleagues to work with on choosing words. First, you'll want to read the text and write a short summary. Then look back and see if you have used key words (but not unknown technical terms) from the text in your summary. If not, do so now. Next, make a list of the key words you did use in your summary, and see if you could write some sentences using those words that would indeed give you an approxima-tion of what's in the text.

   Another method for choosing words is to divide a sheet of paper into four quadrants that are labeled "People," "Places," "Problems," and "Outcomes." As you read, choose words that represent those four categories and write them in the correct quadrant. Some words ought to work equally well in more than one quadrant. For example, in the sample shown, the phrase "no longer attend school" works as well in Problems as in Outcomes. Finally, once you have categorized the words, write some sentences yourself to make sure they get you close to what's happening in the text.

You'll also want to take care not to use proper nouns—especially names of people—unless you're sure students will recognize the name. So we probably would use Martin Luther King, Jr., but not Clara Barton.

3. *What if their sentences aren't at all about the text?*

First, make sure kids are using three or four of the key words in each sentence. Second, make sure you've chosen good words. You should always try writing sentences yourself from the list you've generated. Finally, make sure students are thinking about all the words, not just the three or four they choose for each sentence.

4. *Should I put the words in the order in which they appear in the text?*

That's probably a good idea earlier in the school year or with students who need some extra scaffolding.

KWL 2.0

Understanding This Strategy

KWL 2.0 is what we've named our slight revision to the classic KWL strategy (Ogle 1986). Like KWL, KWL 2.0 asks students to think about what they **k**now about a topic, what they **w**ant to know, and what they **l**earned. And, like KWL, KWL 2.0 begins as a before-reading strategy and moves to an after-reading strategy.

KWL 2.0

Name _____ Date _____

Topic _____

1. Jot down what you know about this topic in column 1. Number them.

2. Think about what else you want to know about what you listed in column 1 and write those questions in column 2. Number your questions so they match the numbers in column 1.

3. Read about the topic. If you found answers to your questions, write those in column 3.

4. If you found new information, write that in column 4.

WHAT DO I KNOW?	WHAT DO I WANT TO KNOW?	WHAT ANSWERS DID I LEARN?	WHAT DID I LEARN THAT'S NEW?

With KWL 2.0, students' "old" knowledge (column 1) is connected to their questions (column 2), answers (column 3), and new knowledge (column 4).

TO GET STARTED

MATERIALS: KWL 2.0 template

TEACHER PREP: Deciding on prompt that will get kids talking about the topic they are about to study.

WHEN TO USE: Before kids read the text; return to it after reading

GROUP SIZE: Small group or large group

VARIATIONS

Math: Use with word problems and change to KWRA—What do I *know*? What do I *want* to know? What are the *rules* that matter? What is my *answer*?

Science: Use with lab experiments and change to KWEL: What do I *know*? What do I *want* to know? What's my *evidence*? What did I *learn*?

FROM KYLENE: When I first began using KWL, I consistently did it wrong. I had kids share what they knew and I'd write their responses in the K (What do I *know*) column. Then, after students had finished sharing all they knew, I'd ask them "What do you *want* to know?" I'd stand ready to write their responses in the second column. But rarely did students offer ideas. Instead, they'd look at me and shrug. They didn't know what else they wanted to know. My favorite response came from a high school student. He studied the responses in the "What do I know?" column and declared, "I'm good." Eventually, I gave up on the strategy.

Then, one time I tried it a different way. After kids would tell me what they knew about a topic and we had listed that information in column 1, I stopped asking "What do you want to know?" Instead, I would choose one item from column 1, point to it, and ask, "What do you want to know about *this*?"

Now students had a hook, something to ask a question about.

With KWL 2.0, the imprecise question, "What do I want to know?" becomes a more specific question: "What do you want to know about what started the Boston Tea Party? Or "What do you want to know about how the phases of the moon affect the tides?"

When you connect what they want to know to something they already know, then they can ask questions.

Teaching the Strategy

This strategy is not a fix-up strategy, so you're offering instructions (directions) more than instruction. What we'll do in the next few sections is share some of the language we used to help an eighth-grade social studies teacher begin a unit on global hunger. This was part of a larger unit on problems of a global society.

We Explain

❝ For the next two weeks, you'll be reading about a growing problem: increasing hunger in the world. Take a moment and talk with your partner about anything you've heard or read about hunger in the world. [We gave students about three to four minutes to talk with one other person.]

OK. Let's come back together. You've been talking some and, as we listened, we heard some interesting thoughts. Let's get those written up here on our chart. Who will share first?

We put up a chart on the whiteboard that looks like what's shown below. We don't put up all four columns because it takes too much space. So we begin with columns 1 and 2 and then add 3 and 4 after students have read. As students report, we insert their responses, numbering each one.

WHAT DO YOU KNOW ABOUT WORLD HUNGER?	
1. It's not just people in India who are hungry. People here are, too.	
2. Droughts are making it harder to have enough food.	
3. Children starve to death in Africa.	
4. The population is getting bigger in the world, so this problem will get bigger.	
5. We waste a lot of food every day here in America.	
6. Grocery stores here throw away a lot of food that hungry people would like to eat.	
7. At restaurants, food that isn't eaten has to be thrown away.	

Notice, the prompt for column 1 is broad enough that many students might be able to offer input, yet specific enough to keep kids thinking about the topic at hand.

> " You have a lot of interesting thoughts about this problem. Let's look back at your first comment, that people are hungry here, too, not just in India. That comment shows us that you realize that this problem isn't just a problem in another country, but it's a problem here, too. That's an interesting thought and we suspect it raises a lot of questions for you. Talk with your partner for a moment about what you're wondering. What do you want to know about hunger here in the U.S.?

We gave students one or two minutes to turn and talk with a partner. Then we had them share their questions about this one idea—that people in the U.S. are hungry. We added their questions to column 2. We numbered their questions with a "1" so they could easily see that these questions referred to the first comment made in column 1. Once students offered their questions for the first comment, we moved on to the next statement in column 1 and asked them what they wondered about droughts and food shortage. The chart below shows you their questions for all their comments.

WHAT DO YOU KNOW ABOUT WORLD HUNGER?	WHAT DO YOU WANT TO KNOW ABOUT . . . ?
1. It's not just people in India who are hungry. People here are too.	1. How can we be such a rich nation and have hungry people? 1. Do we have a larger percentage of hungry people than India? 1. How do you know how many people are hungry in a country? 1. What is "hungry"? Like not eating one meal a day or not eating for days in a week? 1. Who decides who is hungry?
2. Droughts are making it harder to have enough food.	2. What is causing the droughts? 2. Which countries have the worst droughts? 2. Why can't we just take salt out of the oceans and use that water? 2. Which crops don't need much water? Which crops need a lot? 2. Are we using water for things we shouldn't use it for, like for golf courses?
3. Children starve to death in Africa.	3. Do more kids starve in Africa than any other place? 3. Why is it that countries that don't seem to be able to grow a lot of food seem to have more people? 3. Do those charities you see ads for on TV about feeding the children in Africa do any good? Does your money really help? 3. What can we do here to help the children there? 3. How much food do we throw away at our school?

continues

WHAT DO YOU KNOW ABOUT WORLD HUNGER?	WHAT DO YOU WANT TO KNOW ABOUT . . . ?
4. The population is getting bigger in the world, so this problem will get bigger.	4. How many people are there in the world? 4. When did the population really start growing? 4. Why is the population getting bigger? 4. Didn't China make a rule about not having more than one child? Did that help? 4. Should the U.S. say that you can't have more than one child? 4. Is it good for a government to decide how many kids you can have? 4. Do we send our food to other countries? Why do we do that if we have hungry people here? 4. Why do some people say that food stamps are bad?
5. Grocery stores here throw away a lot of food that hungry people would like to eat.	5. Why do grocery stores throw away food? Is that legal? 5. Should grocery stores be required to keep their prices lower so more people can afford to get food? 5. It doesn't seem right that if you're poor, you have to be hungry, too. What can we do about that?

As your students add questions for column 2, don't worry if some comments from column 1 don't elicit many questions. That happens.

After students have generated questions, it's time for them to read. The concern most teachers have at this point is that students have asked questions that the teacher knows won't be answered in the text. That was certainly what happened in this class. We told the students that they would be reading a few articles that would answer some of their questions. If we're with younger students, or students who need extra scaffolding, we might show students which questions will be answered. We tell students that after reading the initial texts, we'll look to see which other questions students still want to explore and we'll point them in the right direction to find information.

After students have read, we return to the chart we've made (so save it!) and add two more columns. In column 3, we put answers to their questions. In column 4, we put information that students have learned that isn't related to the questions they had asked.

> As students read the texts, you'll see that they will let go of some of their initial questions in column 2 as they discover other topics that they want to know more about. That's fine.

Students Reflect

Most students like the structure of seeing their thoughts, their questions, and eventually their answers. In this class, students were old enough that a few remembered trying KWL in earlier grades. One student told us, "I liked it this way better. Before, when the teacher would ask us what we wanted to know, I was always like 'Know about what?' Now, I can think of things I want to know." We like when students recognize that generating the questions is what makes reading the text more interesting. One student pointed out that, "When you start asking your own questions, then your interest goes up."

Listening to Student Talk

We want to take a look at comments from two of the students as they discussed item 5: "Grocery stores here throw away a lot of food . . ." You can hear their interest in the topic grow as they connect what they know to what they want to know. These students clearly are primed to read more attentively and with greater understanding because they see that the issue is relevant even in their own neighborhood.

These two girls were part of a class the principal had told us was for "below-level students." This thinking doesn't look below level to us. What we noticed was that these students have started thinking about what they personally can do to solve the problem in their community: "We could set out big boxes . . ." When you hear that type of comment, you know students are creating relevance.

STUDENT 1: This isn't right. I mean, they just throw away food.

STUDENT 2: Maybe they have to. Like a rule. Like if it is spoiled.

STUDENT 1: Well, yeah, if, like, the milk is rotten, then you would need to. But what if it's just some apples that have set out too long. Those aren't rotten.

STUDENT 2: We could set out big boxes and grocery stores could put "gently bruised fruit," and then people could get it.

STUDENT 1: But then grocery stores wouldn't get paid.

STUDENT 2: But if you think about it, grocery stores are, like, what is it, you know, they should be like public, like for everyone to get what they need.

STUDENT 1: Yeah, but some people, they might come in and get chocolate or beer or ice cream. Things they don't really need.

STUDENT 2: Maybe you could have a part that's for the food you really need, like eggs and milk and apples.

STUDENT 1: Maybe. So, let's ask why grocery stores throw away food. Is that even legal?

Questions You Might Have

1. *Won't some still say, "I don't want to know anything?"*

   Of course. But more often than not, you'll get a few pairs who come up with some good questions, and that will encourage others. And if a couple of comments from column 1 don't generate questions, just move on to the next comment.

2. *What if kids don't ask questions that I know they need to think about as they read?*

   First, pay the most attention to the questions they do ask. They are showing you what interests them about the topic. Second, remember that you are a member of the class. If you need to, you can add something to columns 1 and 2. But we try to keep our own comments and questions to a minimum.

3. *How do kids use this on their own?*

   In the ideal situation, kids would look at a new chapter or a new topic and on their own, with no prompting from you, jot down— or at least think about—a few things they already know and then ask themselves what else they want to know about those things.

4. *What if kids come up with incorrect information for "What I know"?*

   That happens. If what they know is correctable at that moment, we do it. For instance, in a unit on oceans, one fourth grader said, "There are five oceans." We went ahead and corrected him: "That's really close. There are four, not five." (And then later we discovered that, according to The National Oceanic and Atmospheric Administration, most countries now also recognize the Southern Ocean [the Antarctic] as a fifth ocean. We've been unable to find that student to correct the misinformation we gave him.)

   Other times, what students say is so wrong that to leave it in our "What I Know" column would be a distraction. For example, in a unit on frogs' life cycle, one sixth grader said, "Frogs are reptiles." We said, "That's not right. But something has given you that idea. Let's put it here, and put a circle around it. As you read, be looking for the information that will help you clarify this thought."

5. *Can I combine this with Possible Sentences?*

No teacher has actually asked us this question but we wanted to discuss it, so here we are. We often combine Possible Sentences with KWL 2.0. Students take the words we give them, write their sentences, and then use them in column 1 of KWL 2.0 as shown in Figure 33. We then ask what they want to know about the sentences they created. For instance, when students wrote sentences for "Hard at Work," one wrote, "A ten-year-old in Ecuador no longer attends school but works twelve-hour days for as little as $27 per week." We told students that they wouldn't know if this was accurate until they read the article, but if it is true, we wondered what questions they had. They quickly generated questions: Where are their parents? Why don't they go to school? Do they keep the money? What are they doing? Why doesn't the government in Ecuador care if kids go to school?" We listed these questions in column 2 of the KWL 2.0 chart. Before kids read, we showed them which questions this one article would answer.

Figure 33 With KWL 2.0, students' "old" knowledge (column 1) is connected to their questions (column 2), answers (column 3), and new knowledge (column 4).

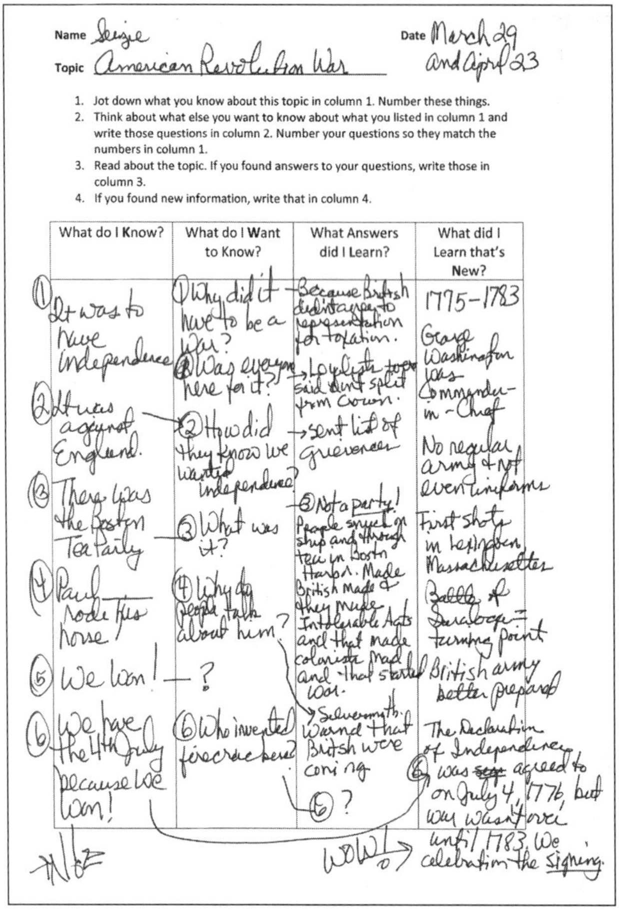
Name Suzie Date March 29 and April 23

Topic American Revolution War

1. Jot down what you know about this topic in column 1. Number these things.
2. Think about what else you want to know about what you listed in column 1 and write those questions in column 2. Number your questions so they match the numbers in column 1.
3. Read about the topic. If you found answers to your questions, write those in column 3.
4. If you found new information, write that in column 4.

What do I Know?	What do I Want to Know?	What Answers did I Learn?	What did I Learn that's New?
(1) It was to have independence	(1) Why did it have to be a war? (1) Was everyone here for it?	Because British didn't agree to representation for taxation. → Loyalists said don't split from Crown.	1775–1783 George Washington was Commander-in-Chief
(2) It was against England.	(2) How did they know we wanted independence?	→ sent list of grievances	No regular army & not even uniforms
(3) There was the Boston Tea Party	(3) What was it?	(3) Not a party! People sneaked on ship and through tea in Boston Harbor. Made British mad & they made Intolerable Acts and that made colonists mad and that started war.	First shots in Lexington, Massachusetts
(4) Paul rode his horse	(4) Why do people talk about him?	→ warned that British were coming	Battle of Saratoga = turning point
(5) We won!	?		British army better prepared
(6) We have the 4th July because we won!	(6) Who invented firecrackers?	(6) ?	(6) The Declaration of Independence was agreed to on July 4, 1776, but war wasn't over until 1783. We celebrate the signing. WOW!

Strategy *3*

Somebody Wanted But So

Understanding This Strategy

Somebody Wanted But So (SWBS) offers students a structure that helps them write a one-sentence summary of a text. First discussed by Macon et al. (1991) and later expanded by Beers (2003), SWBS scaffolds students' thinking as they consider first who the *somebody* of the text is, what that somebody *wanted, but* what happened, and *so* what was the outcome.

Too often when students try to summarize a text, they instead retell it. Retelling, valuable in and of itself, requires that students think through a text and recount what happened in the correct order. Summarizing, by contrast, requires that students think about the text and then distill it to its critical parts. A summary provides the essence; a retelling provides a recounting.

MATERIALS: SWBS template; we model this with a short paragraph shown on page 203.

TO GET STARTED

MATERIALS: SWBS template; we model this with a short paragraph shown on page 203.

TEACHER PREP: If the text is long, choose where students will stop to write their SWBS statements.

WHEN TO USE: During reading/After reading

GROUP SIZE: Individual or pairs of students

VARIATIONS

Science: If avoiding anthropomorphism, you might prefer SHBT (Something Happened But Then)

Somebody Wanted But So

Name _____ Date _____

Text _____ Class _____

SOMEBODY	WANTED	BUT	SO

Developmentally, our youngest students are better prepared to retell than to summarize. These students can use SWBS, but they tend not to internalize the structure, and when you don't remind them to use it, they revert to a "then this happened" retelling.

You easily can tell by their language when students are retelling rather than summarizing. The "this happened and then this happened" language points immediately to a retelling. Students who try to offer a summary ("This is the story of a girl who wants to go to a ball . . .") and then slip into a chronology of events (". . . but first, she had to clean all the rooms, and then her stepmother locked her in an attic, and then her fairy godmother came.") have made a move toward summarizing but need a scaffold to make that move complete. Somebody Wanted But So provides that scaffold.

Teaching the Strategy

In this eleventh-grade classroom, during a Friday seventh-period class when the twenty-nine students were far more interested in getting out for the weekend than having two unknown people teach them a lesson on summarizing, we persevered and introduced them to Somebody Wanted But So.

We began . . .

We Explain

" When your teacher asks you to summarize the article you've just finished reading, he doesn't want a page-by-page recap. Nor does he want a statement about the topic such as "It was about pollution." He wants a summary—something that gives him the essence of what the article was about without making him live through your paragraph-by-paragraph retelling.

But it's easy to fall into the "first this happened and then this happened and then this happened" retelling. To avoid that, you might try using a strategy called Somebody Wanted But So. To do that, write these four words—Somebody Wanted But So—on paper. Then think about each of those words and decide who the *somebody* is you want to discuss. Next, ask yourself what that person *wanted*. Next, think about *but* what happened to that person. Finally, decide *so* what happened. When you are finished, you'll have a one-sentence summary. Let us show you how this works."

We Model

" Take a look at this paragraph from your history textbook. You've been reading about the First World War:

In June 1914, Archduke Franz Ferdinand, heir to the Austrian throne, visited the Bosnian capital, Sarajevo. As the royal
entourage drove through the city Serbian nationalist Gavrilo Princip stepped from the crowd and shot the archduke and his wife
Sophie. Princip was a member of the Black Hand, an organization
promoting Serbian nationalism. The assassinations touched off
a diplomatic crisis. On July 28, Austria-Hungary declared what
was expected to be a short war against Serbia. (From Chapter
19, "First World War," in *The Americans*, McDougal Littell, 2002,
page 580)

Now, to summarize this, let's all get these four words written on
paper:

Somebody   Wanted   But   So

Let's first decide who the the important somebodies are in this
passage. What are your ideas? [The students said Archduke Ferdinand,
his wife Sophie, and Gavrilo Princip. We added those names under Somebody.] **Let's focus first on the archduke and his wife. What did they
want?** [Students discussed this in pairs and eventually reached a decision. We added that information under our Wanted column] **Turn back to
your partner and discuss but what happened to interrupt that visit.**
[Students did and then we turned to the So column. Eventually we had a
sentence written.]

Somebody	Wanted	But	So
The Austrian Archduke Ferdinand and his wife Sophie	to visit Sarajevo	a Serbian nationalist named Princip shot and killed them	this started a war between Austria-Hungary and Serbia.

As we were showing this, one student asked, "How did you know
he was Austrian?" Another student quickly responded, "That's what
heir means. Like Prince William is heir to the English throne. That
means he lives in England." Another student wondered, "How did
you know the war started between Austria and Hungary?" We asked
who could find the answer to that. After a moment, as students reread

Middle school teachers, the vampire bat article works well for modeling and practicing because there are two men (two "Some-bodies") who want very different things. Elementary school teachers, we often use *Chrysanthemum* by Kevin Henkes (which we know is fiction) to teach students how to do this. We can model one SWBS statement using Chrysan-themum as the first some-body and then students can practice writing SWBS statements for her dad, the other students, and the teacher.

the passage, the same student who asked the question said, "Oh, I get it! It says that Austria-Hungary declared what was expected to be a short war." Another student then asked, "How do you know they were killed?" and another spoke up saying, "It says they were assassinated."

After a moment of actual quiet in the classroom, one girl asked, "Can we try it with the Princip guy?"

Students Try

Students paired up and started working on the statement for Princip. As they worked, we circulated. Many students made a typical mistake of trying to do this without rereading the passage. We stopped them and reminded them to reread first. Once we sent them back into the text, kids started reading parts of it aloud to one another. One pair wrote:

Somebody	Wanted	But	So
Princip	Serbia to be its own country	it wasn't	he stepped forward and shot the archduke to start a war.

As students listened to this example, several wondered if Princip intended to start a war. Most of the students mentioned that it was very hard to decide what to put in the Wanted and But columns. We told them that when that happens, they might want to rethink who they have in the Somebody column. In this case, the students had failed to note the importance of the group, the Black Hand.

Several students immediately pointed out that Princip was the other name in the paragraph so that he had to be a Somebody. We nodded and said we agreed that this was a name; then we asked the students if it was critical that the person who did the shooting was named Princip. One student said, "Maybe," and we agreed. "Maybe there is something very important about it being Princip, but do we know that from this paragraph?" They admitted they did not. We asked what else we know about Princip. After a moment one student grinned and began waving his hand, "No! It could have been anyone as long as he was a member of this group called Black Hand, and that group was from Serbia."

"So, we ought to say that the Black Hand wanted something?" another student asked, and before we could say anything they all began working:

Somebody	Wanted	But	So
The Black Hand	to not be under the archduke's rule	they were	one of them shot the archduke.
The Black Hand	Serbia to be its own nation	they were under Austria's rule	a member of The Black Hand assassinated the archduke and his wife.

When the pair that wrote that final statement shared it with the class, another student asked if we really know if they asked Princip to do the assassinating: "The paragraph doesn't say they sent him to do it. It just says he was a member of the Black Hand." This student suggested that the revision ought to be "Princip was a member of the Black Hand, which wanted Serbia to be a nation, but Austria did not want them to be, so Princip assassinated the archduke and his wife." The students who wrote the original statement said they didn't know, and one asked, "Is there something else we can read to find out?" And this is why we use SWBS. As students write statements, they are reading closely and discovering on their own what else they want to know.

Students Reflect

SWBS is a student-directed strategy meaning that once you show them how to use it, they'll continue to use it on their own, whenever they want. For many students, this becomes a go-to strategy that they use often. For that reason, we encourage you to ask students on a regular basis how SWBS is changing the way they think about a text. Here are some comments we've gathered from students:

- ▶ "When I get lost, I stop and do SWBS and that helps me figure out what's going on."

- ▶ "I didn't think I'd use it much, but I use it all the time. It helps me focus on what is really happening."

- ▶ "I used it at home the other night when my little brother was NOT listening to our mom. I finally told him 'Mom wants you to clean your room, but you haven't, and so you are really going to end up in trouble.'"

Listening to Student Talk

These two students worked hard to write their SWBS statement. This passage is a stretch for them, but notice, with the SWBS scaffold, they never gave up.

Notice that this is talk that is creating understanding rather than checking for understanding.

STUDENT 1: What did the Black Hand want?

STUDENT 2: They wanted to be in Serbia? Is that it?

STUDENT 1: I don't think so. Look here. It says they were promoting Serbian nationalism.

STUDENT 2: I don't even know what that is.

Notice the thinking process as this student connects "nation" to "nationalism."

STUDENT 1: Like nation. They wanted Serbia to be a nation.

STUDENT 2: So it isn't a nation? It's, what is Serbia?

STUDENT 1: Maybe it's like a part of Austria and it wants to be its own place.

STUDENT 2: So that's what they want? The Black Hand want Serbia to be its own nation.

STUDENT 1: But maybe the Austrians wouldn't let them.

Student 2 had problems with the vocabulary but as he worked with a peer, he was able to think about what the definitions might be.

STUDENT 2: OK, so that's why they wanted Princip to assassinate the archduke. What's an archduke?

STUDENT 1: Like a duke. Maybe this is what you are before you are a king?

STUDENT 2: No. You're a prince first.

STUDENT 1: Well, anyways, the Black Hand wanted Serbia to be its own nation, but the Austrians wouldn't let them, so they had Princip assassinate the archduke and his wife.

Questions You Might Have

1. *The example you shared was for one paragraph. Can students use this with more than one paragraph?*

   Absolutely! We've seen kids write SWBS statements for chapters, articles, and occasionally novels. When students are learning to use SWBS, however, use a short passage.

2. *Can students do this on their own?*

   This is a great on-your-own strategy, but when we first teach it, we have students work in pairs.

3. *What if the statements students write aren't accurate?*

   Send them back into the text. They'll make mistakes if they don't reread. But don't send them back to rewrite the entire sentence; instead, you might point out the part that needs revision: "I like what you said this person wanted, but I want you to think more about what you said about the problem—what's in the But column."

4. *Does this teach something other than summarizing?*

   As students write their summaries, they are making inferences and seeing cause-and-effect relationships. And as they move from one Somebody to the next, they are noticing how the perspective shifts, which certainly can lead to making comparisons and contrasts. As students move to writing SWBS statements for bigger chunks of texts (entire chapters and then books!) they are making generalizations, looking at theme, and focusing on the main ideas.

5. *I've seen kids change this to "Somebody Wanted But So Then" or "Somebody Wanted Because But So." Are those changes OK?*

   Adding "then" or "because" is fine. We tend to use the SWBS structure, but those additions get kids thinking about causes and effects.

6. *What if students can't get all the information in one sentence?*

   That will happen, especially if the text is complex. We have them write a series of statements and connect them with *then, later, next*, and *finally*.

7. *What do students do with the SWBS statements?*

   You can use these in a variety of ways. Have students write them to show you what they understand about what they read. Let them use them as conversation starters by putting four students in a group and letting them share. There is usually enough difference in statements to get a conversation started. Finally, we often encourage students to use their SWBS statements as their thesis statement for an essay.

8. *What does this look like in math or science?*

   In a math class—across all grades—students use SWBS to think about math concepts as shown in Figure 34.

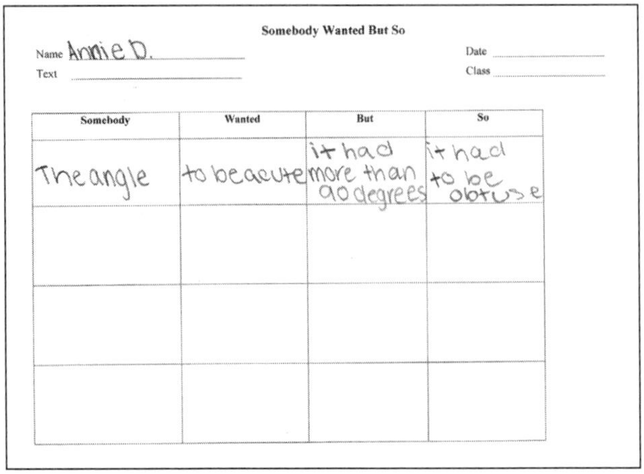
Somebody Wanted But So

Name Annie D. Date

Text Class

Somebody	Wanted	But	So
The angle	to be acute	it had more than 90 degrees	it had to be obtuse

Figure 34 One student had this creative take on defining an obtuse angle.

- "The angle wanted to be acute, but it had more than 90 degrees so it had to be obtuse." (seventh-grade)
- "The fraction wanted to be proper, but the numerator was bigger than the denominator so it had to be improper." (third grade)
- "The Order of Operations wants you to do parentheses first then brackets then braces, but some problems don't have those, so then you just work left to right." (fourth grade)
- "The number one wanted to be a prime number, but it was *only* divisible by itself and not another number, so it cannot be prime." (sixth grade)
- "The figure wanted to be a rhombus, but it had five equal sides instead of four equal sides so it had to be a regular pentagon." (tenth grade)

And in science classes, when teachers are willing to allow for some anthropomorphism students have written:

- The bees wanted to find their way back to their hive, but the pesticides on flowers and plants interferes with the bees' ability to remember where their hive is, and so they can't return." (eighth grade)
- "The plant wanted to eat a hamburger because it was a meat-loving plant and that's how it wanted to get its energy, but it's a plant so it had to convert light energy from the sun into chemical energy through a process called photosynthesis." (a witty eleventh grade)
- "The paramecium wanted to be an amoeba but it had cilia instead of pseudopods for movement and two nuclei instead of only one and can't change shape like the amoeba can and so it is stuck being a two-nuclei, hairy, no-shape-shifting paramecium." (ninth grade)

And from two adolescent eighth-grade boys: "The volvox algae wanted to be anything other than volvox algae because asexual reproduction just isn't that much fun."

Syntax Surgery

Understanding This Strategy

Syntax Surgery is a during-reading fix-up strategy that students use to help clarify confusions that might occur as they are reading. To use Syntax Surgery, students need to be able to write and draw on a text. This is not about jotting notes in the margin. This is about looking for how one part of a text (a word, phrase, sentence, or figure) connects with another part and then drawing lines and arrows to connect those parts.

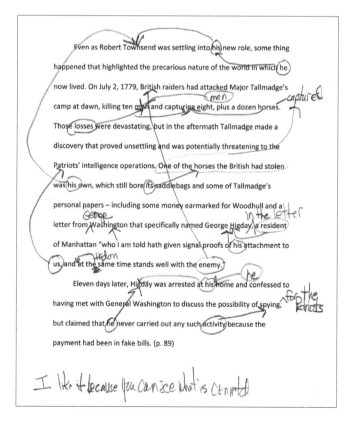

TO GET STARTED

MATERIALS: Model sentences are provided on page 271 of the Appendix.

TEACHER PREP: Put model sentences on whiteboard or chart paper.

WHEN TO USE: During reading

GROUP SIZE: Individuals or pairs

VARIATIONS

Math: The syntax of math is less about connecting pronouns to nouns and more about understanding how math symbols connect words to operations. When kids struggle, be sure they understand how to read the special symbols of math, symbols such as: $( )$, $\{ \}$, $\sqrt{}$, $\approx$, ∞, f, $\geq$.

Students do need to be able to write on a text for Syntax Surgery.

Too often, we teach a student how to do Syntax Surgery, and then a few weeks later when the student says she's stuck, we forget to remind her to use the fix-up strategies we've been teaching! It's easy to fall into the habit of doing the thinking for kids. We've got to remember to let them practice what we preach!

Syntax Surgery was initially envisioned as an instructional strategy to help English language learners understand the word order of English sentences (Herrell 2000). Teachers would write a sentence on a sentence strip, cut it up (thus the name Syntax *Surgery*), and then let their students put the words back into the correct order.

That's a very helpful way to help students think about word order, but used this way it is an instructional strategy that the teacher directs. We've found it is more helpful when instead we show students how this can be a fix-up strategy they can use on their own as needed. You do need to spend some time showing students how to make the various connections we've detailed in the chart below. After that, though, you're mostly reminding students that when they say they are confused or stuck, they might want to try Syntax Surgery.

When students notice that they are confused, we want them to learn to say more than simply "I don't get it." Syntax Surgery becomes the fix-up strategy students use most often. Students find the sentences that are problematic and start underlining or circling pronouns and drawing lines to their antecedents. They might also draw lines connecting words that have similar meanings or referents. They circle unknown words and hunt for clues that will give them some idea of what the words mean. They look for places in which the author has omitted a word, and they try to insert it. They notice signal words and draw lines to what those words signal. The text they are reading might get messy, but their understanding gets sharper.

Teaching the Strategy

Students learn Syntax Surgery through your modeling. You'll choose a passage, put it up on the whiteboard, and then tell students that you are going to read it aloud and think through any confusing parts. As you find those parts, you'll circle the words (or phrases) that are confusing, and then continue reading—or begin rereading—and you'll draw arrows to the words that help you figure out what you didn't understand the first time. It's important that you identify the type of confusion. ("Oh, these two pronouns, even though they are the same, don't refer to the same noun.")

Earlier in the year, we generally use sentences (not long passages) that provide examples for each of the types of problems we showed in Figure 35. Then we begin modeling with longer passages

Follow this QR code, and you'll hear us working with a student who has completely misunderstood a passage. As he uses Syntax Surgery and Sketch to Stretch, he realizes his mistake.

http://hein.pub/readnf8

PROBLEM STUDENTS ENCOUNTER	EXAMPLE OF THIS PROBLEM
Don't see the antecedent The problem: Often, inattentive readers will think the antecedent for a pronoun is the nearest noun. That's not always true. Other times, these readers see pronouns that are similar (*they, them, theirs*) and think they all refer to the same noun.	A geometric proof is a step-by-step explanation that uses definitions, axioms, postulates, and previously proved theorems to draw a conclusion about a geometric statement. There are two of them: direct and indirect. The platoon began marching south. They were tired and their backs hurt. But their orders were clear and they had been delivered with some urgency.
Don't recognize synonyms or similar terms This is a typical problem with social studies texts as authors describe a single event, or a group of people, or a landmass with synonyms or similar terms.	The Americans who remained loyal to the British Crown were often called Tories. These Loyalists stood in opposition to those who wanted independence from England. Seen as "royalists," the King's Men fought against the Patriots, even though they lived alongside them.
Don't recognize context clues We find that trying to define an unknown word with context clues is sometimes easier if students first do Sketch to Stretch (see page 221) and then from their sketch, draw lines that connect words.	The big rock rose straight up from the middle of the fast-flowing water. The boaters had to paddle hard to one side to avoid hitting the monolith.
Don't infer omitted words Authors will omit words that are implied by the context. Struggling readers do not realize that all they need to do is insert the words as they read.	Twelve men volunteered for the mission. Several were chosen. *men*

Don't use signal words to help with meaning
 	
Noticing what signal words actually signal is a critical context clue. Too often we forget that explicitly showing students how signal words work solves many comprehension problems. Here are a few types of signal words you should teach:
 	
    Restatement signal words
 	
    Illustration signal words
 	
    Category signal words
	An isthmus is also called a peninsula.
	
	By way of demonstration, the teacher circled all the pronouns.
	
	There were several species of dogs: collies, labs, poodles, and Rhodesian ridgebacks.
	
	clue!

Don't understand role of dashes, commas, parentheses, or colons Often terms are defined, illustrated, or expanded in information that is found between dashes, commas, or parentheses or after a colon. While highly skilled readers often seem to intuit what these punctuation marks signal, less skilled readers benefit from our showing (not telling) them how they work. NOTE: These same symbols work differently in math, and students need to be taught that. A dash in a math problem is a minus sign. Parentheses suggest which operation occurs first.	Dactylonomy, counting on one's fingers, is what young children might resort to if they forget their math facts. [We could have as easily put dashes or parentheses around "counting on one's fingers"]. Two outcomes were critical: food shortage and water shortage.

Figure 35 This chart shows some of the more common types of connections we teach. For your specific discipline, you might want to add others.

in which we must make a lot of connections and different types of connections.

In the example that follows, we're in a seventh-grade language arts classroom. It's early September, so the students still strike us as young for middle school, perhaps more like sixth graders than seventh graders. They are (mostly) polite, attentive, and ready to learn. We hand them a passage they will be reading later and tell them to take out a pencil. Once that was accomplished (fifteen minutes later) we began . . .

We Explain

" Take a look at this sentence:

> He served juice to all the children in the paper cups.

[Make sure you've written this on chart paper or the whiteboard.] **Now turn to your partner and explain what the author probably meant it to say and what it literally says.** [Students ought to recognize that the juice is what was served in the cups even though it literally says that children were in paper cups.] **Try another sentence:**

> They saw a turtle driving to the park.

| Don't worry! We know we're starting kids off with some poorly written sentences! |

Talk again with your partner. What do you think the author meant, and what does it literally say? [Students ought to fairly quickly recognize that "they" is who was driving to the park even though this says that it's the turtle that's driving.]

Now, write both these sentences on your own paper. If you wanted to show someone what's in the cups and who was driving the car, what words would you connect? Give it a try and show a buddy how you connected words. [Very quickly students underline or circle words and draw lines or arrows to other words.] **OK. What you've just done is called Syntax Surgery.**

When something you've read seems odd, or you're confused, take a moment and underline what was confusing, reread it, and then see if you can draw an arrow to what you think helps you understand it. When you do that, you're fixing up your confusion, on your own, by studying the syntax, which means the structure, of the sentence.

We Model

❝ Over the next couple of days, we're going to talk about the different types of things that might cause confusion, and we'll practice doing some Syntax Surgery that might clear up those different types of confusion. Today, we'll look at one very common problem: connecting pronouns to the correct nouns.

Take a look at this sentence:

> If the girl's aunt could leave work early enough to meet her at the airport, she said she certainly would meet her there.

This sentence has a lot of pronouns, and if I don't read carefully I might end up misunderstanding it. I'll start this Syntax Surgery by circling the pronouns. I see *her*, *she*, another *she*, and then *her* again. [You'll have written this sentence on your whiteboard and can now just circle the pronouns.] If I read too fast or too inattentively I might think that all these pronouns have been substituted for the word *aunt*.

But if I read more carefully, I see that *her* is the substitution for *girl* (the niece). [Draw your arrow from "her" to "girl."] The aunt is at work, so that leaves the girl as the one at the airport. So, who is getting met at the airport? The girl.

Next, I want to read the remainder very slowly. Who said she would get the girl? The aunt did. So the first *she* and the second *she* both refer to the aunt. [Draw your arrows from those two pronouns to "aunt."] As I look at this last pronoun, *her*, I realize that *her* is referring to whoever is being met at the airport, and that takes me back to the girl. [Draw your arrow from "her" to "girl," which takes the form "girl's" in the sentence.] All of these lines and arrows help me make the right connections, and that helps me understand exactly what's happening in the text. The nice thing about Syntax Surgery is that you can use it whenever you're reading. You don't need to wait for a teacher to tell you to use it.

Now let me give you a sentence, and you try it.

Students Try

We give students three or four sentences for them to try on their own. After they have circled pronouns and drawn arrows to the nouns they are replacing, we let them compare their markings with those of another student.

Here are a few sentences we've used with seventh and eighth graders when we're introducing pronoun-to-noun connections. We suggest that you find sentences from the texts that your students are reading.

If this type of problem—pronoun-antecedent—isn't an issue with your content, don't spend any time on it. Often science teachers tell us they need to jump right to inferring omitted words or using signal words.

Example 1:

Breathe through your nose, hold it for a few seconds in your lungs.

We heard a health teacher say this in a class and watched three ninth graders reach up to hold their noses. We've used this sentence with middle and high school students and are always surprised at the number that connect *it* to *nose*. Remind them to replace *it* with the word *nose* and see if the sentence makes sense. When they discover that the sentence doesn't make sense with that substitution, they may realize that the antecedent is the implied "your breath."

Example 2:

The platoon began marching south. They were tired and their backs hurt. But their orders were clear, and they had been delivered with some urgency.

Often, students will correctly identify that the first three pronouns, *they*, *their*, and *their*, refer to the platoon. Then, too many will say that the final *they* also refers to *platoon*. If your students do that, ask them to reread putting *platoon* in the place of that final pronoun. They usually then realize that it was the orders that were delivered with urgency. If they still think that last *they* is substituting for *platoon*, tell them to answer the question "What got delivered?"

Example 3:

The company's bosses decided to let employees decide when they would get to work each day and when they would leave. They decided that as long as workers got in eight hours each day, they really didn't care which eight hours they chose to work.

We ask students to think of this sentence two ways: the first interpretation is that the bosses are letting the employees decide what the employer's hours should be. The second is that the bosses are letting employees choose when the employees' work day starts and stops.

Students Reflect

The example in the opener on page 209 shows a Syntax Surgery an eighth grader completed after several weeks of practicing the various types of syntactical connections that should be made while reading. This student was asked what he thought about Syntax Surgery and hurriedly wrote at the bottom of the page, "I like it because you can see what is connected." In talking with us, he said, "This actually makes thinking about what you don't understand almost fun. It's like the answer was there, but you had to know how to find it."

Listening to Student Talk

Students in an eighth-grade U.S. history class were reading portions of *George Washington's Secret Six*. A small portion of that text was shown on page 209. We had talked with the class about Syntax Surgery, illustrating, in one lesson, several types of syntactical connections one might make in a passage.

> This is from *George Washington's Secret Six: The Spy Ring That Saved the American Revolution*, by Brian Kilmeade and Don Yaeger.

Several weeks later, we were back in that district for a follow-up visit with the teachers. We dropped by that history class and listened in on some of the conversation small groups were having about the first chapter of this book. They had read Chapter 1 and had been told to think about the Big Questions as they read. Now they were in groups sharing passages they had marked. As we moved from group to group, we heard three boys talking:

STUDENT 1: So, I marked this sentence because the author thinks I know what *traversed* means. I have never heard that word.

STUDENT 2: I didn't mark it but, yeah, I don't know what it is either.

> We liked seeing that the students were letting one of the Big Questions help identify problems.

STUDENT 3: Yeah, what does it mean "they traversed"? The boys were, like, pretending to be in a parade. See, one is pretending to play the drums. Maybe it means the men were listening?

STUDENT 2: The men were listening? Like traversed means listening? So then it would say, "as they listened through town." That doesn't make sense.

> This student is wisely inserting the substitution Student 3 offered to see if it makes sense.

STUDENT 1: Wait. [All paused as this student started pointing to the words as he kept rereading.] Look at it again. It says that the boys were parading *in front of* the men. See? The boys are

This student emphasized "in front of" to make the point that it was the boys who were moving. He's come up with a good synonym for traversed (marched) but doesn't yet recognize it.

This is what "talk to create understanding" sounds like in a classroom. You might turn back to the chart that compares talk to create understanding with talk to check for understanding on page 59.

While Student 3 mislabeled *traversed* as a noun, he understood the concept that one word is substituted for another. That's good thinking.

pretending to be the parade, and they, like, marched *in front of* the men. Get it? The men aren't going anywhere. They are standing still.

STUDENT 3: So, is traversed the same as standing still?

[They grew silent as they all begin rereading.]

STUDENT 1: No. I think . . . it's like, I think *traverse* is the same as *parade*, like walking maybe. See, the boys are the ones pretending to be in the parade. So, *they* [now this boy circles "they" on his page] goes to *boys* [and he draws an arrow connecting "they" to "boys"]. And *traversed* [and now he circles "traversed"] goes to *parade*.

STUDENT 2: OK. And see the dash? [He reaches over and circles the dash on Student 1's paper.] See the dash? Remember, a dash [pause] remember it, well what's after it tells you about something before it. So, this [underlining the information after the dash] goes back to *parade* because that's what they did to make the parade.

STUDENT 3: Right! That's what they did. You're right. *They* goes to *boys* and *traversed* must be one of those noun synonyms.

Questions You Might Have

1. *How often do I do a Syntax Surgery lesson with students?*

   Use this often, especially in the first few months of the school year. *Often* means three or four times a week. Students need to see how you are connecting words that might be sentences or paragraphs apart, especially in science texts that have many phrases in single sentences.

2. *When I'm modeling, do the students need a copy of the passage?*

   Yes. When students have a copy, they can work along with you as you model your thinking, or they can work alone and then share what they did. Watching is never as valuable as doing.

3. *How does Syntax Surgery help students make an inference?*

   When authors expect readers to make an inference, some information is often implied but not explicitly stated. For instance, in the May 2015 Scholastic *UpFront* magazine, there is an article titled "Yik Yak & Free Speech." After describing what happened to a college student who read a mean comment about herself on Yik Yak, the author wrote "In response to complaints, a number of colleges have blocked the app on campus servers, which has elicited objections from free-speech advocates" (p. 14). Struggling readers are often reading at such a surface level that they don't catch that the complaints are "complaints about Yik Yak," though authors expect readers to catch that implication. When students are told to "go ahead and finish the thought for the author," they are inserting what was omitted, and that's the inference.

> Skilled readers often don't realize there was an omission, they so quickly infer the omitted phrase.

CLASSROOM CLOSE-UP

The Syntax of Science Texts

We think some of the most challenging texts students will encounter in school will be science texts. If disciplinary literacy skills—those literacy skills needed for one specific discipline—are ever needed, it might be in the reading of science texts.

Science texts written for other scientists tend to be highly specialized, highly informational, and highly technical (Biber and Gray 2013). When those texts are translated to a science magazine that nonscientists read, they are somewhat specialized, still highly informational, but less technical. And by the time that science news makes it to the daily newspaper, that information is not specialized, is somewhat informational, and is not technical.

For example, here are a couple of sentences from a journal article published by the United States National Academy of Sciences. This article addressed a topic that should interest most people, ensuring proper food production to feed the climbing population of the world:

> The persistence of food insecurity does not reflect so much a lack of capacity of the world as a whole to increase food production to whatever level would be required for everyone to have consumption levels assuring satisfactory nutrition. The world already produces sufficient food. The undernourished and the food-insecure persons are in these conditions because they are poor in terms of income with which to purchase food or in terms of access to agricultural resources, education, technology, infrastructure, credit, etc., to produce their own food. (Alexandratos 1999, p. 5908)

And from an op-ed piece in the New York Times:

> Yet obviously not all poor people feed themselves well, because they lack the essentials: land, water, energy and nutrients. Often that's a result of cruel dictatorship (North Korea) or war, displacement and strife (the Horn of Africa, Haiti and many other places), or drought or other calamities. (Bittman 2013)

It's easy to see why some teachers would turn to the second passage over the first. The vocabulary and the syntax in the second make the passage more accessible. The language of the scientist in the first passage is what one might expect from the National Academy of Sciences: detached, unemotional, measured, and highly specific.

For example, the people simply called "poor" in the second passage are more specifically described in the first as "undernourished and food-insecure persons." We can easily see a tenth grader's eyes glazing as he reads that first passage, and we can see that same student wanting to organize food drives after reading the second.

Teachers react to that, and in high school science classes we've visited, too many completely turn away from the texts written by scientists for scientists. As a result, many students in science classes mostly read science that comes from popular magazines or newspapers, which means they are reading science written in nonscientific vernacular. Then, when we do hand them a science textbook, one written by scientists for an audience expected to be thinking deeply about science, the syntax and vocabulary shift. Furthermore, this shift usually occurs with no warning to students. We don't stop to explain that because the language will be specific, more modifiers will be used, thus making sentences longer. We don't explain that scientists tend to put as much information as possible in a single sentence—again to achieve some sort of specificity—and most of us don't spend time showing students how to chunk sentences so they become navigable.

As we discussed this idea with some high school science teachers, all who had been teaching fewer than ten years, they admitted that although they read science texts in college, they no longer read texts written by scientists for scientists. These teachers said they weren't sure how to explain to students how to read the complicated syntax and technical talk of science texts. We appreciated their honesty.

Suddenly, the science textbook is "too hard" or "dumb" or "impossible" from the students' point of view. So the teacher returns to the less technical articles, those written with the nonscientist in mind, the vocabulary demands go down, and the syntax becomes easier to follow.

Later, those students will struggle on the mandated tests as they read science passages that are often written by scientists for scientists. Scores are lower than all had hoped they would be, and concern goes up that students don't know enough science. But the problem is more likely to be that students simply haven't had enough practice with these texts to figure out how to navigate the syntax.

FROM BOB: Kylene says that kids can't write what they haven't read; I'd add that they can't read with fluency what they haven't practiced reading.

What You Can Do

The most important thing you can do to help students read science texts is to actually give them science texts to read. Most science teachers have told us that they "tell students what they need to know" rather than expecting them to read about what they need to know. We think it's important that students actually read science texts, and know how to think about the technical language.

Vocabulary

When we look at these specialized, highly informational, technical texts, we see that vocabulary causes most of the problems for two reasons. First, science texts often give common words a specific science meaning. For instance, we talked with a tenth grader who was confused by the word *charge* in the sentence "The electric charges were a type of kinetic energy." He said, "I thought charge meant to buy something, you know how you charge it with a credit card." While it's easy to focus on the technical language of a science text, it is just as important to focus on those more common words that have a specialized meaning in science such as *bond, charge,* and *stress*.

Second, in addition to common words used in a specific way, scientific texts are filled with highly technical language. While new terms might be explained (depending on the expertise that the author assumes of readers), other technical terms may not.

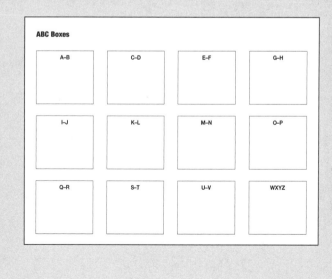

ABC Boxes

A–B	C–D	E–F	G–H
I–J	K–L	M–N	O–P
Q–R	S–T	U–V	WXYZ

Figure 36 As students record the technical language from a particular chapter or topic here, they are building their own personal word wall.

For example, readers are expected to understand cell division before they begin reading the paragraph about meiosis. So, meiosis is explained, but not the broader topic of cell division, which was probably explained previously. Science textbooks define a technical term the first time it is used. Then the word simply is applied to various other situations. Students are expected to remember what they've read and put that to use in future sections. We all know how well that works for some students.

We've found it helpful to have students use the ABC chart (see Figure 36) to create their own personal word wall as they are learning information about one topic. As they start a new chapter, they begin collecting the terms they need to know and placing them on the chart. We find it helpful if students include the page number (or article name) where they found that word. Then, when students say to you, "I don't get it," if the problem is a term they have supposedly already learned, send them to their ABC chart so they can look up the page where they read it, turn back to that page, and review.

Sketch to Stretch

Understanding This Strategy

Often, when students declare that a text is confusing, they begin their laments with comments such as "I don't see what it means," or "I wish there was a picture." Those comments are clues that the problem in comprehending that text is with visualizing what the author is saying. When visualizing is the problem, encourage kids to use a fix-up strategy called Sketch to Stretch.

TO GET STARTED

MATERIALS: Model passages: Dyson Bladeless Fan and portion of Viet Nam Declaration of Independence. See Appendix page 272.

TEACHER PREP: Practice your sketch for the Dyson Bladeless Fan passage.

WHEN TO USE: During reading

GROUP SIZE: Individuals or pairs

VARIATIONS: None needed.

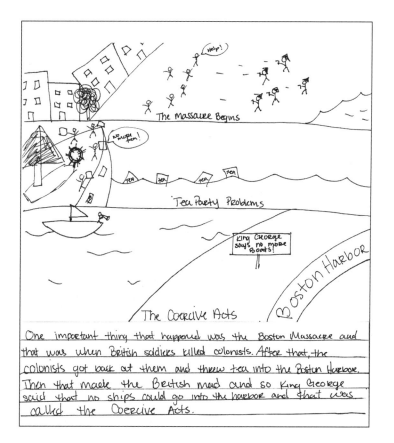

An excellent article that will provide many other references on transmediation is "The Art of Learning to be Critically Literate." This appeared in *Language Arts,* Volume 92, Number 2, Nov 2014 and can be retrieved at www.ncte.org /library/NCTEFiles/ Resources/Journals/LA /0922-nov2014/LA0922Art .pdf.

In the mid 1980s, Jerry Harste and colleagues began looking at a body of research called transmediation. Transmediation is the changing of one medium to another. Harste's work looked at transforming text into art. He thought that readers could stretch their understanding of a written text if after they read it they would draw either a literal or metaphorical representation of that text. For several years after his initial work, some very smart doctoral students focused their dissertations on this idea, giving us now a robust body of knowledge about the power of transmediation, and, in particular, a strategy Jerry called Sketch to Stretch.

Although we've long been fans of Sketch to Stretch as an after-reading strategy, we only recently began to consider it as a during-reading strategy students might use to fix up confusions. When we noticed that many of the confusions students faced had to do with trying to visualize what the author was describing, we began to have students do three things:

1. Underline the specific parts of the text causing the confusion.

2. Reread those parts and, while rereading, try to draw in the margin what the author was describing.

3. Label their drawing with terms the author used in the text.

More times than not, when students would begin sketching they would focus on signal words (*for example, after, before, as an effect*) as they looked carefully at describing words ("*flat* pedestal," "*small* opening," "*drawn* bayonets"). Most often, their marginal drawings gave them enough of a scaffold for understanding that they could continue reading with a sense that they had, as one student told us, "figured out it myself."

Teaching the Strategy

In this tenth-grade classroom of mostly reluctant and struggling readers, we introduced Sketch to Stretch, modeling it with a text they were unlikely to have seen and then turning to a text the district had chosen. *We* found both texts confusing and worried how the students would fare. We thought this would be a fine time to test out Sketch to Stretch as a fix-up strategy. We began our lesson with the students.

We Explain

“ There's a saying that a picture is worth a thousand words. We've always taken that to mean that photos, videos, paintings—all the images we see—offer us so many details that if we wanted to write about what we saw, it would take a thousand words. Seeing an image always makes a powerful impression.

Perhaps that's why visualizing what we see as we read is so important. The author tries to paint a picture in our minds with her words. Sometimes, though, that picture just doesn't emerge. When that happens, we often feel a little lost in all those words. We say to ourselves, "If I could just see it," or "I wish the author had drawn a picture," or "I can't image what she means," and then we stop reading, saying to ourselves, "I just don't get it."

We want to show you a way you *can* get it, a way you can figure out what the author means *on your own*. This is a fix-up strategy you can use with almost any text, almost any time you're confused. It's called Sketch to Stretch.

We Model

" We were reading about a new type of fan called the Dyson Bladeless Fan—which is an electric fan that doesn't have the blades you normally see in a fan. These blades are hidden in the pedestal of the fan, and that's why Dyson calls it bladeless. We thought we understood how this fan worked until we got to this paragraph:

> The fan appears to be a circular tube mounted on a pedestal. . . . The air flows through a channel in the pedestal up to the tube, which is hollow. As air flows through the slits in the tube and out through the front of the fan, air behind the fan is drawn through the tube as well. This is called inducement. The flowing air pushed by the motor induces the air behind the fan to follow. Air surrounding the edges of the fan will also begin to flow in the direction of the breeze. This process is called entrainment.

Well, that was a bit confusing. I had been able to picture what it looked like up to this point. I didn't have any problem with this part that said that the fan sits on a pedestal and that a circular tube is mounted on the pedestal. And I didn't have any trouble with visualizing this part that says that the tube has slits in it, and that's where the air comes out.

This new information, though, about air coming in and out, and something called inducement and entrainment slowed me down a

You're going to want to mark this up in front of the students, so project it on your whiteboard leaving some space between the lines and some margin space for sketching. The entire article about this fan can be found at http:// electronics.howstuffworks .com/gadgets/home/dyson -bladeless-fan.htm /printable9/2/2014

Draw your own for kids on your whiteboard. They'll love seeing you give this a go.

You can see Bob's sketch on page 95.

We're not providing Bob's step-by-step description of how specific words helped him draw the picture he did because we don't want his language to replace yours. Students need to hear you be hesitant, start, stop, reread, and rethink. They need to see you start a sketch, start over, label parts, put question marks beside parts (in the text and in your sketch) you aren't sure of. In other words, they need to see you struggle—successfully. Be sure to end by labeling on your sketch the parts that clarify what you had found confusing.

bit. So, the first thing I'm going to do is underline the specific parts that were confusing. For me, it's the word *this* in the sentence "This is called inducement." This what? Also, I'll underline "This process" in the last sentence because I'm not sure about the process. Now I know what I really need to reread—the sentence that explains inducement and the sentence that explains entrainment. [At this point, Bob— the teacher in this lesson—began reading the final paragraph aloud several times. One time he would point to words; another time he would slow down; another time, he was almost doing Syntax Surgery as he underlined words and drew arrows to others. As he was talking, he was drawing a sketch of what he saw on the whiteboard.]

I'm not positive [Bob explained] that this is 100% accurate, but I have enough of an idea to keep on reading. Notice, I'm not worried about how great this fan looks. I'm just trying to get a sketch of this in my head so I can see—literally—what the author is describing.

Students Try

" Although we want you doing this with any text you're reading, we'd like you to try it right now with a text that we'll share with you. Take a look at this short paragraph. It's from the Declaration of Independence of the Democratic Republic of Vietnam. Just as the United States of America declared its independence from England in writing, the Democratic Republic of Vietnam declared its independence from France. An introduction to Vietnam's Declaration of Independence says:

This text is from an online history course called "History Matters." This is part of the introduction to the actual Declaration of Independence of the Democratic Republic of Vietnam. We've changed the word *granaries* to *warehouses* and *famine* to *hunger*. If your students can handle the more advanced vocabulary, you should use it.

> With the support of rich and poor peasants, workers, businessmen, landlords, students, and intellectuals, the Viet Minh [people fighting for independence] had expanded throughout northern Vietnam where it established new local governments, redistributed some lands, and opened warehouses to alleviate the hunger.

Read this again to yourself, and then, on your paper, do three things. First, underline any parts that are confusing; second, sketch out what you see happening; and third, label your drawing using words from the text. Once you have a sketch, turn to a partner and share your drawing. Be sure to label as many parts of your drawing as you can, using the words from the text." (See Figure 37)

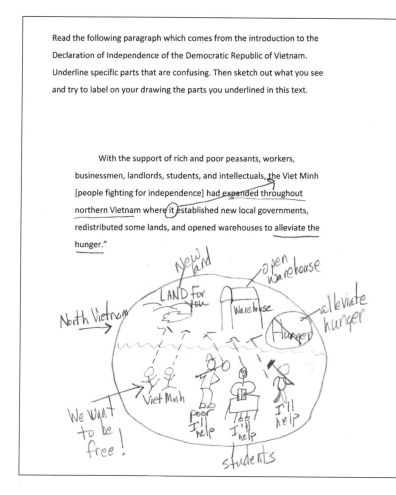

Read the following paragraph which comes from the introduction to the Declaration of Independence of the Democratic Republic of Vietnam. Underline specific parts that are confusing. Then sketch out what you see and try to label on your drawing the parts you underlined in this text.

With the support of rich and poor peasants, workers, businessmen, landlords, students, and intellectuals, the Viet Minh [people fighting for independence] had expanded throughout northern Vietnam where it established new local governments, redistributed some lands, and opened warehouses to alleviate the hunger."

If you are working with younger students, this example isn't appropriate. You might choose paragraph 3 from the article, "Garana's Story," which is on page 265 of the Appendix.

Figure 37 This student's sketch is quite sophisticated, but your students' needn't be.

Circulate as students are drawing, and remind them that they don't have to artistically draw people. Stick figures are great. If students tell you that they don't know what the country of Vietnam looks like, tell them to just draw a box or a rectangle and label it Vietnam. You want them to recognize that the effort started in the south and then moved northward, so look for drawings that focus on the phrase "expanded throughout northern Vietnam."

Students Reflect

If we're ever going to hear students say they "hate" a particular strategy, it's this one. The first time we heard two students talking about how much they "despised this" we almost set aside the strategy. When the boys showed us their sketch (everyone had paired up, found a part of a short text that they found difficult, and sketched out their

The other boy replied that he was pretty sure he'd never use it again. "Nah. I hate to draw so I pretty much still hate this." So, this was valuable for 50%. If batters had a 500 batting average . . .

understanding of that section of the passage), we asked them if Sketch to Stretch had helped them understand the passage better. Both fourth graders nodded, and one replied, "It was awesome."

We then mentioned that we had heard them say that they didn't enjoy this—actually hated it—and we wondered what had changed their minds. The other boy didn't pause for a moment, "Oh, I said that because I am such a bad drawer. I was like really hating having to draw." His partner chimed in, "Yeah, and I hated it because to do it, you like really really really have to keep rereading what was confusing and I hate to read ." We asked that boy if he'd ever use this again on his own:

> "Yeah, I will. I get tired of not understanding and always
> having to say to the teacher that I didn't get it and this, I mean it
> was hard, but this was like showing me that I could figure it out
> a little and I liked that."

We highlight these two boys because they represent the most common responses (minus the "I hate it" part). Many students worry about how well they draw. For that reason, we always model this all year long. They see our drawings don't get much better, but our ability to understand the text faster does. Another group of students—your reluctant or struggling readers—will resist because this requires them to identify the problem, reread, sketch, reread some more, and label what they've learned. When students first begin doing this, you might hear them say that they like it better when the teacher tells them what it means. Eventually, though, most students find that the self-satisfaction they feel from figuring this out on their own is motivating. As a senior in high school told us, "It's like eating your vegetables. At first you don't want to. But then you do and discover they don't taste that bad and eventually you realize that they really are good for you, even if you still don't really like them."

So, Sketch to Stretch: the strategy that is good for you even if you don't really like it.

Listening to Student Talk

Some students will skip the first step—underlining exactly what's confusing. These students did not skip that step. Because they didn't skip that step they both realized that location of places was the problem.

No matter the age of students, we notice that when they begin sketching what they are "seeing," they return to the text repeatedly. It's the rereading that gives them the evidence they need for the drawing they are creating. Here are two seventh-grade girls discussing a text about southern South America, specifically Paraguay, Uruguay, southern Chile, and Argentina. A map would have been nice, but without one it became perfect for Sketch to Stretch.

STUDENT 1: I underlined "not many live there" because I couldn't figure out where "there" was.

STUDENT 2: And I marked here, about Uruguay being the smallest country because it didn't say where it was.

STUDENT 1: Yeah, but I think it has to be in the east. Or at least more east than Paraguay. See, it says that people live east of there.

STUDENT 2: Right. So Uruguay is east of Paraguay. OK. I get it. So how are you going to draw it?

STUDENT 1: Well, like South America, it's, like, long, so I'm just going to draw, like, a long box. And this is all about just southern South America. So I'm just going to put a line across here.

STUDENT 2: Yeah, and label everything under it as southern South America.

STUDENT 1: And this part, see, it says that Chile runs down the west coast. So we could draw it here.

STUDENT 2: I think you have to make it skinny because, see, it says it runs all the way down the west coast.

STUDENT 1: So, then Uruguay has to go over here.

STUDENT 2: Yeah, and put Paraguay more to the west, or maybe in the middle?

> Student 1 has embraced our point that if we don't know the exact shape of something, draw a box or a rectangle or a circle. This keeps the process moving.

As you can see, the students begin discussing far more than they initially said they had underlined. We see that often. Kids mark as little as possible, but then their conversation takes them to other places. Reread this transcript looking specifically for points at which students returned to the text. Sketch to Stretch pushes students back into the text and rereading improves comprehension.

Another Conversation

Two fifth graders were reading a math word problem. They approached their teacher complaining that the problem was too hard. These boys struggle more than the girls in the previous transcript because they skipped that critical first step of underlining what is confusing. The

> This problem is from www .mathplayground.com. Our go-to math guy, Will LaRiccia, from Solon, Ohio, suggested the site to us for its word problems. We sure appreciate all his help in all things math!

teacher realized that, reminded them what they needed to do, and then smartly told them they might use Syntax Surgery to help them figure out their sketch.

Here is the problem the boys were trying to solve: "An airplane can hold forty passengers. If there are four rows of seats on the airplane, how many seats are in each row?"

STUDENT 1: This problem makes no sense.

TEACHER: What's confusing?

STUDENT 2: It says forty passengers, and then it asks about seats. This is about forty *passengers.*

TEACHER: Why don't you boys go circle the parts that are confusing, and if you can do a Syntax Surgery to help you connect everything, try that, too. After that, see if you can sketch out what is confusing.

STUDENT 1: [back at his desk with student 2] So, what does the forty passengers connect to?

STUDENT 2: You could draw an arrow from seat to seat, and from row to row, but nothing to forty passengers.

STUDENT 1: Wait! You draw an arrow from four rows to forty passengers because, see, the passengers sit in seats that are in rows.

STUDENT 2: Oh! So, if we draw it, it looks like this.

[After a moment of drawing the boys return to the teacher.]

STUDENT 2: Look! We did it. The forty passengers sit in the seats. You have four rows. So we put a X for each seat. Usually planes have the same number of seats in each row, so when you draw it, you have to have ten seats in each row.

STUDENT 1: That seems like a lot of seats in a row. I think no plane would be that wide.

STUDENT 2: It could be a really big jet. Then it would be that wide.

STUDENT 1: Yeah, but it wouldn't just have forty seats. It would have more like 400. This is a stupid problem. But we got it!

Questions You Might Have

1. *Is it important that kids underline the confusing parts before they start sketching?*

   Yes! Struggling readers live in generalities. They encounter one confusing paragraph and declare of the entire book, "I don't get it." We want them to define the "it" before they begin sketching. Just recognize that they will underline as little as possible. If you notice that Sketch to Stretch isn't helping clear up confusions, then it might be that students are underlining too few parts, or the vocabulary is too demanding.

2. *If a student is confused, does it make sense to tell him to draw what he can't see?*

   That seems logical, but research has consistently shown that rereading is a powerful way—perhaps the most powerful way—to clear up confusions. So Sketch to Stretch pushes kids back into the text. Also, as students begin to sketch what the text says, they focus on words or phrases, and that helps them figure out what's going on.

3. *Is Sketch to Stretch as you use it really any different from the Sketch to Stretch that Harste first wrote about?*

   Yes and no. It's the same principle of transmediation. But when kids use Sketch to Stretch after reading (as Harste suggested), we agree that a metaphorical representation of what the text meant to them is fine. Consider the student who drew a picture of the Nazi swastika and then drew a book and placed it on top of the swastika and labeled the book *Diary of Anne Frank* and wrote, "The hope Anne wrote about crushed the prison the Nazis tried to put her in." That student has truly stretched her understanding, as shown in her metaphorical drawing. That's perfect for *after* reading.

   When students are confused *while* reading, we want literal drawings from the words in the text. This is when they do go directly back into the text and use the author's words to create the scene that's causing the confusion.

Strategy 6

Genre Reformulation

TO GET STARTED

MATERIALS: *Everything You Need to Know about American History Home-work* passage, found on Appendix page 269. *Brown Bear, Brown Bear*; *If You Give a Mouse a Cookie*; *The Napping House*; and any ABC book (available at any library or book store)

TEACHER PREP: You should practice this with the Christopher Columbus passage.

WHEN TO USE: After reading

GROUP SIZE: Individuals or pairs

VARIATIONS

Social studies: Much of social studies is about noticing the causal con-nections. For that rea-son, reformulating with the text *If You Give a Mouse a Cookie* in mind is helpful.

Math: This is most helpful in math as a review and students should use the ABC text structure for reformulation.

Understanding This Strategy

Genre Reformulation, also called Text Reformulation or Story Recycling (Feathers 1993/2004) is an after-reading strategy that students use to help solidify content—and while doing so clarify any confusions. They write about what they have read, using a particular text structure. Whether students turn the expository text into a narrative text structure, an ABC book, or a rap song, Genre Reformulation almost always helps kids think deeply about what they've read.

> If this sounds a bit like the transmediation that was discussed with Sketch to Stretch, that's because it is. Although students aren't moving from one medium (print) to another (image), they are moving from one text structure (expository) to another (narrative).

> Abraham Lincoln, Abraham Lincoln, what do you see?
> I see unhappy slaves looking at me.
>
> Unhappy slaves, unhappy slaves, what do you see?
> I see Northern soldiers fighting to rescue me.
>
> Northern soldiers, Northern soldiers, what do you see?
> I see my Southern brother shooting at me.
>
> Southern brother, Southern brother, what do you see?
> I see all my slaves being freed and taken from me.
>
> Slaves, slaves what do you see?
> I see some people fighting hard to make sure all are really free.

Two middle school students in a resource classroom created this reformulation about the Civil War. They used the text structure found in the children's picture book *Brown Bear, Brown Bear.*

Research consistently affirms that we tend to remember narrative texts with more detail and with more accuracy than we remember expository texts. There are many reasons for this, with the most often-cited being that we tend to talk using a narrative structure (what's been called a "story grammar"). We tell the story of our day; we tell the story of what happened to someone else; we teachers tell stories of how we taught a lesson. This means we give our accounts a beginning, a middle, and an end. We place events in a chronological sequence. We provide characters (ourselves and others), and we often build toward a particular moment that we know will delight our listeners in some way (or we end up telling a rather dull story).

Other researchers point out that we tell bedtime stories to our youngest—whether that means telling children a favorite fairy tale or reading that tale to them. Either way, from an early age children learn the narrative text structure of beginning, middle, and end. We think we might remember narratives more easily because this text structure carries the reader along in a user-friendly way as a character explains the setting, describes the problems, and eventually shares the outcome. The reader only needs to come along for the ride. Expository text, by contrast, leaves the reader on his own as he navigates various text structures (causal, comparative, descriptive, sequential), with no friendly narrator pointing the way.

Whatever the reason, most people process information better when it has a narrative structure to it and then tend to remember it more easily and longer.

> Rather than cite a dozen or more articles for this section, we're going to encourage you to go online and read "Harnessing the Power of Story," by Steven Nathanson. It is excellent for all our content teachers and has plenty of references cited at the end that you can turn to if this is a research area of interest. You can find it at http://scholarworks.wmich.edu/cgi/viewcontent.cgi?article=1124&context=reading_horizons.

Patterns to Use in Genre Reformulation

Genre Reformulation uses the power of narrative as students take an expository structure and reformulate it into a narrative structure (see the opening figure). We usually give students a narrative structure to follow, and often we choose from the following:

1. **The if/then structure.** This can be modeled with *If You Give a Mouse a Cookie* and the other books in that series, by Laura Joffe Numeroff.

2. **The repetitive book structure.** Your best model for students is *Brown Bear, Brown Bear*, by Bill Martin, Jr.

3. **The ABC structure.** A is for _____ because _____.

4. **The cumulative tale structure.** You might choose the old tale "The House That Jack Built" or a newer cumulative tale such as *The Napping House*, by Audrey Wood, or *The Cake That Mack Ate*, by Rose Robart.

Particular text structures focus students' attention on specific skills. For instance, if students reformulate the text into an if/then structure, they tend to be focused on reading for causal relationships. If they choose a repetitive structure like the one used in *Brown Bear, Brown Bear*, their focus is a bit more on sequencing. The ABC structure pushes kids to think more about big ideas and details as well as inferences. The cumulative tale structure encourages students to, as the name suggests, think about all those skills: sequencing, causal relationships, main ideas, and details.

No matter what structure students use, they are also analyzing, synthesizing, and evaluating as they choose which parts of the text to include in their reformulation. Additionally, as they work on their reformulation they must return to the text repeatedly. That constant close rereading, often one or two sentences at a time, is critical for improving students' comprehension.

Teaching the Strategy

We have erred on the side of overexplaining this strategy to students, spending far too much time talking about types of texts they can use for their reformulation or showing far too many examples. After too many glazed eyes from kids, one day we hit upon the right amount of instruction: next to none. So as you read these next sections, if they look sparse, that's because we're encouraging you to say less, giving kids the time to do more. That's what we found actually works best for us.

We Explain

❝ Often, when we try to remember something from a text we've just read, we just repeat to ourselves what was in the text. That works for a while, but then later we notice we've forgotten what we had worked so hard to memorize.

If instead we take that text and rewrite it into a different format, we have a better chance of remembering it. Today, you're going to see for yourself how text reformulation affects your thinking about a passage as you reformulate a text we're about to give you. You'll work with a partner, but both of you will write, so go ahead and take out paper and pen while we distribute the passage you will reformulate."

Students Try

You'll notice that we're skipping the "We Model" section. That's done purposefully because we've found that our modeling of this always restricted what students did. When we simply gave students instructions and then turned them loose, while some might have asked a lot of questions, most created something smarter than what we would have modeled. But when we provided a model first, most worked only to that low level.

    “ Before we look at the short passage you now have on your desks, let's look at a picture book I bet some of you remember hearing when you were little. It's called *Brown Bear, Brown Bear*. Take a moment and listen while I read it to you. [We encourage you to find a copy of this book to read aloud to students. We don't reproduce it here because the cost for doing so was prohibitive.]

One reason little ones enjoy this so much is that while they can anticipate how each page begins—always with the animal that was mentioned on the previous page—they have no idea what animal they'll meet next. So, the brown bear sees a red bird; then the red bird sees a yellow duck; then the yellow duck sees a blue horse, and so on. The author, Bill Martin, Jr., used a very simple pattern when he wrote this book and that pattern lets readers easily predict what's happening next and be surprised at the same time. We call this a *repetitive text structure*.

> Reading the story aloud is important, but then you still must go back and point out how the specific pattern for that book works.

    “ Now, keep that text structure in mind and take a look at this short passage about Christopher Columbus. Follow along as I read aloud:

> In 1492, Native American life began to change dramatically. Christopher Columbus, an Italian who was captain of three Spanish ships, "discovered" what Europeans called a New World. He thought he had reached the Spice Islands near India. He called the people he met "Indians." Soon after, other European nations sent explorers to the Americas.

> We're using a short passage about Christopher Columbus that you'll see below. You can find this in the Appendix. You should make sure each student has a copy of whatever passage you choose to use.

continues

At first, Native Americans welcomed the Europeans. They introduced the Europeans to tomatoes, corn, potatoes, and tobacco. Europeans introduced Native Americans to guns, sugarcane, and horses. They also brought diseases new to the Americas—the common cold, measles, and smallpox, to name a few—which killed many Native Americans.

When Europeans began to explore and later settle in North America, they used guns to take whatever they wanted. They thought they had the right to do this. When they built villages and cities, they often cleared forests. These forests were the homes of many of the wild animals the Native Americans hunted.

Some groups, like the Cherokee, took on European ways, but the settlers wanted their land anyway. Most tribes that survived were forced to move west. Today, most of the remaining American Indians live there. Some have sued the government to repay them for the land that was taken from them or granted to them by treaties that were broken. (From *Everything You Need to Know about American History Homework*, Scholastic)

You ought to give it a try before you do this with students—using all the different text patterns. Figure 38 is an example of one teacher's reformulation from a workshop we ran in Florida.

> ❝ This passage has some interesting information, some of which you probably already know and some that might be new. Now, I want you and one partner to think more carefully about this passage by rewriting it into the format used in *Brown Bear, Brown Bear*. So, let's look again at the first couple of lines of *Brown Bear*. See the pattern? The animal mentioned at the end of the one page becomes the one mentioned at the beginning of the next. This means, if you begin your rewrite "Native Americans, Native Americans/What do you see?/I see three ships sailing toward me," then your next part must begin with "Three ships, three ships what do you see?"
>
> Talk with your partner, decide how you want to get started, and see what you two create.

As you start circulating, students will ask, "Does it need to rhyme?" No. "Do we have to always use the line "What do you see?" No. You could say "What did you hear?" or "What did you want?" or "What did you do?" And some will ask the typical "How long does this need to be?" Long enough to include all that you see as important.

Students Try

When students do this for the first time, you'll see a long wait time as they reread and wonder how to start. We usually keep a few stanzas of *Brown Bear, Brown Bear* up on the whiteboard for students to look at. You'll want to circulate and answer again those same three questions you've already addressed. Soon, though, you'll see kids begin writing. Some will write themselves into a circle. When that happens, send them back into the text to figure out what happened next so that they move forward. As you circulate, if you see students skipping information you want included, just point them to the paragraph and tell them to include information from that section.

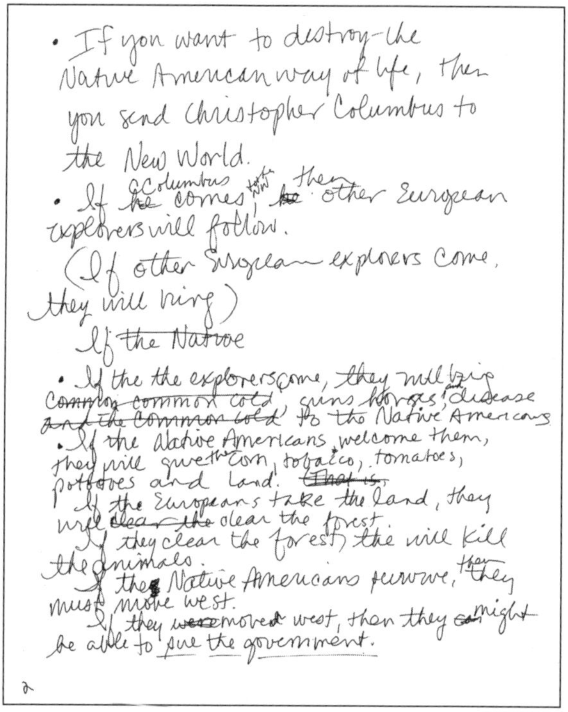

• If you want to destroy the Native American way of life, then you send Christopher Columbus to the New World.
• If Columbus comes, then other European explorers will follow.
(If other European explorers come, they will bring)
~~If the Native~~
• If the the explorers come, they will bring ~~Common~~ ~~common cold~~, guns, horses, disease ~~and the common cold~~ to the Native Americans
• If the Native Americans welcome them, they will give the corn, tobacco, tomatoes, potatoes and land. ~~That is,~~
If the Europeans take the land, they will ~~clear the~~ clear the forest.
If they clear the forest, the will kill the animals.
If the Native Americans survive, then they must move west.
If they ~~were~~ moved west, then they ~~can~~ might be able to sue the government.

Figure 38 Notice the false starts—shown via the strikethroughs—as the teacher must figure out how the original text fits into this new format. She said later, "I learned much about this passage I had not noticed on my first fast read as I kept going back to it."

Students Reflect

Ninth graders, after reformulating a portion of a science text on light waves, said, that they thought "this was cool," "hard to do," "something that really made me think," "really smart because you have to really think" and "hurting my brain because of all the thinking." One second grader told us "My redo is better than the first one [a short text on beetles] and now it is in my brain and I'm just remembering it all the time."

In a sixth-grade class, a quiet girl spoke up almost immediately, surprising everyone. She said, "I liked it and didn't like it. I liked making a story that had a pattern, so I didn't have to worry about the pattern, but I didn't like that to get in all the details. I had to keep rereading what was in the book. It was, like, write then read then write then read. You have to keep reading, and I do not like reading so much." This strategy does push kids back into the text a lot, and that's the reason it's so powerful. But don't overuse it. Kids don't want to think that they will have to rewrite everything they read.

A high school student said he uses the ABC reformulation often to help him think about content. Figure 39 is his ABC reformulation of his history textbook chapter that discussed the Silk Road, Sand Road, and Sea Road.

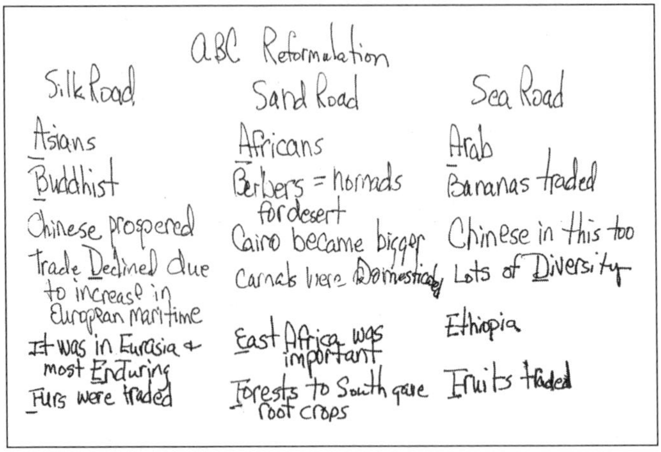
ABC Reformulation

Silk Road	Sand Road	Sea Road
Asians	Africans	Arab
Buddhist	Berbers = nomads for desert	Bananas traded
Chinese prospered	Cairo became bigger	Chinese in this too
Trade Declined due to increase in European maritime	Camels were Domesticated	Lots of Diversity
It was in Eurasia & most Enduring	East Africa was important	Ethiopia
Furs were traded	Forests to South gave root crops	Fruits traded

Figure 39 This student's side-by-side reformulation allowed him to make a quick comparison of these three routes.

Listening to Student Talk

We want to share a few comments from one eighth-grade class that worked on the Christopher Columbus reformulation. Then we'll shift to another class, this time a high school class that reformulated a science text.

The Middle School Students

STUDENT 1: How are we going to start?

STUDENT 2: I think "Columbus, Columbus what do you see? I see Native Americans looking at me."

STUDENT 1: Yeah. That would work. But wait. Look here at the beginning. See, it says that "In 1492, Native American life began to change." That makes it seem like this is really more about the Native Americans than Christopher Columbus.

STUDENT 2: Well, the next three sentences are all about Christopher Columbus.

STUDENT 1: Yeah. But I think it should start, "Native Americans, Native Americans, what do you see? I see three ships sailing toward me. Three ships, three ships what do you see? We see Indians waving at us."

STUDENT 2: That doesn't rhyme. But OK. Then "Indians, Indians, what do you see? We see Europeans bringing tomatoes, corn, potatoes, and tobacco to us."

STUDENT 1: Then the next would have to be "Tomatoes, corn, potatoes, and tobacco what do you see?" That doesn't make sense. Corn can't see something.

STUDENT 2: Well, a blue horse doesn't exist either. It's OK. Let's do, "Tomatoes, corn, potatoes, and tobacco what do you see? We see other 'gifts' of guns, sugarcane, and horses–"

STUDENT 1: [interrupting] Wait. Look. The Europeans didn't bring the food. They brought the diseases. Look. See! Read it again.

These students then went back into the text and discovered their initial misreading. That happens with students often—they read something quickly and only once. They know someone brought something, and they're content to let their first draft of understanding become their final draft. Genre Reformulation pushes them back into the text repeatedly so that, often, they catch their misunderstandings and revise their thinking. It's not only the text they reformulate, but also their own thinking.

High School Students

In a ninth-grade health class, students were reading about the various body systems. The teacher told them to break into groups of two and to reformulate a section of the chapter (each pair was assigned a different section) using the if/then structure (based on *If You Give a Mouse a Cookie*), the cumulative structure (based on "This Is the House That Jack Built"), or the repetitive structure (back to *Brown Bear, Brown Bear*).

One group wrote:

If you eat, you're going to swallow. If you swallow, your throat muscles open. If food is in the throat, the epiglottis has a job to do and routes food to the esophagus. If the esophagus does its job, food ends up in the stomach. If the food just stays in your stomach, your body won't get nourishment. If your body is going to get nourishment, then the small intestine is going to have to absorb the nutrients from the food. If the nutrients are going to be pulled out of the food, then the liver and gallbladder and

We've purposefully used the phrase "first draft of understanding" and "revise their thinking" here, and we use those terms with kids. As often as possible we use terms from the writing process with the reading process. A process is a process whether with reading or writing. We draft, revise, draft, revise . . .

One group wrote: "The mouth is connected to the epiglottis, which is connected to esophagus, which is connected to stomach, which leads to small intestines, which leads to liver, gallbladder and pancreas, which leads to large intestine, which leads to 'Man I got to go.' It's like an assembly line, like for making cars. Hey, they ought to call it Digestive Motors."

pancreas will have to help out. If they do their job, then the large intestine will only need to absorb some water and some smaller amounts of nutrients and then send the rest on to your exit system. In other words, what goes in, will eventually come out.

Questions You Might Have

1. *Do you tell students which structure to use, or do you let them choose?*

   Most often, we tell students. But after some practice, we want students to choose the structure that helps them the most.

2. *Is one structure harder than others?*

   Well, the ABC structure is probably the easiest. The repetitive structure (*Brown Bear, Brown Bear*) is probably harder, followed by if/then, with the cumulative structure being the most demanding.

3. *How often should I encourage kids to use this?*

   We find that students are quite willing to use the ABC structure often. The other structures require more time, and therefore we wouldn't encourage this more than once every several weeks.

4. *Should I ask students to reformulate an entire chapter?*

   We think it's important to use this for a part of a text that is complex and demanding. This gets kids rereading, and rereading always improves understanding. So this isn't an activity to be done to show someone has read a certain amount of text; it's a fix-up strategy to be used to go over a section of a text that's presenting some challenges.

5. *Should students do this on their own or with others? Is there a preference?*

   When kids first try this, we always encourage them to work with a partner. Talking with another student is almost always what helps students think through confusions, choose main points, double-check causal connections, and confirm the correct sequence.

After students have learned the basic text reformulation patterns, we find that they often begin to do this on their own, especially the ABC pattern. So have some flexibility and perhaps remind students that if working collaboratively isn't helpful, they should give it a go on their own; likewise, if working alone is too hard, they should find a buddy.

6. *Can I use this with fiction?*

   Yes! While we've restrained ourselves from discussing fiction in this book about reading nonfiction, we can't avoid it here. ELA teachers, please use the QR code in the margin to see a video of a high school student who reformulated "The Tell-Tale Heart" using the *Brown Bear, Brown Bear* structure. (Actually, all teachers will enjoy watching this student share his reformulation.) The teacher told us that the students in this class performed as well as (and some did better than) the kids in the honors class on the exam on this story. He was sure it was because they reread the story so often while creating their reformulations.

http://hein.pub/readnf9

Poster

TO GET STARTED

MATERIALS: A short passage of your choosing taped in center of flip-chart paper. Make one for every four students.

TEACHER PREP: Choosing the passage; taping onto flip-chart paper

WHEN TO USE: After reading

GROUP SIZE: Small groups of four

VARIATIONS

Math: Put problem of the day in center of poster. Tell students to write or draw the process they would use on the poster. Tell them they are not to solve the problem. You circulate and when students have a correct process, let them, then, on their own solve the problem.

Understanding This Strategy

Poster is a simple strategy that encourages talk by prohibiting talk. Students read a short passage and then, with three or four others, write responses to the passage which has been taped in the middle of a sheet of flip-chart paper. Groups of four or five students gather around that large sheet, listen while you read the passage aloud, and then begin to write their reactions to the passage all over the flip-chart paper. They are asked to do this silently—no talking at all during the writing.

> You might prepare the passage in large font, sixteen to eighteen points or even larger, so that it can easily be read at a distance of three to six feet.

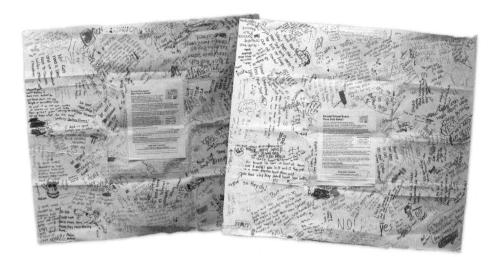

After they have had ten to twenty minutes to annotate the passage, the ideas generated can be immediately discussed, or they can be used to set an agenda for further conversation, or perhaps further reading or writing, over the next day or two.

Teaching the Strategy

Although this is not a strategy that students will do on their own, the habits it encourages—slowing down, rereading a short section of a longer text, and jotting notes—will transfer to reading they do on their own. You'll need to find the passage and decide if you agree with us that this is best used as an after-reading strategy. We've had several teachers tell us that they use it before reading to help students begin to think about a topic. As with Genre Reformulation, say as little as possible about what students will be doing; instead, get them doing it.

We Explain

❝ I'm about to give you a short text, which we are going to read in a somewhat unusual way. This will require you to follow one simple ground rule: You won't be able to talk. Here's how it's going to work:

First, you won't each have a copy of the text. Instead, there'll be one copy for four of you. You will have to share it. It will come to you on a large sheet of flip-chart paper so that it will be surrounded by big margins on all four sides. So, let's first put ourselves in groups of roughly four, and someone come get one sheet of flip-chart paper for

FROM KYLENE: Bob has been doing this activity for many years now, using it first with short poems and more recently with nonfiction passages. He should have written about it in *Response and Analysis*, but, negligently, didn't do so. He did, finally, write about Poster in an article titled "Literature as Invitation" in the December 2000 issue of *Voices from the Middle.*

your group. [Ideally, you'll also have felt-tip pens available to distribute so that each student within the group has a unique color.]

Now that you have the poster, I'm going to read the passage to you one time. Then that no-talking ground rule takes effect. Instead, you're going to have your conversation on paper. What do you write? Whatever comes to you. Write about why you agree or disagree with something in the passage. List questions. Draw what you see. Make a connection. Write a response to what others have said. [Some students benefit from seeing this list of options on an anchor chart.]

OK. Get started.

Students Try

We've omitted the "We Model" section because this isn't a fix-up strategy you need to model. Just tell kids what to do and get them writing.

After you've read the passage once to students, remind them of their vow of silence, grab a marker yourself, and begin to wander around the room, joining groups briefly to add your own comments to the poster. At the same time, remember that this is a strategy, not an activity. So you're looking to see which students are asking questions, which are making connections, which are perhaps sketching out what they visualize, which are clarifying others' confusions. Watch this thinking emerge, and you will learn a lot about your students.

After sufficient time, whatever that turns out to be, has gone by, you'll have a choice to make. One possibility is to invite the students to wander around the room, visiting other posters, adding their comments to them or making notes about comments they find there. Doing so may show students that there were possible readings of the text that their group simply didn't discover. This may enable you later to ask the students how their group differed from others that they visited, although not every class will have students who are alert to that subtlety.

The other possibility is to skip the tour of the room and go directly into full-group conversation, which you might begin by simply asking, "What ideas came up as you were reading and writing?"

Encourage the conversation. It is this conversation, after all, that we were hoping for when we forbade talking. We hoped that the pressure to talk would come from the need to say something, rather than from our pointing finger. We wanted students to react to the text, see how others reacted to it, and out of that to generate the thoughts and feelings that would later sustain the full-group conversation.

Take notes on this conversation. It should provide you with ideas for further reading, with issues that might serve as the agenda for subsequent class discussions, possibly with problems or questions that the class—or small groups within the class—might research further, and perhaps for writing the students might undertake.

Students Reflect

When you debrief with students, ask them either the general question "What did you think of this?" or the more specific "How did this change your thinking?" When we ask students what they thought of doing this, we hear these responses and we suspect you will, too.

- ▶ "I liked that I could write my ideas and then read the ideas others wrote. When we have discussions in class, if I'm thinking about what I want to say, then I'm not listening to others. Or, if I'm listening to others, I forget what I want to say."

- ▶ "I liked that I had a chance to say something. When the teacher lets us have discussions, it's always just two or three people who do all the talking. With this, everyone gets to talk."

- ▶ "I was afraid at first to write, because it is, like, it is writing and everyone will see it. But then, we just all started writing and it gave you time to think before you started writing. I liked it a lot."

- ▶ "I thought it was like harder in a way than just talking about it because you had to really think about what you wanted to say so people would be understanding you."

Listening to Student Talk

First, we encourage you to take a look at the images you can find by following the QR code shown here. You will see eighth graders in Linda Rief's school in New Hampshire doing Poster for the first time.

If you don't have access to a computer right now, read this short exchange that comes from students in a ninth-grade classroom. These students read a short passage about climate change written by a scientist who postulates that in about 100 years humans will cease to exist because the warming climate will have made the Earth uninhabitable.

After about fifteen minutes of very intense writing, we called students back together and told them to circle the comments they found

http://hein.pub/readnf10

most intriguing. Then we asked them to share those comments with the entire class. Conversation began immediately:

STUDENT 1: I can't believe that people have only 100 years left. Is that right?

STUDENT 2: Well, it won't matter to me. I'll be dead by then, anyway.

STUDENT 3: Yes, but if you have kids, they won't be dead.

STUDENT 4: Why does he say it's too late? How does he know? I mean, shouldn't this be like on the news every day or something if it is too late?

STUDENT 5: How could he know that?

STUDENT 6: Well, he is a scientist, so he probably has, like, some scientific experiments.

STUDENT 3: Can you imagine what it would be like to be around when humans go extinct? Could that actually even happen?

In just those seven comments, you can see the possibility for further reading, research, writing, and conversation. Consider the issues that these students have raised:

> ▶ The accuracy of the prediction. They wonder if the human species will be gone in a century.

> ▶ The possibility that it is too late to change anything and to prevent our extinction.

> ▶ The evidence upon which the scientist has based his estimate.

> ▶ The question about what life will be like in the last days for the last humans on earth.

In those four points there is the potential for a great deal more thinking, reading, and writing. More importantly, the students raised these questions, so these are the things that are relevant to them.

Questions You Might Have

1. *Why should I do this?*

   This is one of the best ways we've seen for the teacher to be privy to students' thinking. In oral conversation, you can hear one student at a time. In this written conversation, you can watch the thinking of all your students.

The writing students do around the poster actually is serving for the thinking they will share in oral conversation once the silent writing time has ended. These students move from incredulity to skepticism to confusion as they wonder what would happen if humans become extinct. This type of conversation is engaging and leads to deeper analysis.

2. *How do I choose the passage?*

As you read the piece you are about to assign to your students, be looking for a passage that strikes you as discussable. *Discussable* is an ambiguous term, but it is meant to refer to anything evocative or provocative, debatable or startling. If you think the passage is likely to awaken strongly held feelings, remind them of personal experiences, surprise them with a novel thought or a new perspective, or encourage them to take opposite sides on an issue, then it is likely to work. We watched this fail quickly when the passage chosen was a short poem about the beauty of butterflies. Students wrote, "Nice" and "They are pretty." There must be something worth discussing for students to, well, have something to discuss.

3. *Could I use this in math class?*

We enjoyed working with groups of math teachers in Akron, Ohio, and Orlando, Florida. They said that Poster had become their go-to strategy for "Problem of the Day." They would put a problem in the center of the paper and have students "discuss" the process they would use. They would not solve the problem, but write out (and draw if needed) how they would solve it. Once they had agreed on a process, they would return to their individual seats and actually solve the problem. Teachers in both locations said that students really enjoyed working this way, and students began to report that they understood the problems better.

4. *How do we move from the small groups clustered around the flip-chart paper to full-class conversation?*

One way to do that is simply to ask, "What ideas have come up that you would like to discuss further?" Often, that invitation alone is sufficient to get a discussion started. If, however, you are using this strategy to begin a unit of work on some complicated issue, then you might want to use the ideas that have poured out on the flip-chart paper to generate an agenda for further research, writing, and conversation to take place over the next few days or weeks. A passage on climate change, for instance, awakened the interest of one group in figuring out just what natural resources we are going to lose first. To answer that, some research was required, so it became the guiding question for several days of further reading, writing, and discussion.

5. *What if I have some students who are reluctant to write so publicly?*

We've had students ask if spelling counted. Clearly, it does not; we remind students that this is writing to explore, not writing to be published. They've asked if they can use text-message symbols, and we tell them, "Certainly. Use symbols, sketches, diagrams—whatever helps you capture your thoughts." And no one will be marked down for bad handwriting in this activity.

If you have some students who, you predict, will be very intimidated by the public nature of this writing, you might even give them the passage the night before, encouraging them to read it over and think of what they might write the next day. That way they can come in prepared for the activity, able to join in even if at a somewhat lower level than their classmates.

C o n c l u s i o n

And Now You Begin

Louise Rosenblatt once told us that she had considered the title *The Journey Itself* for the book that ultimately became *Literature as Exploration* (1935/1995). She liked the metaphor of reading as a journey. It suggested that you were on an adventure, not knowing what you'd see on the roadside but alert and watchful so that you wouldn't miss it, not sure whom you'd meet along the way but willing to travel in their company for a while, not certain where you'd land at the end of the trip but curious to discover what this new place might be like.

But she was afraid that the book, if titled *The Journey Itself*, might be shelved by some careless librarian or bookstore clerk in the travel section, in between *To Kill a Mockingbird on $5 a Day* and *Frommer's Guide to Heart of Darkness*, so she settled for *Literature as Exploration*. That captured at least some of the essence of a journey.

The idea that reading was an *exploration* suggested that the reader would encounter something new, something at least potentially surprising and novel, something unknown. It was not like the drive to school in the morning. You know that route; you could drive it with your eyes closed—you may actually have done that on a Monday morning after a long hard weekend reading student papers. How many times have you arrived at school and realized that you hadn't seen many of the landmarks that you know lie along the route? You drove automatically, mechanically, barely aware of the traffic and the turns. Any surprises were likely to be unpleasant and annoying. The drive to work isn't a journey, an adventure—it's just a routine obligation, one you barely pay attention to.

Reading a book, whether it's fiction or nonfiction, should be more than just routine, though sadly, much of it does become just that. We may read through part of the morning paper simply because it's what we always do over our breakfast cereal. Unless some article strikes a particularly responsive chord, very little of what we read may sink in.

Louise Rosenblatt, a friend of John Dewey's, was a force in literacy education. Her first book, published in 1935, remains a touchstone text today. Her last book was published in 2005 when she was 101, several months before her death. She was a tireless advocate for reading education, always asserting that the success of our democracy was dependent upon all being literate to the highest levels.

And the novel we pick up just to pass time on the airplane may have little more effect upon us.

But both the novel and the morning paper have the potential for being more and doing more. Novels (and poems, plays, and movies) have the potential for refining our insights into human experience and deepening our sympathies. Newspapers (and magazine articles, scientific papers, editorials, and all the other texts that fall into the vast realm of nonfiction) have the potential for sharpening our understanding of the world around us, providing us with new information, new insights, or new ways of reasoning. Reading, whether in the realm of fiction or that of nonfiction, should be something of an adventure. It should be an exploration, a journey that offers some possibility for reflection, rethinking, and discovery. The journey through fiction and the journey through nonfiction are, however, slightly different. As we explained in previous pages, we found that difference to be one of invitation and intrusion:

> Fiction invites us into the imaginary world the author has created; nonfiction intrudes into our world, and purports to tell us something about it.

That is not to say that fiction doesn't tell us something about our world. Certainly it does. But it does so by inviting us into that invented world and asking us to observe, listen, notice what's happening, pay attention to the patterns we see, weigh what we find there against the understandings and insights that we have brought to the text from our other readings and from our lives beyond books, and draw our own inferences. *Notice and Note* was our effort to help students journey through those imaginary worlds paying attention to them in ways that would generate deeper thought and good conversation.

Nonfiction operates in a somewhat less subtle, somewhat more direct fashion. Of course, nonfiction can be subtle and indirect, but it seldom denies that it is attempting to tell us about what *is*, not about what the author has imagined or invented. Nonfiction *purports to tell us something about our world*. Nonfiction acknowledges that it has the goal of shaping our understanding. It does that in countless different

Reading Nonfiction has been our effort to help students take control over their own journeys through nonfiction so that, guided by reason and evidence, they get safely to a destination for which they can take responsibility.

ways, from the simplicity of a to-do list, to the complexity of a report on a scientific experiment, but it almost always makes some assertion about the way things are.

And we have to decide what to make of that assertion. We have to decide whether to accept it or reject it, or—more likely—we have to figure out how to integrate it into our thinking so that our vision of the world is sharper, clearer, better than it was before we read. In a sense, nonfiction takes us to a destination, and that destination matters.

With nonfiction . . . it isn't the journey itself that matters quite so much as where you end up.

So, perhaps if Rosenblatt had been thinking more of nonfiction and less of fiction and poetry when she was struggling to find the title for her book, she might have had other reasons for rejecting *The Journey Itself*. With nonfiction, although obviously we would prefer to enjoy, rather than endure, the trip from the opening to the concluding paragraph, it isn't the journey itself that matters quite so much as where you end up.

Reading Nonfiction has been our effort to help students take control over their own journeys through nonfiction so that, guided by reason and evidence, they get safely to a destination for which they can take responsibility. And so now we give it to you. It's your book now. It's you who will transform these ink blots on the page into meaningful practices for your students. You will take these ideas, make them yours, and in doing so will make them better.

We watch you remind students that what they cannot do, they simply cannot do *yet*.

We don't expect the journey to be easy. We know that it's a tough time to be a teacher, with policies shifting almost daily and the focus more often on the test than on the child. We watch you stand boldly against the practices you know are not best, not even good, and we watch you remind students that what they cannot do, they simply cannot do *yet*. We have always said the best hope for many children is a great teacher.

We so look forward to watching your journey with your kids and these ideas. It's your time to begin.

Appendix A **Surveys**

In this section, we present two surveys.

http://hein.pub/readnfres1

Survey 1: Teaching Nonfiction, Grades 4–12

Results for this survey were presented in Part I, Issue 4. Here, we provide some demographic data for who responded and then on page 251, you'll find the actual survey.

Demographic Data for Teaching Nonfiction Survey

We received 1,627 responses. Of that group, about 200 were administrators, and their responses were omitted in many questions. We saw remarkably even distribution across the grades, with the fewest responses coming from fourth grade (191) and fifth grade (189). The remaining grades had between 266 and 290 responders.

The largest group of responders had six to ten years of experience (341); 308 had eleven to fifteen years; and 237 had one to five years. We also had 229 teachers with sixteen to twenty years of experience, and 336 teachers had more than twenty years' experience. The rest skipped the questions. Most of the teachers who responded, predictably, were language arts/English and reading teachers (918).

About 275 of the respondents reported teaching about 75 students each day, while 226 teach only about 30. Nearly twice that number (450) teach more than 125 students each day.

An overwhelming 87% of our respondents said that English is the home language of the students in their school, and 60% described the majority of their students as white. Only 11% of our respondents said that most were Hispanic or Latino, and 4% said the majority of their students were black or African American.

Nearly 45% described their schools as having between 200 to 750 students, and over half described their students as coming from homes "where finances are tight."

Survey 2: Let's Talk About It

The survey you'll find on page 256 is for helping you assess your own practices and dispositions toward the role of talk.

Teaching Nonfiction, Grades 4–12

1. What do you primarily teach?

- [ ] I teach all content subjects
- [ ] Language Arts/English
- [ ] Reading
- [ ] Science

- [ ] Social Studies/History
- [ ] Technical subjects
- [ ] Fine Arts
- [ ] Resource

- [ ] Special Education
- [ ] Mathematics
- [ ] I am not a classroom teacher. I am an administrator, coach, supervisor, or university professor.

2. What grade do you primarily teach? Check all that apply.

- [ ] Grade 4
- [ ] Grade 5
- [ ] Grade 6

- [ ] Grade 7
- [ ] Grade 8
- [ ] Grade 9

- [ ] Grade 10
- [ ] Grade 11
- [ ] Grade 12

3. How long have you taught?

- [ ] 1–5 Years
- [ ] 6–10 Years
- [ ] 11–15 Years

- [ ] 16–20 Years
- [ ] 21–25 Years
- [ ] 26–30 Years

- [ ] More than 30 years

4. How many students are in your school?

- [ ] Fewer than 200
- [ ] 200–500
- [ ] 500–750

- [ ] 750–1000
- [ ] 1000–1500

- [ ] 1500–2000
- [ ] More than 2000

5. How many students do you teach each day? (Round to the closest number.)

- [ ] About 15 students
- [ ] About 30 students
- [ ] About 50 students

- [ ] About 75 students
- [ ] About 100 students
- [ ] About 125 students

- [ ] About 150 students
- [ ] More than 175 students

6. The majority of my students speak. . . .

- [ ] English as their home language

- [ ] English as a second language

7. The majority of my students are. . . .

- [ ] Hispanic or Latino
- [ ] White
- [ ] Black or African American

- [ ] Native Hawaiian or Other Pacific Islander
- [ ] Asian

- [ ] American Indian or Alaskan Native
- [ ] My school is roughly equally divided between 2 or more ethnicities

If split between or among groups, list them here using the terms we used above

8. **The majority of my students. . .**

☐ Appear to come from homes where finances are tight.

☐ Appear to come from homes where financial issues do not negatively affect a student's work and concentration.

☐ Appear to come from homes where students have many advantages.

9. **How often do you spend time specifically teaching students TO READ your subject matter, as opposed to teaching them the content itself?**

☐ Never

☐ Not very often (once a month)

☐ Once every couple of weeks

☐ Once a week

☐ Several time a week

☐ Every day

10. **On average, about how many minutes per week do students read assigned nonfiction material during class time? This is silent reading that they do with no support of buddy reading, you reading aloud to them, or the CD playing the text they are reading.**

☐ None

☐ About .5 hour

☐ About 1 hour

☐ About 1.5 hours

☐ About 2 hours

☐ More than 2 hours

11. **About how much at-home reading of nonfiction do you assign each week?**

☐ None

☐ Fewer than 10 pages

☐ 11–20 pages

☐ 21–40 pages

☐ 41–60 pages

☐ More than 60

12. **What is most of the nonfiction reading your students do for your class? Choose one.**

☐ Primary source documents

☐ Trade books on a particular topic (such as *Earthquakes* by Seymour Simon or *We've Got a Job: The 1963 Birmingham Children's March* by Cynthia Levinson)

☐ Textbooks

☐ Newspapers

☐ Materials from the web

☐ Articles from magazines

☐ Workbooks and/or worksheets

13. **I believe that I should be expected to teach students not only the content itself, but also how to read the content.**

☐ Yes

☐ No

14. **When it comes to teaching students who struggle with reading the texts for my content, I . . .**

   ☐ Know a lot about teaching reading to struggling readers.

   ☐ Know some things about teaching reading to struggling readers.

   ☐ Know little about teaching reading to struggling readers.

15. **In choosing texts for your teaching of nonfiction, which of these is most problematic?**

   ☐ Planning instruction that accommodates diverse and unrelated interests of students.

   ☐ I have no choice. The school system specifies what is to be taught.

   ☐ Not knowing enough about the students' reading levels.

   ☐ Finding and organizing several texts on a particular topic in order to teach students to look at multiple sources of information.

   ☐ Identifying or funding (purchasing) texts at the students' levels.

   ☐ Finding the time to select appropriate texts.

   Other (please specify)

16. **Where do you spend the majority of your instructional time when working with struggling readers? Choose up to 3.**

   "I spend my time helping struggling readers to. . ."

   ☐ Recognize the importance of text features—bold-faced words, maps, figures, diagrams, charts, headings, etc.

   ☐ Use context clues to understand unknown vocabulary.

   ☐ Identify the main idea, details, and summarize or paraphrase what was read.

   ☐ Think about the author's purpose, arguments, and bias.

   ☐ Make logical inferences from the text and cite evidence for interpretations and inferences they offer about the text.

   ☐ Offer questions about the author, the text, and their responses to the text.

   ☐ Simply comprehend and retain the material.

17. **The preceding question asked you to identify the area where you must spend the majority of your instructional time when working with struggling readers. Consider these same options in this question and tell us where you must spend the majority of your instructional time when working with skilled and highly skilled readers. Choose up to 3.**

    "I spend the majority of my instructional time helping skilled and highly skilled readers. . ."

    ☐ Recognize the importance of text features—bold-faced words, maps, figures, diagrams, charts, headings, etc.

    ☐ Use context clues to understand unknown vocabulary.

    ☐ Identify the main idea, details, and summarize or paraphrase what was read.

    ☐ Think about the author's purpose, arguments, and bias.

    ☐ Make logical inferences from the text and cite evidence for interpretations and inferences they offer about the text.

    ☐ Offer questions about the author, the text, and their responses to the text.

    ☐ Simply comprehend and retain the material.

18. **What do you perceive as your students' biggest stumbling blocks when it comes to understanding the nonfiction you assign? Select up to 3.**

    ☐ Lack of ability to identify main idea and key details

    ☐ Lack of vocabulary needed to access the text

    ☐ Lack of knowledge about transition words and phrases ("before this," "so as to," "as a result") and how they indicate text structure

    ☐ Lack of background knowledge on the topic

    ☐ Poor decoding abilities

    ☐ Lack of strategies for getting through difficult texts

    ☐ Lack of interest in, or reason for, reading about the topic

19. **How do students in your class primarily get the information about the topic you are teaching?**

    ☐ Through reading   ☐ Through my class lectures, explanations, presentations   ☐ Through class discussions

20. **Do you think your students, as a group, mostly like to read about your content or mostly do not like to read about your content?**

    ☐ I think most of them do not enjoy reading about the content we are studying.

    ☐ I think most of them enjoy reading about the content we are studying.

    ☐ I do not know what most of my students think about the reading they must do.

21. **Do you think readers use different strategies for reading various types of nonfiction texts? In other words, do you think we need different strategies for reading, for instance, a science text and a social studies text?**

    ☐ Yes ☐ No ☐ I'm really not sure

    If you answered yes, please offer examples of strategies that you think are more appropriate for one content or another. . .

22. **If there is one work of nonfiction that you have students read every year, what is it? (This could be a magazine that you rely on; if so, please tell us its title.)**

Let's Talk About It Survey

A Survey of How Talk Is Used in Your Classroom

First, in this space, write your definition of "classroom discussion."

Second, complete the survey below.

STATEMENT	STRONGLY AGREE	AGREE	NEUTRAL	DISAGREE	STRONGLY DISAGREE
Practices and Dispositions					
Students who struggle with content benefit from first answering questions that reveal their understanding of basic information before trying to consider higher-level questions.					
Students seem to listen to one another as they answer questions I ask of the class.					
When discussing content, I generally know the answers to the questions I ask students.					
I plan the order of questions I will ask during a classroom discussion.					
My classroom discussions look a lot like great conversations: Students look at one another, listen intently, build on comments each other make, and reach aha's about the text through their discussions.					
In my classroom discussions I ask most of the questions, students respond to me, and I evaluate their responses.					
I mostly keep kids in a large group for discussions.					

continues

STATEMENT	STRONGLY AGREE	AGREE	NEUTRAL	DISAGREE	STRONGLY DISAGREE
I believe that student-led discussions about a confusing part of a text can improve understanding of the text.					
I believe I am responsible for telling students the accurate information that they must learn regarding the content I teach.					
I set the topic for discussion in my classroom.					
I believe my students mostly approach classroom discussions as a way to show that they read and understood the material rather than as a tool for improving understanding.					
I would like to have more classroom discussions in my classroom that are student-led.					
I remind students that talk is a powerful way to clarify confusions or expand thinking about a topic.					
I do not have time in my classroom to do much more than ask questions about what students have read.					

Next Steps

1. Do your answers reveal any patterns or dispositions you would like to change?

2. What's your plan for changing your practices in those areas?

3. Discuss your survey results with other colleagues. Are there patterns of response in your school that suggest areas of growth for the entire faculty?

Appendix B **Teaching Texts**

On the next few pages, you'll find copies of the teaching texts we used and have permission to reprint here for you.

http://hein.pub/readnfres2

To access these files digitally, you need a Heinemann account.

1.   Enter the URL http://hein.pub/readnfres2 or scan the QR code and enter your email address and password.

2.   Click "Sign In."

If you need to set up a new account, click "Create a New Account."

3.   Enter the key code **READNF** and click "Register."

Hard at Work

By Ritu Upadhyay. Reported by Lucien Chauvin/Ecuador

Ten-year-old Wilbur Carreno is less than four feet tall and weighs only 50 pounds. He is small for his age. That's exactly what makes him good at his job.

From the pages of

Wilbur spends his afternoons climbing banana trees four times his height. He expertly ties the heavy stalks of bananas so the trees won't droop from the weight of the fruit. "I've been working since I was 8," he told TFK. "I finish school at noon and then go to the field."

In Wilbur's poor country of Ecuador, one in every four children is working. An estimated 69,000 kids toil away on the vast banana plantations along the country's coast. Ecuador is the world's largest banana exporter. Kids working in the industry are exposed to harmful chemicals, pull loads twice their weight, and use sharp, heavy knives.

Do Kids Belong on the Job?

Child labor is certainly not limited to Ecuador. The United Nations estimates that 250 million kids around the world are forced to work. Many countries don't have laws limiting kids' work.

A concerned group called Human Rights Watch conducted a study of Ecuador's banana plantations last April. They found that most children begin working on plantations around age 10. Their average workday lasts 12 hours! By age 14, 6 out of 10 no longer attend school. Many families face the difficult choice of either putting food on their tables or sending their kids to school.

The family of Alejandro, 12, struggles with that choice. Alejandro has had to work beside his father, Eduardo Sinchi, on a plantation. "I don't want my kids to work," says Sinchi. "I want them in school, but we have few options." Sinchi has nine children and earns as little as $27 a week. "It isn't even enough for food, let alone school, clothes, transportation."

Hard Work for Little Pay

Sinchi's pay is typical in Ecuador. The average banana worker earns just $6 a day. One reason pay is so low is that Ecuadorians are not allowed to form work groups called unions. In countries like Costa Rica, where laws allow unions, some banana workers earn $11 a day. Such countries have fewer child workers because better pay means parents can afford to keep their kids in school.

Ecuador's big banana companies have begun to do something about child labor. Last year, they signed an agreement not to hire kids younger than 15 and to protect young workers from chemicals. "We need to eliminate child labor," says Jorge Illingworth, of Ecuador's Banana Exporters Association. But small plantations did not sign the agreement, and, he says, they employ 70% of the kids.

Banning child labor is a start, but it doesn't really help families like the Sinchis. Now that Alejandro can't work, his family suffers more. The answer, most believe, is better pay for Ecuador's adult workers. For that to happen, U.S. shoppers would have to put up with higher banana prices or stop buying Ecuador's bananas to make their point. Guillermo Touma fights to help Ecuador's workers. "If we could raise awareness," he says, "we could raise wages and invest in education for our children."

From *TIME for Kids* January 24, 2003 Vol. 8 No. 14

TIME FOR KIDS and the *TIME FOR KIDS* logo are registered trademarks of Time Inc., used under license.

Vampires Prey on Panama

By Chris Kraul, Tribune Newspapers: *Los Angeles Times*

Originally published May 27, 2005

TONOSI, Panama — Cattleman Francisco Oliva was on a round-up—of vampire bats. After a swarm of the blood-slurping creatures dive-bombed his herd and drank their fill one recent night, he corralled several dozen of them in special contraptions that look like giant badminton nets.

He put each bat in a cage and then applied a poison called vampirin to their backs with a brush before releasing them. Back in the bat roost, the animals would be groomed by about 20 other bats, causing their deaths. Or so Oliva hoped.

"We have to look for answers, because this little animal is very stubborn," Oliva said days after the capture, surveying his 300-head herd, most of them bearing bat-fang markings and red stains from the nightly bloodletting. Oliva said he would exterminate every bat if he could.

Stefan Klose begged to differ. He not only stuck up for the common vampire bat, but described the animals as boons to humanity. Bat-based research led to the development of sonar and anti-coagulant medicines that prevent heart attacks, he pointed out, and scientists are only beginning to understand the creatures.

"I certainly defend vampire bats' right to a place in the ecosystem," said Klose, a young German zoologist. People's irrational reaction to vampires, he said, reflects "our primal fear of being someone else's food object."

Klose also confessed a fondness for the creatures. The scientist said feeding time, when the bats accept bits of banana from his hand, is a "really sweet and peaceful sight. It always reminds me of how close these animals are to us and how incredibly intelligent they are—certainly more exotic and wilder than my neighbor's dog, but no less smart or cuddly."

Few animals inspire the repugnance and fascination of vampire bats, and perhaps nowhere are opinions more divided than in Panama.

Bats thrive in the tropical rain forests that cover much of Panama because of a plenitude of animal and plant foods, abundant shelter and the lack of seasons to inhibit regeneration.

"Bats have developed a radar system that can distinguish the tiniest insect in the middle of dense bush in the dead of night," said Todd Capson, a Smithsonian staff scientist who tracks the development of technology derived from tropical flora and fauna. "It's inconceivable there isn't something more to learn from that."

Rancher Oliva can be forgiven for feeling antagonistic. Here in the remote and hilly southwest corner of Panama, he and other cattlemen wage a continual battle against a variety of livestock pests such as coyotes, crocodiles, ticks, worms and a host of tropical diseases. But he has been driven to the edge of desperation by the increasing bat attacks. During the month of April, Oliva said, he lost 10 calves to anemia caused by successive bloodlettings.

While sympathizing with the cattlemen, Klose says further study of bats might yield more technological breakthroughs. "Vampires could hold the key to a problem we want to solve, like AIDS or cancer. But if you destroy them, they are lost for eternity."

The Dung Beetle as a Weapon Against Global Warming

By Jennifer S. Holland, for *National Geographic*

Originally published September 06, 2013

Published online at http://news.nationalgeographic.com/news/2013/09/130904
-dung-beetles-global-warming-animals-science/

It may seem like an unlikely environmental hero. But the dung beetle, with its sordid habit of laying eggs in and eating cow poo, might just be a weapon in the battle against global warming.

Agriculture, you see, is a gassy business. The 1.3 billion large ruminants—dairy cows and beef cattle, buffalo, sheep, goats—that burp, fart, and poop around the world emit more greenhouse gases than does the transportation industry, according to the UN.

These animals are responsible for about a third of global emissions of methane, a gas that makes up half of farming's contribution and is even more potent than the much-maligned CO_2. (The other big methane offenders: the natural gas/petroleum industries and landfills.)

So any animal helping to quell gas release invites investigation. In a paper published August 7 in the journal *PLOS ONE*, Atte Penttilä and colleagues from the University of Helsinki report on experiments designed to see whether dung beetles affect how much methane is released from cow patties, the dung heaps that dot farm pastures.

Dung beetles, by the way, dig burrows into pasture feces and feed on the droppings of cows and other ruminants. They also deposit their eggs in the excrement, and their hatchlings feed on the same stuff.

The answer to the methane question was yes. The scientists found that cow patties with beetles, specifically *Aphodius* species, rummaging around in them released nearly 40 percent less methane over a summer period than beetle-free cowpats did.

Do Beetles Really Help?

The beetles' good work happens mainly as they dig around in the poop. Methane is born under anaerobic, or oxygen-free, conditions. So as the insects tunnel through the dung, they aerate it, changing the conditions so that less methane is produced within the pats. This translates to less methane gas released into the atmosphere.

Importantly, the study also showed that the presence of the beetles in aging cowpats increased the release of another greenhouse gas, nitrous oxide. More studies will help clear up whether this cancels out their methane-related efforts.

"In terms of the net effect on global warming, I'd say the jury is still out," said study co-author Tomas Roslin. "Much of the methane emission from cattle escapes from the front and rear of the animal; less escapes from the dung pats. But the beetles' actions should be weighed into any calculations of net effects, so we don't miss the mark," he said.

Declining Dung—and Beetles

Sadly, like many animals these days, dung beetles are in decline. Roslin said that in Finland, for example, more than half of dung beetle species are threatened or near endangered.

The reasons include the lack of diversity in both dung and pasture that goes with fewer but more intensively managed farms, and the reduced quality of the dung—which nowadays contains more chemicals, such as anti-parasite drugs given to farm animals.

That's troubling, in part because even as the farm industry has suffered due to droughts, higher input costs, and the like, the worldwide demand for beef is only growing.

In the developing world in particular, emissions are on the rise as farms expand. Beetles alone can't contain greenhouse gases, of course, but "we do need to understand and account for the effects of such live agents in changing gas fluxes from dung," Roslin said. "We can't just think of [pats] as passive objects."

The best way to help beetles thrive and "do their thing on the gas fluxes" is to let cattle graze on variable types of outdoor pasture, Roslin said.

"If we lock our cattle into barns and treat their dung as waste, we will be blocking the very cycles" that might make a silent, but still significant, contribution to one of the world's hottest problems.

Garana's Story
A Day in the Life of a Young Afghan Refugee

by Kent Page, for *National Geographic Explorer*

Originally published September 1, 2002

The sun has not yet risen over the rocky hills outside the city of Peshawar, in Pakistan. Loudspeakers from the top of a **mosque** (mahsk), or **Muslim** house of worship, call out to the people, "God is great! It is better to pray than sleep! Come to prayers!"

Ten-year-old Garana rises from a mat on the dirt floor of her family's house. She puts on her black robe and covers her head with an old shawl. Then she walks to the mosque to pray.

Garana and her family have lived in their one-room house for two years. It's one of thousands of mud-brick homes in Shamshatoo **Afghan** Refugee Camp. The camp holds about 50,000 Afghan **refugees.** They are people who have fled from war or **drought** in Afghanistan.

Garana works hard. Her father left the family several years ago. Her mother can't see very well and can do little to help. Her older brother works all day weaving carpets. And her younger brother is too small to do many chores. So Garana does most of the household tasks. But her day is not all work. She has time for school, friends, and even a little mischief.

Early Morning

After prayers, Garana begins her morning chores. She walks to the camp's water pump to fill two bottles. After bringing them home, she eats breakfast, which is usually hot tea and bread. Then she washes the dishes in the backyard, using cold pump water. Next she sweeps the floor of the one-room house.

Then it's time to walk to the bakery. There she leaves a small amount of flour. The bakers will use it to make a loaf of bread. Garana's family will eat that loaf for their next three meals.

Now it's time to walk to school.

Class Time

Children in the refugee camp go to school six days a week. Boys and girls attend separate classes. Garana is in first grade, although she is ten years old. That's because when she lived in Afghanistan, Garana and other girls were not allowed to go to school. She has a lot of catching up to do. Classes in Garana's school go only through the second grade for girls and the third grade for boys. Still, it's an important start.

Garana gets to school just before classes begin at 8:30. The concrete building has six classrooms. These rooms have no windows, but there is paint on the walls.

Thirty-five girls are in Garana's class. The students sit on mats on the floor. They study mathematics, the Afghan languages of Pashto and Dari, and the English alphabet. There is also class time for singing and drawing. Garana enjoys school.

"My favorite subject is English," she says. "If you can speak languages, then you can understand what people are saying. It's easier to get things done."

Today Garana stands at the chalkboard with a ruler and leads the class through the English alphabet. She mixes up *b* and *d*. Otherwise, she recites the alphabet perfectly.

Lunch Break

Classes end before lunch. The students race out to the small dirt playground to play on the swings, the slide, and the merry-go-round. Garana usually visits with her friends. But soon it's time for more chores.

She heads to the bakery to pick up the bread. Then she walks along the mud streets to her house. After a quick hello to her mother, Garana goes to the pump to collect water. When she returns, she fills the teapot and puts it on the small fire. Garana sits on her mat on the floor and eats her lunch with her hands. Today her mother has prepared potatoes along with the bread and tea.

"Some days we have potatoes. Some days we have rice. And some days we have beans," Garana says. "Whatever we eat for lunch, we have again for dinner. Rice is my favorite food."

Afternoon and Evening

After lunch, Garana trudges back to the pump for water to wash the plates and cups. Then she sweeps the house, cleans the yard, and feeds her family's four chickens. Once in a while, when there is money, she goes to the local shop to buy food. After she finishes her chores, she does her homework.

Soon it's time for dinner. Because the houses in the refugee camp have no electricity, the family eats the evening meal before it gets dark. Then, if there is any daylight left, Garana plays with her best friend, Assia. Sometimes they get into a little trouble.

"Garana saw some of the older girls with jewelry in their noses," Assia explains. "She said that looked beautiful. She asked me to pierce her nose. So I took a long sewing needle, and I did it."

Garana's mother was not pleased. But she helped Garana put a string through the hole to keep it open. Garana hopes that someday she can replace the string with jewelry.

A Wish for Peace

Garana has a hard life in the refugee camp. But at least there is no fighting. "I would like to go back to Afghanistan," she says, "but not until there is peace everywhere. We are told at school that some parts of Afghanistan are safe. But there is still fighting in other parts."

Many others share Garana's wish. For more than 20 years, the nation has suffered from war and unrest. Now the Afghan people, with the help of countries around the world, are trying to make changes. They hope to bring peace to Afghanistan.

Excerpt from **George Washington's Secret Six**

by Brian Kilmeade and Don Yaeger

Originally published by Sentinel, an imprint of Penguin Group USA, © 2013

Even as Robert Townsend was settling into his new role, something happened that highlighted the precarious nature of the world in which he now lived. On July 2, 1779, British raiders had attacked Major Tallmadge's camp at dawn, killing ten men and capturing eight, plus a dozen horses. Those losses were devastating, but in the aftermath Tallmadge made a discovery that proved unsettling and was potentially threatening to the Patriots' intelligence operations. One of the horses the British had stolen was his own, which still bore its saddlebags and some of Tallmadge's personal papers—including some money earmarked for Woodhull and a letter from Washington that specifically named George Higday, a resident of Manhattan "who I am told hath given signal proofs of his attachment to us, and at the same time stands well with the enemy."

Eleven days later, Higday was arrested at his home and confessed to having met with General Washington to discuss the possibility of spying, but claimed that he never carried out any such activity because the payment had been in fake bills.

Excerpt from **Everything You Need to Know about American History Homework**

Originally published by Scholastic Inc., ©1994, 2005

In 1492, Native American life began to change dramatically. Christopher Columbus, an Italian who was captain of three Spanish ships, "discovered" what Europeans called a New World. He thought he had reached the Spice Islands near India. He called the people he met "Indians." Soon after, other European nations sent explorers to the Americas.

At first, Native Americans welcomed the Europeans. They introduced the Europeans to tomatoes, corn, potatoes, and tobacco. Europeans introduced Native Americans to guns, sugarcane, and horses. They also brought diseases new to the Americas—the common cold, measles, and smallpox, to name a few—which killed many Native Americans.

When Europeans began to explore and later settle in North America, they used guns to take whatever they wanted. They thought they had the right to do this. When they built villages and cities, they often cleared forests. These forests were the homes of many of the wild animals the Native Americans hunted.

Some groups, like the Cherokee, took on European ways, but the settlers wanted their land anyway. Most tribes that survived were forced to move west. Today, most of the remaining American Indians live there. Some have sued the government to repay them for the land that was taken from them or granted to them by treaties that were broken.

Excerpt from **Up Before Daybreak**

by Deborah Hopkinson

Originally published by Scholastic Inc., © 2006

Like most children, Mary turned her pay over to her parents for a long time. "Papa set me free when I was nineteen and after that what I made was mine," she said. After years of work, Mary managed to save $1,400. "Then the bank went busted and I lost my money."

Emma Willis spent a lifetime in mills, from age twelve until seventy-five. "I worked in a cotton mill for sixty-three years, but I never did care for it much," Emma said when she was eighty-one.

In the beginning, Emma worked from six in the morning until seven at night, earning thirty-five cents a day. "Every pay day that come, I brought my money home and laid it in my mother's hand; then after she died, I turned every cent over to my sister who kept house for almost fifty years. I worked steady, too, once while I was at the Cannon Mill I went eleven years without missing a day's pay. Back then if you didn't go, they'd send for you because they didn't have anyone else to do your work."

Model Passages for Teaching Syntax Surgery

1. He served juice to all the children in the paper cups.

2. They saw a turtle driving to the park.

3. If the girl's aunt could leave work early enough to meet her at the airport, she said she certainly would meet her there.

4. Breathe through your nose, hold it for a few seconds in your lungs.

5. The platoon began marching south. They were tired and their backs hurt. But their orders were clear and they had been delivered with some urgency.

6. The company's bosses decided to let employees decide when they would get to work each day and when they would leave. They decided that as long as workers got in eight hours each day, they really didn't care which eight hours they chose to work.

7. Even as Robert Townsend was settling into his new role, something happened that highlighted the precarious nature of the world in which he now lived. On July 2, 1779, British raiders had attacked Major Tallmadge's camp at dawn, killing ten men and capturing eight, plus a dozen horses. Those losses were devastating, but in the aftermath Tallmadge made a discovery that proved unsettling and was potentially threatening to the Patriots' intelligence operations. One of the horses the British had stolen was his own, which still bore its saddlebags and some of Tallmadge's personal papers—including some money earmarked for Woodhull and a letter from Washington that specifically named George Higday, a resident of Manhattan "who I am told hath given signal proofs of his attachment to us, and at the same time stands well with the enemy."

   Eleven days later, Higday was arrested at his home and confessed to having met with General Washington to discuss the possibility of spying, but claimed that he never carried out any such activity because the payment had been in fake bills. (From *George Washington's Secret Six* by Brian Kilmeade and Don Yaeger, p. 89)

Model Passages for Sketch to Stretch

The fan appears to be a circular tube mounted on a pedestal. . . . The air flows through a channel in the pedestal up to the tube, which is hollow. As air flows through the slits in the tube and out through the front of the fan, air behind the fan is drawn through the tube as well. This is called inducement. The flowing air pushed by the motor induces the air behind the fan to follow. Air surrounding the edges of the fan will also begin to flow in the direction of the breeze. This process is called entrainment. (From "How the Dyson Bladeless Fan Works" found at http://electronics.howstuffworks.com/gadgets/home/dyson-bladeless -fan.htm/printable9/2/2014)

****

With the support of rich and poor peasants, workers, businessmen, landlords, students, and intellectuals, the Viet Minh [people fighting for independence] had expanded throughout northern Vietnam where it established new local governments, redistributed some lands, and opened warehouses to alleviate the hunger. (From the Viet Nam Declaration of Independence)

Appendix C **Teaching Resources and Booklists**

The next two pages provide the lists of magazines and websites we collected from our surveys.

Following those pages, you'll see booklists provided by three of the smartest folks we know when it comes to thinking about books! Teri Lesesne, Franki Sibberson, and Mary Lee Hahn.

Franki and Mary Lee put together a list of 30 books they'd share in elementary school. Teri created a list of 40 nonfiction picture books that we'd all want to use at any grade.

All of these resources are available online.

http://hein.pub/readnfres1

Magazines Most Often Used*

NAME	URL	FOCUS
Time for Kids	timeforkids.com	Current Events
Scholastic Scope (6–8)	weeklyreader.com/read -classroom-magazine-online	Language Arts
Scholastic News (editions for grades 1 through 5–6)	sni.scholastic.com	Current Events
National Geographic Kids	kids.nationalgeographic.com	Nature and Science
Junior Scholastic	junior.scholastic.com	Current Events
Sports Illustrated for Kids	SIKids.com	Current Events/Sports
The New York Times Upfront (9–12)	weeklyreader.com/nyt-upfront	Current Events
Popular Science	popsci.com/tags.kids	Science
Dig into History (9–14 history and archeology)	diagnosite.com/	History and Archeology
Choices: Current Health (7–12)	choices.scholastic.com/	Health and Life Skills
Discover Girls (Preteen)	popsci.com/tags/kids	Girls' Interests
Highlights (2–12)	Highlights.com	World Around Us
Science World: Current Science (6–10)	weeklyreader.com/current -science-magazine	Science

*These are shown in order of frequency mentioned in our survey.

Websites Most Often Used*

NAME	URL	INFORMATION
Beyond Penguins and Polar Bears	beyondpenguins.ehe.osu.edu	Free: YES Levels texts: No Focus: Polar regions
Beyond Weather & the Water Cycle	beyondweather.ehe.osu.edu	Free: YES Levels texts: No Focus: Climate Issues
Brightstorm Math	brightstorm.com/math/	Free: YES Levels texts: No Focus: Mathematics, K–12
CNN Student News	cnn.com/studentnews/	Free: YES Levels texts: No Focus: Current events
DOGOnews: Fodder for Young Minds	dogonews.com	Free: YES Levels texts: No Focus: Current events
Great Websites for Kids	gws.ala.org/tags/nonfiction	Free: YES Levels texts: No Focus: animals, arts, history and biography, literature and language, mathematics and computers, sciences, social sciences, reference desk.
Iluminations: Resources for Teaching Math	illuminations.nctm.org/	Free: YES Levels texts: No Focus: Mathematics K–12
In the News	hmhinthenews.com	Free: YES Levels texts: No Focus: Language arts and mathematics, K–12
IXL	ixl.com	Free: YES Levels texts: No Focus: Language arts and mathematics, K–12
newseum	newseum.org	Free: YES Levels texts: No Focus: support for teachers interested in news (This site is largely about the Newseum in D.C.)
Nick News with Linda Ellerbee	news.nick.com	Free: YES Levels texts: No Focus: Current events
ReadWorks.org—The Solution to Reading Comprehension	ReadWorks.org	Free: YES Levels texts: No Focus: Provides passages students can read with information for teachers on linking passages to standards.
The Nonfiction Minute	nonfictionminute.com	Free: YES Levels texts: No Focus: Short items and support for teachers on range of topics in news, science, history.
The Why Files: The Science Behind the News	whyfiles.org	Free: YES Levels texts: No Focus: Science and news

*These are shown alphabetically because we did not do a frequency count.

Thirty of Our Favorite Nonfiction Books

Compiled by Mary Lee Hahn and Franki Sibberson

TITLE	AUTHOR
A Home for Mr. Edison	Barbara Kerley
A Leaf Can Be…	Laura Purdie Salas
Africa Is My Home	Monica Edinger
Balloons over Broadway	Melissa Sweet
Bill the Boy Wonder	Marc Tyler Nobleman
Brave Girl: Clara and the Shirtwaist Makers' Strike of 1909	Michelle Markel
Can We Save the Tiger?	Martin Jenkins
Cowboy Up! Ride the Navajo Rodeo	Nancy Bo Flood
Eye on the Wild: Gorilla	Suzi Eszterhas
Face to Face with Dolphins	Flip Nicklin
Feathers: Not Just for Flying	Melissa Stewart
Handle with Care	Loree Griffin Burns
I Am Rosa Parks	Brad Meltzer
Ivan: The Remarkable True Story of the Shopping Mall Gorilla	Katherine Applegate
Kakapo Rescue (Scientists in the Field Series)	Sy Montgomery
Locomotive	Brian Floca
Look Up! Bird-Watching in Your Own Backyard	Annette LeBlanc Cate
My Light	Molly Bang
Neighborhood Sharks	Katherine Roy
Over and Under the Snow	Kate Messner
Separate Is Never Equal	Duncan Tonatiuh
Snakes	Nic Bishop
That's a Possibility	Steve Jenkins
The Animal Book	Steve Jenkins
The Day-Glo Brothers	Chris Barton
The Right Word: Roget and His Thesaurus	Jennifer Bryant
The Tree Lady	Joseph Hopkins
Timeless Thomas: How Thomas Edison Changed Our Lives	Gene Baretta
We Are the Ship	Kadir Nelson
Winter Bees and Other Poems of the Cold	Joyce Sidman

Forty of My Favorite Nonfiction Picture Books

Compiled by Teri Lesesne

TITLE	AUTHOR
28 Days: Moments in Black History That Changed the World	Charles R. Smith
About Penguins: A Guide for Children	Cathryn P. Sill
All Different Now: Juneteenth, The First Day of Freedom	Angela Johnson
Aviary Wonders Inc. Spring Catalog and Instruction Manual: Renewing the World's Bird Supply Since 2031	Kate Samworth
Bad for You: Exposing the War on Fun!	Kevin C. Pyle
Benny Goodman & Teddy Wilson: Taking the Stage as the First Black-and-White Jazz Band in History	Lesa Cline-Ransome
Bone Collection: Animals	Rob Colson
Dare the Wind	Tracey E. Fern
Dear Malala, We Stand with You	Rosemary A. McCarney
Eye—How It Works	David Macaulay
Fly Guy Presents: Sharks	Tedd Arnold
Flying Solo: How Ruth Elder Soared into America's Heart	Julie Cummins
Go: A Kidd's Guide to Graphic Design	Chip Kidd
Grandfather Gandhi	Arun Gandhi
Gravity	Jason Chin
Growing Up Pedro	Matt Tavares
Ivan: The Remarkable True Story of the Shopping Mall Gorilla	Katherina Applegate
JFK	Jonah Winter
Lifetime: The Amazing Numbers in Animal Lives	Lola M. Schaefer
Locomotive	Brian Floca
Migrant	Jose Manuel Mateo
Nelson Mandela	Kadir Nelson
Papa Is a Poet: A Story About Robert Frost	Natalie Bober
Parrots over Puerto Rico	Susan L. Roth
Pluto's Secret: An Icy World's Tale of Discovery	Margaret A. Weitekamp
President Taft Is Stuck in the Bath	Mac Barnett

TITLE	AUTHOR
Queen Victoria's Bathing Machine	Gloria Whelan
Reptiles: The Coolest and Deadliest Cold-Blooded Creatures	Penelope Arlon
That's a Possibility A Book About What Might Happen	Bruce Goldstone
The Boy Who Loved Math: The Improbable Life of Paul Erdos	Deborah Heiligman
The Iridescence of Birds: A Book About Henri Mattise	Patricia MacLachlan
The Mad Potter: George E. Orh, Eccentric Genius	Jan Greenberg
The Mystery of Darwin's Frog	Martha L. Crump
The Noisy Paint Box: The Colors and Sounds of Kandinsky's Abstract Art	Barb Rosenstock
The Right Word: Roget and His Thesaurus	Jennifer Bryant
The Tree Lady: The True Story of How One Tree-Loving Woman Changed a City Forever	H. Joseph Hopkins
Triangles	David A. Adler
Tuesday Tucks Me In: The Loyal Bond Between a Soldier and His Service Dog	Luis Carlos Montalvan
Viva Frida	Yuyi Morales
When the Beat Was Born: DJ Kool Herc and the Creation of Hip Hop	Laban Carrick Hill

Signal Words

Words that signal a category

Categories	Kinds	Sets	Species
Classes	Parts	Sorts	Type
Divisions			

Words that signal a cause or an effect

Causes	Were caused by	For that reason	Therefore
As	Effects	Hence	Thus
Because	Accordingly	Since	
Due to	As a result	So	
Given that	Consequently	Subsequently	

Words that signal comparison

Additionally	As well as	Furthermore	Resembling
Alike	Both	In common	Similar (similarly)
Also	Comparable	Like	Too
Analogous	Compared with	Moreover	
As good as	Equivalent	Related (to)	

Words that signal a conclusion

As a Result	Finally	In summation	So
Conclusively	Findings	Last of all	Therefore
Consequently	Hence	Lastly	Thus

Words that signal a continuation

Additionally	Further	Likewise	Similarly
Also	Furthermore	Moreover	In addition to

Words that signal contrasts

Although	Even though	Nothing like	Though
As opposed to	However	On the other hand	Unlike
Conversely	In spite of this	Otherwise	Yet
Different from	Instead of	Still	
Dissimilar	Nevertheless	Then again	

Words that signal emphasis

A key idea	Important to note	Namely	The crux of the matter
A main focus	It all boils down to	Of course	
A primary concern	Most of all	Remember that	
Above all	Most significantly	Should be noted	

Words that signal an exception

Even though	Instead of	Otherwise	The opposite
In contrast	On the other hand	Still	Though

Words that signal an illustration or example

By way of demonstration	To illustrate	Specifically	Such as
For example	Particularly		

Words that signal main idea

There are several reasons for	A major development	The critical point(s) is (are)	Remember that

Words that signal the author is qualifying his thinking

Alleged	Looks like	Reported	Supposedly
Almost	Might	Seems like	Was reported
Assumed	Mostly	Some	
Except	Purported	Sort of	

Words that signal a restatement or a definition

Also called	Also referred to as	Sometimes called	That is to say
Also known as	In other words	That is	

Words that signal a sequence or chronology

After	Following	Prior to	Today (yesterday, tomorrow)
Always	Initially	Subsequently	While
At last	Later	Since	Without further delay
During	Next	Then	
First (second . . .)	Preceding		

Words that signal spatial proximity

About	Between	Contiguous	Near
Across	Bordering	End-to-end	Neighboring
Adjacent	By	Far	Upon
Around	Closest	Flanking	

All of these resources are available online.

http://hein.pub/readnfres1

Word Knowledge

Semantic Map

Chemistry Notes

Math Notes

Social Studies Notes

Possible Sentences

KWL 2.0

Somebody Wanted But So

ABC Boxes

Acknowledgments

If any book was ever written within the embrace of a community, it was this one.

The community we must thank first is our national teaching community—you. So many teachers answered our questions, lent us their students, shared their thinking, tried these strategies, and never stopped asking for the nonfiction signposts. That encouragement meant much to us, and it gave us a small hint of the support you must offer your students. We've said it before, but it's worth repeating: We are proud to stand beside you in all that you do; but actually, we stand in awe of all that you do. Thank you.

In particular, we offer our deepest thanks to classroom teachers and literacy leaders Jen Ochoa, Lindsey Jones, Jeff Williams, Tara Smith, Eileen Ours, Will LaRiccia, Paul Hankins, Angie Rosen, Elizabeth Snevily, Lauren Maynes, and Kim Kooista. Each of you helped us in the journey of this book. Additionally, Allison Jackson and Shannon Clark, you two amaze us. Your work with the Facebook Notice and Note Book Club page has helped thousands of teachers share the literary signposts with their students. What a vision you two had. Thank you. Franki Sibberson and Mary Lee Hahn, when we needed more books, you gave us great ideas. Your own professional work helps so many of us, and the time you shared with us for this project meant much to us.

Teri Lesesne, well, you make us—meaning *all* of us—smarter, and your ideas and suggestions and the great list of books you provided made this book smarter. Thank you, Teri. Thank you, thank you.

Our community of friends and colleagues at Heinemann support *all* our work. Vicki Boyd and Eric Chalek, you both offered advice at important junctures. Patty Adams and Sarah Fournier, thank you both for juggling the hundreds of details that must be attended to as a manuscript becomes a book. You both took on tasks that more organized authors would have handled themselves and your assistance was invaluable. Sherry Day and Michael Grover, you made our videos look great.

Lisa Fowler, we couldn't imagine getting through this project without your constant, unwavering support, your brilliant ideas, and that ever-ready "What a good idea," even when we had just suggested something anyone else would have labeled impossible.

And Debra Doorack, our dear editor. Is there a relationship more important in the creation of a book than that of author and editor? You made this book better, and where it is not, it's because we were too stubborn to listen to you.

Our smallest communities of our own families were our strongest supporters. In particular, Meredith Beers and Baker Beers stepped up and put aside their own tasks to help us out. Meredith offered critical eyes reading this manuscript when hers were tired—we are sure—from writing her dissertation. When you are ready for readers, Mer, we owe you some serious time. Baker reviewed manuscripts, rewrote student work that had arrived in pencil and could not be read, created some of the lists in the Appendix, and catalogued hundreds of books that arrived for us to review. When you need help moving furniture to New Orleans as you get settled to start at Tulane Law School, Baker, we owe you lots of help.

FROM KYLENE: And one final community that helped us make sure this book was (eventually) finished. In December 2014, Bob suffered a stroke. A small group of friends—Linda Rief, Penny Kittle, Chris Crutcher, Lester Laminack, and Brad Beers—kept Bob laughing with funny emails that first scary week. Friends are there when you need them, and you were all there. "Bob is Back" in part because you never left.

And there is one more person I must thank: Bob, himself. It's not typical to thank a coauthor in an acknowledgment page, but it's also not typical for the coauthor to have a stroke right before being scheduled to give a keynote to nearly 1,000 people. Bob's first question to the doctor while still in the emergency room was, "I realize I probably won't be able to join Kylene to give the morning keynote, but do you think I can make it back in time for our afternoon workshops?" The doctor looked at me and I said, "He's serious." I have said all along, if anyone could come back from a stroke to resume a grueling speaking schedule, finish this book, and juggle all the other demands of life, it would be Bob Probst. And I was right. You did it, Bob. Thanks for refusing to do less when there was more to be done. Many, many thanks.

References

ACT, Inc. 2006. *Reading Between the Lines.* Iowa City, IA: ACT.

Allen, Janet. 1999. *Words, Words, Words.* York, ME: Stenhouse.

Allington, Richard L. 2002. "What I've Learned About Effective Reading Instruction from a Decade of Studying Effective Literacy Elementary Classroom Teachers." *Phi Delta Kappan* 83: 740–47.

American Academy of Pediatrics. 2013. "The Crucial Role of Recess in School." *Pediatrics* 131: 183–88. doi:10.1542/peds.2012-2993. Retrieved from http://pediatrics.aappublications.org/content/131/1/183.full.

American Heritage Dictionary of the English Language, The, 4th ed. 2000/2003. New York: Houghton Mifflin.

"American High School Students Are Reading Books at Fifth-Grade-Appropriate Levels: Report." 2012. *Huff Post Education.* Retrieved from www.huffingtonpost.com/2012/03/22/top-reading_n_1373680.html.

Anand, Sowmya, and Jon A. Krosnick. 2003. "The Impact of Attitudes Toward Foreign Policy Goals on Public Preferences Among Presidential Candidates: A Study of Issue." Publics and the Attentive Public in the 2000 U.S. Presidential Election. *Presidential Studies Quarterly* 20 (10): 31–71.

Anderson, Richard C., Elfrieda H. Hiebert, Judith A. Scott, and Ian A. G. Wilkinson. 1985. *Becoming a Nation of Readers: The Report of the Commission on Reading.* Champaign, IL: The Center for the Study of Reading.

Anderson, Richard C., Paul T. Wilson, and Linda G. Fielding. 1988. "Growth in Reading and How Children Spend Their Time Outside of School." *Reading Research Quarterly* 23 (3): 285–303.

Angelos, Susan, and Nancy McGriff. 2002. "Tracking Students' Reading Progress." *Knowledge Quest* 30 (5): 44–46.

Baumann, James F., and Edward J. Kame'enui. 2004. *Vocabulary Instruction: Research to Practice.* New York: Guilford.

Beck, Isabelle L., Margaret G. McKeown, and Linda Kucan. 2002. *Bringing Words to Life: Robust Vocabulary Instruction.* New York: Guilford.

Beers, Kylene. 1996. "No Time, No Interest, No Way: The Three Voices of Aliteracy." *School Library Journal* 42: 30–33.

———. 2002. *When Kids Can't Read: What Teachers Can Do. A Guide for Teachers 6–12.* Portsmouth, NH: Heinemann.

Beers, Kylene, and Lee Odell. 2003. Holt Literature and Language Arts: First Course. *Mastering the California Standards: Reading, Writing, Listening, Speaking,* Calif. ed. Austin, TX: Holt, Rinehart and Winston.

Beers, Kylene, and Robert E. Probst. 2013. *Notice and Note: Strategies for Close Reading.* Portsmouth, NH: Heinemann.

Berkman, Michael, and Eric Plutzer. 2012. "An Evolving Controversy: The Struggle to Teach Science in Science Classes." *American Educator* Summer: 12–40. Retrieved from www.aft.org/sites/default/files/periodicals/berkman_plutzer.pdf.

Biber, Douglas, and Bethany Gray. 2013. "Nominalizing the Verb Phrase in Academic Science Writing." In *The Verb Phrase in English: Investigating Recent Language Change with Corpora*, ed. Bas Aarts, Joanne Close, Geoffrey Leech, and Sean Wallis, 99–132. Cambridge, UK: Cambridge University Press.

Blachowicz, Camille L. Z., and Peter Fisher. 2004. "Keep the 'Fun' in Fundamental: Encouraging Word Awareness and Incidental Word Learning in the Classroom Through Word Play." In *Vocabulary Instruction: Research to Practice*, ed. James F. Baumann and Edward J. Kame'enui, 218–38. New York: Guilford.

Braddock, Richard, Richard Lloyd-Jones, and Lowell A. Schoer. 1963. *Research in Written Composition*. Urbana, IL: National Council of Teachers of English.

Brenner, Devon. 2009. "Supporting Struggling Readers in Social Studies Education." Apex Learning, Inc. Retrieved from www.apexlearning.com /documents/Research_LiteracyAdvantage_SocialStudies_2009-05(2).pdf.

Brulle, Robert J., Jason Carmichael, and J. Craig Jenkins. 2011. "Shifting Public Opinion on Climate Change: An Empirical Assessment of Factors Influencing Concern Over Climate Change in the U.S., 2002–2010." Retrieved from www .pages.drexel.edu/~brullerj/02-12ClimateChangeOpinion.Fulltext.pdf.

Buehl, Doug. 2011a. *Developing Readers in the Academic Disciplines*. Newark, DE: International Reading Association.

_____. 2011b. "Mentoring Students in Disciplinary Literacy." In *Developing Readers in the Academic Disciplines*, 1–30. Newark, DE: International Reading Association. Retrieved from www.reading.org/Libraries/books/bk845-1-Buehl.pdf.

Cheney, Richard. 2002. "In Cheney's Word." *New York Times*, 26 August 2002. Retrieved 9/16/2014 from www.nytimes.com/2002/08/26/international /middleeast/26wb-cheney.html.

Chin, Beverley. 2000. "The Role of Grammar in Improving Student's Writing." Retrieved from http://people.uwplatt.edu/~ciesield/graminwriting.htm.

Cipielewski, Jim, and Keith E. Stanovich. 1992. "Predicting Growth in Reading Ability from Children's Exposure to Print." *Journal of Experimental Child Psychology* 54: 74–89.

Clark, Christina, and Kate Rumbold. 2006. "Reading for Pleasure: A Research Overview." National Literacy Trust. Retrieved from http://files.eric.ed.gov /fulltext/ED496343.pdf.

Clark, Herbert. 1996. *Using Language*. Boston, MA: Cambridge University Press.

Coleman, David, and Susan Pimentel. 2012. "Criteria for the Common Core State Standards in English Language Arts and Literacy, Grades 3–12." Retrieved from www.corestandards.org/assets/Publishers_Criteria_for_3-12.pdf.

Common Core State Standards: English Language Arts & Literacy in History/Social Studies, Science, and Technical Studies. 2010. "Appendix B: Task Exemplars and Sample Performance Tasks." Retrieved from www.corestandards.org /assets/Appendix_B.pdf.

Cotton, Kathleen. 1988. *Instructional Reinforcement*. Portland, OR: Northwest Regional Educational Laboratory.

Criscuola, Margaret M. 1994. "Read, Discuss, Reread: Insights from the Junior Great Books Program." *Educational Leadership* 51 (5): 58–61.

Cullinan, Bernice E. 2000. "Independent Reading and School Achievement." *School Library Media Research* 3. Retrieved from www.ala.org/ aasl/sites/ala.org.aasl/files/content/aaslpubsandjournals/slr/vol3/ SLMR_IndependentReading_V3.pdf.

Dweck, Carol. 2006. *Mindset: The New Psychology of Success*. New York: Ballantine.

Dyer, Wayne. 2009. "When You Change the Way You Look at Things." Retrieved from www.youtube.com/watch?v=urQPraeeY0w.

"ELA/Literacy Grade-Level Instructional Materials Evaluation Tool." Retrieved from www.cgcs.org/cms/lib/DC00001581/Centricity/Domain/72/ELA_Rubric_Grade%208.pdf (textbook evaluation tool from the Council of Great City Schools)

Elley, Warwick B., ed. 1994. *The IEA Study of Reading Literacy: Achievement and Instruction in Thirty-Two School Systems*. Oxford: Pergamon.

Feathers, Karen. 1993/2004. *Infotext: Reading and Learning*. Portsmouth, NH: Heinemann.

Fielding, Linda G., Paul T. Wilson, and Richard C. Anderson. 1986. "A New Focus on Free Reading: The Role of Trade Books in Reading Instruction." In *Contexts of School-Based Literacy*, ed. Taffy E. Raphael. New York: Random House.

Frey, Nancy, and Douglas Fisher. 2013. "Close Reading: The Common Core State Standards Have Brought New Attention to a Long Respected and Valuable Reading Strategy Called Close Reading." *Principal Leadership* 13 (January): 57–59. Retrieved from http://fisherandfrey.com/uploads/posts/Close_read.pdf.

Graves, Michael F. 2000. "A Vocabulary Program to Complement and Bolster a Middle-Grade Comprehension Program." In *Reading for Meaning: Fostering Comprehension in the Middle Grades*, ed. Barbara M. Taylor, Michael F. Graves, and Paul van den Broek, 116–35. New York: Teachers College Press.

Greaney, Vincent. 1980. "Factors Related to Amount and Type of Leisure Reading." *Reading Research Quarterly* 15 (3): 337–57.

Greaney, Vincent, and Mary Hegarty. 1987. "Correlates of Leisure Time Reading." *Journal of Research in Reading* 10 (1): 3–20.

Gross, Wendy, Tobias H. Stark, Jon Krosnick, Josh Pasek, Gaurav Sood, Trevor Tompson, Jennifer Agiesta, and Dennis Junius. 2013. "Americans' Attitudes Toward the Affordable Health Care Act: Would Better Public Understanding Increase or Decrease Favorability?" Retrieved from https://pprg.stanford.edu/wp-content/uploads/Health-Care-2012-Knowledge-and-Favorability.pdf.

Guthrie, John T. 2004. "Teaching for Literacy Engagement." *Journal of Literacy Research* 36 (1): 1–28.

Guthrie, John T., and Donna E. Alvermann. 1999. *Engaged Reading: Processes, Practices, and Policy Implications*. New York: Teachers College Press.

Hafner, Lawrence, Barbara Palmer, and Stan Tullos. 1986. "The Differential Reading Interests of Good and Poor Readers in the Ninth Grade." *Reading Improvement* 23: 39–42.

Halliday, Michael. 2004. *An Introduction to Functional Grammar*. London and New York: Routledge.

Harste, Jerome. 2014. "The Art of Learning to Be Critically Literate." *Language Arts* 92 (2): 90–102. Retrieved from www.ncte.org/library/NCTEFiles/Resources/Journals/LA/0922-nov2014/LA0922Art.pdf.

Herrell, Adrienne. 2000. *Fifty Strategies for Teaching English Language Learners*. Columbus, OH: Merrill.

Hiebert, Elfrieda H., Kathleen M. Wilson, and Guy Trainin. 2010. "Are Students Really Reading in Independent Reading Contexts? An Examination of Comprehension-Based Silent Reading Rate." In *Revisiting Silent Reading: New Directions for Teachers and Researchers*, ed. Elfrieda H. Hiebert and D. Ray Reutzel, 151–67. Newark, DE: International Reading Association.

Hillocks, George Jr. 1986. *Research on Written Composition: New Directions for Teaching*. Urbana, IL: ERIC Clearinghouse on Reading and Communication Skills and the National Conference on Research in English.

Improving Online Education Blog. 2015. "10 Salient Studies on the Arts in Education." Online Colleges. Retrieved from www.onlinecolleges.net/10-salient-studies-on-the-arts-in-education/.

Iyengar, Shanto, and Kyu S. Hahn. 2009. "Red Media, Blue Media: Evidence of Ideological Selectivity in Media Use." *Journal of Communication* 59: 19–39. doi:10.1111/j.1460-2466.2008.01402.x.

Jamail, Dahr. 2014. "Evidence of Acceleration of Anthropogenic Climate Disruption on All Fronts." *Truth-Out*, April 10. Retrieved from http://truth-out.org/news/item/22999-evidence-of-acceleration-on-all-fronts-of-anthropogenic-climate-disruption.

Johnston, P. 2004. *Choice Words: How Our Language Affects Children's Learning*. Portland, ME: Stenhouse.

Keene, Ellin Oliver. 2012. *Talk About Understanding: Rethinking Classroom Talk*. Portsmouth, NH: Heinemann.

Koch, Wendy. 2006. "New Citizen Exam Is Democracy 101." *USA Today*, December 1, 2006. Retrieved from http://usatoday30.usatoday.com/educate/reading/20061228_GAFRcitizen.pdf.

Krashen, Stephen D. 1993. *The Power of Reading: Insights from the Research*. Englewood, CO: Libraries Unlimited.

Krosnick, Jon A. 1988. "The Role of Attitude Importance in Social Evaluation: A Study of Policy Preferences, Presidential Candidate Evaluations, and Voting Behavior." *Journal of Personality and Social Psychology* 55: 196–210.

Krosnick, Jon A., and Bo MacInnis. 2010. "Frequent Viewers of Fox News Are Less Likely to Accept Scientists' Views of Global Warming." Retrieved from https://woods.stanford.edu/sites/default/files/files/Global-Warming-Fox-News.pdf.

Laminack, Lester, and Reba Wadsworth. 2012. *Bullying Hurts: Teaching Kindness Teaching Kindness Through Read Alouds and Guided Conversations*. Portsmouth, NH: Heinemann.

Langer, Judith A., Arthur N. Applebee, Ina V. S. Mullis, and Mary A. Foertsch. 1990. *Learning to Read in Our Nation's Schools*. Princeton, NJ: National Assessment of Educational Progress, Educational Testing Service.

Lauter, David. 2015. "App Aims to Show Chinese People Polluters Who Are Fouling China's air." Newsela. Retrieved from https://newsela.com/articles/china-pollutionapp/id/6833/.

Lester, Emile. 2014. "A Triumph of Ideology over Ideas: A Review of Proposed Textbooks for High School U.S. Government in Texas." Texas Freedom Network Education Fund. Retrieved from www.tfn.org/site/DocServer/FINAL_Lester_GOV.pdf?docID=4621.

"Lie Algebra." 2015. Retrieved from http://en.wikipedia.org/wiki/Lie_algebra. (Last modified May 20, 2015.)

Lupia, Arthur, and Tasha S. Philpot. 2005. "Views from Inside the Net: How Websites Affect Young Adults' Political Interest." *Journal of Politics* 67: 1122–42. doi:10.1111/j.1468-2508.2005.00353.x.

Macon, James M., Diane Bewell, and MaryEllen Vogt. 1991. *Responses to Literature: K–8*. Newark, DE: International Reading Association.

McCarthey, Sarah J., and Elizabeth Birr Moje. 2002. "Identity Matters." *Reading Research Quarterly* 37: 228–37.

McConachie, Stephanie M. 2010. "Disciplinary Literacy: A Principle-Based Framework." In *Content Matters: A Disciplinary Literacy Approach to Improving Student Literacy*, ed. Stephanie M. McConachie and Anthony R. Petrosky, 15–32.San Francisco: Jossey-Bass.

McKenna, Michael C., and Dennis J. Kear. 1990. "Measuring Attitude Toward Reading: A New Tool for Teachers." *The Reading Teacher* 43: 626–39.

Miller, Donalyn. 2009. *Book Whisperer: Awakening the Inner Reader in Every Child*. San Francisco: Jossey-Bass.

Moore, David W., and Sharon Arthur Moore. 1986. "Possible Sentences." In *Reading in the Content Areas* (2d ed.), ed. Ernest K. Dishner, Thomas W. Bean, John E. Readence, and David W. Moore, 174–79. Dubuque, IA: Kendall/Hunt.

Moss, Joy F. n.d. "Literature, Literacy & Comprehension Strategies in the Elementary School." Urbana, IL: National Council of Teachers of English. Retrieved from https://secure.ncte.org/library/NCTEFiles/Resources/Books /Sample/29900chap01x.pdf.

Mutz, Diana C., and Paul S. Martin. 2001. "Facilitating Communication Across Lines of Political Difference: The Role of Mass Media." *American Political Science Review* 95: 97–114.

Nagy, W. E. 1990. *Teaching Vocabulary to Improve Reading Comprehension*. Newark, DE: International Reading Association.

Nathanson, Steven. 2006. "Harnessing the Power of Story: Using Narrative Reading and Writing Across Content Areas." *Reading Horizons* 47(1): 1–26. Retrieved from http://scholarworks.wmich.edu/cgi/viewcontent.cgi?article=1124& context=reading_horizons.

Nystrand, Martin, and Adam Gamoran. 1991. "Instructional Discourse, Student Engagement, and Literature Achievement." *Research in the Teaching of English* 25 (3): 261–90.

Nystrand, Martin, Lawrence L. Wu, Adam Gamoran, Susie Zeiser, and Daniel A. Long. 2003. "Questions in Time: Investigating the Structure and Dynamics of Unfolding Classroom Discourse." *Discourse Processes* 35 (2): 135–96.

Ogle, Donna M. 1986. "K-W-L: A Teaching Model That Develops Active Reading of Expository Text." *Reading Teacher* 39: 564–70.

Pearson, P. David, and Elfrieda H. Heibert. 2013. "The State of the Field: Qualitative Analyses of Text Complexity." *Reading Research Report* #13.01. Santa Cruz, CA: TextProject, Inc. Retrieved from http://textproject.org/assets/publications/ TextProject-RRR-13-01-Qualitative-Analyses-of-Text-Complexity-v.1.0.pdf.

Probst, Robert E. 2000. "Literature as Invitation." *Voices from the Middle* 8 (2): 8–15.

Probst, Robert E. 2004. *Response and Analysis: Teaching Literature in Secondary School*. Portsmouth, NH: Heineman.

"Reading Between the Lines: What the ACT Reveals About College Readiness in Reading." 2006. Iowa City: ACT, Inc. Retrieved from www.act.org/research/ policymakers/pdf/reading_report.pdf.

Reiter, Ashley. 1998. "Helping Undergraduates Learn to Read Mathematics." Mathematical Association of America. Retrieved from www.maa.org/node /121566.

Rosenblatt, Louise. 1935/1995. *Literature as Exploration.* New York: Modern Language Association.

Rupley, William H., and William Dee Nichols. 2005. "Vocabulary Instruction for the Struggling Reader." *Reading and Writing Quarterly* 21 (3): 239–60. Retrieved from http://literacyconnects.org/img/2013/03/Vocabulary -Instruction-for-the-Struggling-Reader.pdf.

Searls, Donald T., Nancy A. Mead, and Barbara Ward. 1985. "The Relationship of Students' Reading Skills to TV Watching, Leisure Time Reading, and Homework." *Journal of Reading* 29 (2): 158–62.

Schiffman, Richard. 2011/2012. "The Truth About Thanksgiving: What They Never Taught You in School." *Huffington Post Politics*, November 21, 2011, updated January 21, 2012. Retrieved from www.huffingtonpost.com/richard -schiffman/the-thanksgiving-truth_b_1105181.html.

"Sentence Completions: Contrast vs. Continuation." Retrieved from http://grockit .com/blog/sentence-completions-contrast-vs-continuation/.

Sethna, Melissa, compiler. 2010/2011. *Literacy Skills and Strategies for Content Area Teachers: Comprehension and Vocabulary.* Retrieved from www.valrc.org /resources/docs/MHS_Literacy_Strategy_Book.pdf.

Shanahan, Timothy, and Cynthia Shanahan 2008. "Teaching Disciplinary Literacy to Adolescents: Rethinking Content Area Literacy." *Harvard Educational Review* 78: 40–59.

———. 2012. "What Is Disciplinary Literacy and Why Does it Matter?" *Topics in Language Disorders* 32 (1): 7–18.

Simonson, Sara D. 1995. "A Historical Review of Content Area." In *Content-Area Reading* (7th ed.), ed. Richard T. Vacca and Jo Anne L. Vacca. Boston: Allyn & Bacon.

Stahl, Steven A. 1999. *Vocabulary Development: From Reading Research to Practice.* Newton Upper Falls, MA: Brookline Books.

Stahl, Steven A., and Charles H. Clark. 1987. "The Effects of Participatory Expectations in Classroom Discussion on the Learning of Science Vocabulary." *American Educational Research Journal* 24: 541–56.

Strauss, Valerie. 2014. "Texas Approves Social Studies Textbooks Criticized As Inaccurate and Biased." *The Washington Post*, November 21. Retrieved from www.washingtonpost.com/blogs/answer-sheet/wp/2014/11/21/ texas-approves-social-studies-textbooks-criticized-as-inaccurate-and-biased/.

Stroud, Natalie Jomini. 2008. "Media Use and Political Predispositions: Revisiting the Concept of Selective Exposure." *Political Behavior* 30 (3): 341–66.

Taylor, Barbara, Barbara Frye, and Geoffrey Maruyama. 1990. "Time Spent Reading and Reading Growth." *American Educational Research Journal* 27 (2): 351–62.

VanDeWeghe, R. 2003. "Classroom Discussion of Literature." *English Journal* 93 (1): 87–91.

Watkins, Marley W., and Vicki A. Edwards. 1992. "Extracurricular Reading and Reading Achievement: The Rich Stay Rich and the Poor Don't Read." *Reading Improvement* 29 (4): 236–42.

"Yik Yak & Free Speech." 2015. *UpFront*, May.

"Young Earth Creationism." 2015. Wikipedia (modified June 16, 2015). Retrieved from http://en.wikipedia.org/wiki/Young_Earth_creationism.

Adler, David. 2014. *Millions, Billions, and Trillions: Understanding Big Numbers*. New York: Holiday House.

Alexandratos, Nikos. 1999. "World Food and Agriculture: Outlook for the Medium and Longer Term." *Proceedings of National Academy of Science of the United States of America* 96 (11): 5908–14. Retrieved from www.ncbi.nlm.nih.gov/pubmed/10339517.

"A Little Disconnect Goes a Long Way to Learn Motor Tasks, Brain Study Says." Retrieved from https://newsela.com/articles/brain-learning/id/8508/.

Alifirenka, Caitlin, and Martin Ganda. 2015. *I Will Always Write Back: How One Letter Changed Two Lives*. New York: Little, Brown.

"Archduke Franz Ferdinand Assassinated." Retrieved from www.history.com/this-day-in-history/archduke-franz-ferdinand-assassinated.

Armstrong, Jennifer. 2000. *Shipwreck at the Bottom of the World: The Extraordinary True Story of Shackelton and the Endurance*. New York: Knopf Books for Young Readers.

Barnard, Bryn. 2015. *Outbreak: Plagues That Changed History*. New York: Dragonfly Books.

Bartoletti, Susan Campbell. 2005. *Hitler Youth: Growing Up in Hitler's Shadow*. New York: Scholastic.

Bial, Raymond. 1999. *The Underground Railroad*. New York: Houghton Mifflin.

Bittman, Mark. 2013. "How to Feed the World." *New York Times*, p. SR9. Retrieved from www.nytimes.com/2013/10/15/opinion/how-to-feed-the-world.html?pagewanted=all&_r=0.

Blackburn, Laura. 2015. "Baltimore Is Quiet After Curfew." *Time for Kids*, April 29.

"Bottled Water: 10 Shockers 'They' Don't Want You to Know." www.cbsnews.com/pictures/bottled-water-10-shockers-they-dont-want-you-to-know/2/.

Campbell, Scott. 2012. *The Great Showdowns*. London: Titan Books.

Crane, Cody. 2015. "Antarctica's 'Bleeding' Glacier." *News for Your Classroom*, May 8. Retrieved from http://magazines.scholastic.com/news/2015/05/Antarctica-s-Bleeding-Glacier.

"Curious Chimp Swats Down Drone." 2015. *National Geographic for Kids*, April 16. Retrieved from http://kids.nationalgeographic.com/explore/nature/curious-chimp-swats-down-drone/.

Deverell, William and Deborah Gray White. 2009. *United States History: Beginnings to 1877*. Austin, TX: Holt, Rhinehart and Winston.

"First Thanksgiving." Retrieved from http://kids.nationalgeographic.com/explore/history/first-thanksgiving/.

Fitzgerald, Brian. 2015. "Flying on Sunlight." *News for Your Classroom*, May 1. Retrieved from http://magazines.scholastic.com/news/2015/05/Flying-on-Sunlight.

"4-Year-Old Finds 94-Million-Year-Old Fossil of an Armored Dinosaur?" 2015. *Fort Worth Star-Telegram*, April 20. Retrieved from https://newsela.com/articles/dinosaur-find/id/8643/.

Gibbons, Gail. 1983. *New Road.* New York: HarperCollins.

Goudarzi, Sara. 2015. "Dino Eggs by the Dozen." *Scholastic News*, May 4. Retrieved from http://magazines.scholastic.com/news/2015/05/Dino-Eggs-by-the-Dozen.

Hakim, Joy. 2007. *The History of US: Ten Volume Set*, 3d ed.. New York: Oxford University Press.

Henkes, Kevin. 1991. *Chrysanthemum.* New York: HarperCollins.

Herbert, Janis. 1999. *The Civil War for Kids: A History with 21 Activities.* Chicago: Chicago Review Press.

Holland, Jennifer. 2003. "The Dung Beetle as a Weapon Against Global Warming." *National Geographic*, September 6. Retrieved from http://news.nationalgeographic.com/news/2013/09/130904-dung-beetles-global-warming-animals-science/.

Hoose, Philip. 2015. *The Boys Who Challenged Hitler: Knud Pedersen and the Churchill Club.* New York: Farrar, Straus & Giroux.

Hopkinson, Deborah. 2006. *Up Before Daybreak: Cotton and People in America.* New York: Scholastic.

Humenik, Zachary. 2015. "Mummy Mystery." *Time for Kids*, March 11. Retrieved from www.timeforkids.com/news/mummy-mystery/223161.

Iasevoli, Brenda. 2015. "Debate! Should the Sale of Tropical Fish Be Banned?" *USA Today*, February 27. Retrieved from www.timeforkids.com/news/debate/219786.

Jarrow, Gail. 2015. *Fatal Fever: Tracking Down Typhoid Mary.* Honesdale, PA: Calkins Creek.

Johnson, Renée, and M. Lynn Corn. 2014. "Bee Health: Background and Issues for Congress." November 3. Retrieved from https://www.fas.org/sgp/crs/misc/R4311.pdf.

Kamoji, M. A. n.d. "Forced Vibrations." http://elearning.vtu.ac.in/14/enotes/Mech%20vib/4&5-MAKamoji.pdf.

Kilmeade, Brian, and Don Yaeger. 2013. *George Washington's Secret Six: The Spy Ring That Saved the American Revolution.* New York: Sentinel.

Kraul, Chris. 2005. "Vampire Bat Debate: To Kill or Not to Kill." *Los Angeles Tribune*, May 27.

Manning, Molly Guptill. 2014. *When Books Went to War: The Stories That Helped Us Win World War II.* New York: Houghton Mifflin Harcourt.

Martin, Bill Jr., and Eric Carle. 2010. *Brown Bear, Brown Bear, What Do You See?* New York: Henry Holt.

McDougal Littell. 2002. "First World War." Chapter 11 in Unit 2, *Reconstruction to the 21st Century* of *The Americans*, p. 580. Boston: McDougal Littell/HMH.

McPherson, James M. 2002. *Fields of Fury: The American Civil War.* New York: Atheneum Books for Young Readers.

Micucci, Charles. 1997. *The Life and Times of the Honeybee.* New York: HMH.

Numeroff, Laurie Joffe. 2005. *If You Give a Mouse a Cookie.* New York: HarperColllins.

Page, Kent. 2002. "Garana's Story: A Day in the Life of a Young Afghan Refugee." *National Geographic Explorer* (September 1): 18–23.

Perkovich, Adedayo. 2015. "The Long March to Freedom." *News for Your Classroom*, May 1. Retrieved from http://magazines.scholastic.com/kids-press/news/2015/05/The-Long-March-to-Freedom.

Robart, Rose. 1991. *The Cake That Mack Ate*. New York: Little, Brown.

Romain, Hailee. 2015. "Tornado Terror." *News for Your Classroom*, May 13. Retrieved from http://magazines.scholastic.com/news/2015/05/Tornado-Terror.

St. George, Judith. 2004. *So You Want to Be President?* New York: Philomel Books.

Schwartz, David M. 2004. *How Much Is a Million?* (20th anniversary ed.) New York: HarperCollins.

"Scientists Say Jupiter Muscled Its Way Through Solar System to Form Earth." Newsela. April 24, 2015. Retrieved from https://newsela.com/articles/jupiter-earth/id/8747/.

Serna, Joseph. 2014. "Privacy Fears at Heart of Drone Debate." *Los Angeles Times*, July 7. Retrieved from https://newsela.com/articles/drones-privacy/id/4463/.

Sesink Clee, Paul R., and Mary Katherine Gonder. 2012. "Macroevolution: Examples from the Primate World." *Nature Education Knowledge* 3 (12): 2. Retrieved from www.aft.org/sites/default/files/periodicals/berkman_plutzer.pdf.

Silverstein, Shel. 2003. "I Cannot Go to School Today." In *Where the Sidewalk Ends*. New York: HarperCollins.

Stanchak, John. 2011. *Eyewitness Civil War*. New York: DK Publishing.

Stickland, Jonathan, and Nathan Chandler. n.d. "How the Dyson Bladeless Fan Works." Retrieved from http://electronics.howstuffworks.com/gadgets/home/dyson-bladeless-fan1.htm.

Tarshis, Lauren. 2013. *I Survived the Battle of Gettysburg 1863*. New York: Scholastic.

Upadhyay, Ritu. 2003. "Hard at Work." *Time for Kids* 8 (14): 44–47.

Vick, Karl, and Dolly Mascareñas. 2015. "Cuba on the Cusp." *Time/Edge*. Retrieved from www.timeedge.com/article/cuba-on-the-cusp/teacher.

"Virginia Woolf Biography." Retrieved from www.biography.com/people/virginia-woolf-9536773.

Walters, Jennifer Marino. 2015. "A Volcano Erupts in Chile." *Scholastic News*, April 29. Retrieved from http://magazines.scholastic.com/news/2015/04/A-Volcano-Erupts-in-Chile.

"Why Is the Divergence of a Magnetic Field Equal to Zero?" Retrieved from http://physics.stackexchange.com/questions/108224/why-is-the-divergence-of-a-magnetic-field-equal-to-zero.

Willing, Richard. 2006. "Study: Cats Have More Than Nine Lives, and Plenty of Cousins." *USA Today*, January 6. Retrieved from http://usatoday30.usatoday.com/educate/reading/GreatAmer3.pdf.

Wood, Audrey. 2015. *The Napping House*. Boston: HMH Books for Young Readers.

Zeman, Anne, and Kate Kelly. 1997. *All You Need to Know about American History Homework*. New York: Scholastic.

Index

Credits

Text Credits

continued from page iv

"Vampires Prey on Panama" by Chris Kraul from *Los Angeles Times* (May 18, 2005). Reprinted with permission from the publisher.

"The Dung Beetle as a Weapon Against Global Warming" by Jennifer S. Holland from *National Geographic Magazine* (September 6, 2013). Reprinted with permission from the publisher.

"Garana's Story: A Day in the Life of a Young Afghan Refugee" by Kent Page from *National Geographic Explorer* (September 1, 2002). Reprinted with permission from the publisher.

Photo Credits

Front cover: © Michael Grover, Heinemann

Charts on inside front cover and pages 78, 81, 91, and 100

Lindsey Jones; Pages 10-11: © Tim Pannell/Corbis/HIP

Page 13 (top left): © Don Couch/Houghton Mifflin Harcourt/HIP

Pages 76–77: © Mohamed Syaheir Azizan/iStockphoto.com/Getty Images/HIP

Page 91 (top right): © Steve Skjold/Alamy/HIP

Page 100 (top left): Jupiterimages/Getty Images/HIP

Pages 112–113: © Don Mason/Blend Images/Corbis/HIP

Page 123 (top left): © Stock 4B/Getty Images/HIP

Charts on pages 123, 136, 148, 158, 168, and inside back cover: Jennifer Ochoa

Page 136 (top left): © Stock 4B/Getty Images/HIP

Page 148 (top left): © bo1982/iStockphoto.com/HIP

Page 158 (top left): © Peopleimages/E+/Getty Images/HIP

Page 168 (top left): © Don Couch/Houghton Mifflin Harcourt/HIP

Pages 180–181: © Corbis Super RF/Alamy/HIP

Page 193: © Jose Luis Pelaez, Inc./Blend Images/Corbis/HIP

Page 221 (top right): © Apeloga/Maskot/Getty Images/HIP

About the Authors

Kylene Beers, Ed.D., is a former middle school teacher who has turned her commitment to adolescent literacy and struggling readers into the major focus of her research, writing, speaking, and teaching. She is the author of the bestselling *When Kids Can't Read/What Teachers Can Do*, co-editor (with Bob Probst and Linda Rief) of *Adolescent Literacy: Turning Promise into Practice*, and co-author (with Bob Probst) of *Notice and Note: Strategies for Close Reading*, all published by Heinemann. She taught in the College of Education at the University of Houston, served as Senior Reading Researcher at the Comer School Development Program at Yale University, and most recently acted as the Senior Reading Advisor to Secondary Schools for the Reading and Writing Project at Teachers College.

Kylene has published numerous articles in state and national journals, served as editor of the national literacy journal *Voices from the Middle,* and was the 2008–2009 President of the National Council of Teachers of English. She is an invited speaker at state, national, and international conferences and works with teachers in elementary, middle, and high schools across the U.S. Kylene has served as a consultant to the National Governor's Association and was the 2011 recipient of the Conference on English Leadership Outstanding Leader Award.

Robert E. Probst, Ph.D., author of *Response and Analysis* (Heinemann, 2004) is a respected authority on the teaching of literature. Bob's focus on engagement and literary analysis helps teachers learn the strategies to help readers approach a text with more confidence and greater skill.

Professor Emeritus of English Education at Georgia State University, Bob's publications include numerous articles in *English Journal, Voices from the Middle,* and professional texts including co-editor with Kylene Beers and Linda Rief of *Adolescent Literacy: Turning Promise into Practice* (Heinemann, 2007), and the co-author of *Notice and Note: Strategies for Close Reading* (with Kylene Beers). He speaks at national and international conventions including the International Literacy Association (ILA), the National Council of Teachers of English (NCTE), the Association of Supervisors and Curriculum Developers (ASCD), and the National Association of Secondary School Principals (NASSP). He has served NCTE in various leadership roles including the Conference on English Leadership Board of Directors, the Commission on Reading, column editor of the NCTE journal *Voices from the Middle*, and is the 2007 recipient of the CEL Outstanding Leadership Award.